God Stories

FOUR

The Regional Church of Lancaster County
www.theregionalchurch.com

Photo by Lisa Hildebrand

God Stories 4

© 2009 by The Regional Church of Lancaster County
Lancaster, Pennsylvania, USA
www.regionalchurch.com

ISBN: 978-0-9760387-4-0

Printed in the United States of America

Dedication

This book is dedicated to the people of
South Central Pennsylvania.

Photo by Sarah Sauder

Photo by Janet Medrow

Acknowledgments

Thank you to the many contributing authors who made this book possible.

Edited by Karen Boyd, Lisa Dorr, Sharon Neal, Cindy Riker, Tracy Stoltzfus and Keith Yoder.

House To House Publications Team: Brenda Boll, Karen Ruiz and Sarah Sauder.

Proofreaders: Sharon Neal and Denise Sensenig

Cover photos: Sarah Sauder, Mark Van Scyoc and Mandi Wissler

Photo by Christina Ricker

Introduction

Throughout my life, it always has blessed me whenever I witness moments of Christian unity, perhaps, in part, because my family background includes Presbyterian, Catholic, Evangelical, Anabaptist, Episcopal and Lutheran. It is as though, at such times, we can feel God smiling on us! Indeed, Psalm 133 reminds us that dwelling together in unity, which Jesus prayed for in John 17, is "good and pleasing to God" and upon such dwelling the Lord bestows His blessing (Psalm 133:1, 3b).

In this 4th Volume of *God Stories* you will be blessed to read accounts of the living God acting in the present lives of everyday folk like you and me—your brothers and sisters in Christ...family! It is my hope and prayer that throughout the coming year, as you spend time daily with the Lord, you will hear "God's still, small voice" and recognize the fingerprint of God's hand on your life, just as God has acted in the lives of the writers of these stories. We hear throughout the Bible that God is not a respecter of persons (Acts 10:34), meaning, God does not show partiality or favoritism in wanting a personal relationship with His children.

It is also my hope and prayer that all of us will more deeply value the significance of our participation in the One Body of Christ as we daily share in the personal stories of our brothers and sisters in Christ. As God's children, may we be led to thank God daily for each other, even as we pray for one another. May we also pray that God will manifest visibly what we already are spiritually in Christ: One Body, One Spirit, (with) One Hope, One Baptism, One Faith, One Father in Heaven, One God, and One Lord...one day at a time...

...so that "we will in all things grow up into Him who is the Head, that is Christ...joined and held together by every supporting ligament, growing and building itself up in love, as each part does its work" (Ephesians 4:15-16).

—Scott Fischer
Executive director of Lancaster County Council of Churches and member of the Regional Council of the Regional Church of Lancaster County

January

My Choice

"I know, my God, that you test the heart and are pleased with integrity. All these things have I given willingly and with honest intent...." 1 Chronicles 29:17

I sat across from the CEO. This conversation had been brewing for months, and today was the day. People were interceding; we had prepared for this conversation. As the company's chief analytic officer, I was responsible for demonstrating the value of our business strategy. The issue: the results were not showing the promised financial return.

The CEO's offer was clear. For the "right" results, I could become wealthy, and I could connect to prominent not-for-profit agencies. It was seductive. Perhaps this offer for connections was His plan. Was the cost of delivering right results in order to do kingdom work so large? Would I choose the world's way or God's way? The Scripture came to me—God is pleased with integrity; He does not use deceit in order to further His purposes. I made my choice.

I thanked the CEO and turned down the offer. Painfully we discussed how I would leave the company. I wish I could say that I had complete peace. I realized I'd be unemployed within three months. I struggled to hold on to faith, sometimes by my fingertips. In the midst of holding on, one thing I was sure of—I had chosen for my Father. There was a true joy in that.

Two years later it remains a powerful moment, choosing to walk in His will despite the cost. He blessed me with a wonderful new job which has opened up many avenues to know Him and live for Him. Through it all, I am abundantly aware of my Father's unending love and provision for me.

Heavenly Father, Your ways are so much higher than mine, may Your will and not mine be done in my life. Amen.

Sarah Davies is a business professional in the financial services sector. She serves on the board of Teaching the Word Ministries and leads a women's marketplace ministry, The Lydia Network.

An Answer to Prayer

"And in that day you will ask me no question. Truly truly I say to you if you shall ask the Father for anything, he will give it to you in My name." *John 16:23*

I once heard this comment and it stuck with me, "Coincidence is God working anonymously." It is a neat way of admitting that God's hand is in all things, that there is no such thing as coincidence. Knowing this, it is very important for us to notice the activities of God in our daily lives. When we notice what God is doing, we will grow in our personal relationship with Him.

I recently came across an intense situation in which God jumped onto the scene. A member of the congregation had fallen into temptation and had gotten himself into trouble. His family was not sure where he was, but knew he was somewhere in Lancaster City. I was concerned for him and decided to do a little cruising to see if I might spot him, or the car, or something. Lancaster is a large city, and I knew it was a needle in a haystack situation, but I needed at least to look. Sitting at a red light, I prayed very specifically, "God, somehow in your power let me see the car, that it may lead me to my friend." Before long, a car passed me. You guessed it; my friend drove past me. In less than three minutes, God answered my prayer; the needle in the haystack was found. Though I did not catch up to my friend that afternoon, God sent me a message of comfort that all was going to be okay. God's hand was over my friend, his family, and me. He is a God who can give immediate responses to our prayers, no coincidence.

If God can answer my prayers to find a specific car in the middle of Lancaster City, then He is more than sufficient in caring for my friends. God does answer our prayers in His time. It is important for us to notice His answers that we may be constantly turning more and more of our lives over to His sovereign power.

God, open my eyes to see You acting in my daily life. Amen.

Tom Weber is the pastor at Akron Church of the Brethren.

No Longer an Orphan

"...I have loved you with an everlasting love...." *Jeremiah 31:3*

I can still recall, as a little girl, crying under the bathroom sink after another beating from my mother. Sobbing, I asked God why this kept happening to me and why He didn't send someone to rescue me. My "little girl" mind reasoned the beatings were my own fault, because my mother always said I was "bad." Needless to say, the emotional scars were much worse than the physical. The marks left by the leather whip disappeared over time, but the emotional scars lasted into adulthood.

I was born again in my twenties, but struggled with the concept of the Father's love. My earthly father did not intervene to stop the physical abuse, and I thought my heavenly Father would be the same—distant and uninvolved. Why would God the Father get involved with a "bad" girl, anyway? I spent the first twenty-five years of my Christian life believing that God would either abandon me or punish me for every infraction of His rules.

One day a friend advised me to listen to a teaching tape by Pastor Jack Frost. Returning home after our breakfast, I visited his website and began reading his biography. Suddenly, one word leapt off the computer screen: *orphan*. Then, very clearly, I heard these words deep within my spirit. "Ellen, you feel like an orphan, but I'm telling you that you are not an orphan. You are My daughter and I love you. You have gifts and talents, and faults and flaws just like everyone else, but you are My daughter and I have work for you to do."

For the first time in my life I knew who I was and why I was created. I was not a "bad" girl; I was the Father's daughter! My life changed radically that day—I have never been the same!

Abba, words cannot express my gratitude for You calling me Your daughter.

Ellen Dooley is assistant pastor at Crossroads Wesleyan Church.

Draped in White

"For we who are alive are always being given over to death for Jesus' sake, so that His life may be revealed in our mortal body."
2 Corinthians 4:11

Newly fallen snow is truly beautiful. Winter is one of my favorite seasons after a snowfall (as long as I don't have somewhere to drive). But when it is not snowing, the winter scene is quite different. Deciduous trees are barren and look empty. Their lives seem somewhat useless, since the leaves and fruit they have spent the summer growing have left. They are bare and can hide nothing. That is when God bejewels them with a lovely cape of white snow, and never do they look more peaceful or serene. They wear their snow with honor.

God wants us to be exactly where those trees are before the snow—completely empty and hiding nothing. If the trees still held their leaves, the snow would slide off, and the tree would miss out. If we abandon everything and wait on Him, He will cover us with the same glorious robe of purity and give us peace. Did you also notice how silently this happens? God usually does not announce His glory with a loud show, yet it is obvious, nonetheless, for all to see.

Lord, please empty me of myself so that I might have room to be filled with Your Spirit. I desire the glory You have waiting for me. Amen.

Tracy Slonaker is a wife, mother of three, and Director of Christian Education at Harvest Fellowship in Colebrookdale.

Love Your Enemies

"But I tell you who hear Me, love your enemies, do good to those who hate you." *Luke 6:27*

I was serving with a group from Lancaster Bible College at a Bible camp in Hungary, where I had been several summers in a row. I had developed friendships with staff, counselors, and campers and looked forward to building relationships with them this year. The young man I had built the deepest friendship with was a Hungarian counselor named Dezso. We were helping to register campers on Sunday afternoon, when someone told us there were Iraqi kids coming to camp.

I left registration later in the day without seeing them. In my mind I had already labeled them "the enemy" because of the war in Iraq. Without even meeting these kids, I was already thinking of how I could avoid them and hoped they wouldn't come to our volleyball sessions.

I met Dezso later and he told me with great excitement about how many of the Iraqi kids were assigned to his dorm. He said these kids were Iraqi refugees and heard about the camp and its teaching of soccer. They were all Muslims, could speak English, and he couldn't believe that they came to a Christian camp. Dezso said, "This week we *must* tell them about Jesus. We *must* show them His love. This may be the only time they are ever exposed to Jesus." His words were like getting hit by a truck. I quickly came to my senses and agreed with him. I worked on showing these kids respect, talking with them, and trying to be a Christ-like example.

Several evenings we had the opportunity to go to the dorm and talk with these kids, hear their stories, share our testimonies and fellowship (of course with snacks). The following year, one of the kids told me that he hated Americans before he met us, but now he knows at least a few are good.

Thank You, Lord, for the ways You teach us and show us the right way. Continue to teach us to love our enemies and our neighbors as ourselves. Thank You for Your unchanging love for all.

Randy Wingenroth is vice president of E.F. Martzall, Inc. He also serves on the Discovery Commission at Mohn's Hill Evangelical Congregational Church.

Approaching the Throne of Grace

"Let us then approach the throne of grace with confidence, so that we may receive mercy and find grace to help us in our time of need."
Hebrews 4:16

Little Kitty showed up on my doorstep a few months ago. He was tired, cold, hungry, but mostly he seemed scared. He ate from the bowl of food I put in front of him but wouldn't come close enough for me to touch him. The whole time he was eating he would look over at me and over each shoulder. It was hard for him to receive my kindness and to build trust.

After patiently feeding him every day and talking to him, I was eventually able to reach out my hand, and he accepted my strokes. "L.K." even seemed to enjoy the attention by the sound of his purring!

I began inviting Little Kitty into my home by holding open my door to him. He would come close but wouldn't cross the threshold. One day L.K. appeared on the porch, and he was soaking wet from the rain. This time when I opened the door he stepped into a warm dry home where I welcomed him, dried him off with a towel, fed him and loved him.

My recent adventures with Little Kitty reminded me that sometimes I am a little afraid, a little mistrustful, a little tired to boldly step into the throne room and receive what I need.

Father, thank You that I can enter Your throne room with confidence and receive all that I need because of Your great love.

Sharon Blantz serves as regional pastor of single parents and support and care ministries at The Worship Center.

God at Work

"And I am certain that God, who began the good work within you, will continue his work until it is finally finished…." *Philippians 1:6*

I'm sure you have seen a temporary sign at a construction site "Men at Work." You look around and don't see anyone. "Where are they working?" you wonder, "It's certainly not here." Too quickly, you may mentally accuse someone of slacking on the job or of being lazy when the boss is away. However, it could be those workers are taking a needed break to eat, to rest or to seek a supervisor's input.

To work at our fullest potential, occasionally we need to stop to renew our strength, to gain a fresh perspective or to evaluate our future steps. At such times, we could display a "God at Work" sign. The promises in His Word renew our vision and purpose in life. The refreshment of others' encouraging words may spur us on to good works.

Has a good friend confided that she wants to improve in a specific discipline such as patience or self control? While she is going through the transformation, be assured "God [is] at Work." Share a truth from God's Word to edify her. Offer grace. Forgive when failure happens. Be supportive when change seems slow.

Whether a "God at Work" sign is displayed or not, we can be sure He is faithfully constructing behind the scenes. By acknowledging that God is at work, we can freely offer mercy and forgiveness to others. After all, we want grace extended to us because God is also at work in us.

May a "God at Work" sign be displayed at the construction site of my life. Father God, I yield to the work of the Holy Spirit. I'm grateful Jesus intercedes for me. With integrity, I accept insights and encouragement from others. Amen.

Nancy Leatherman resides in Manheim Township. Both of her children are married, so she is now delighted to be a mother of four.

My Timing or God's Timing?

"In his heart a man plans his course, but the Lord determines his steps." *Proverbs 16:9*

"So, what are you doing after you graduate?" It was the query I heard after high school and then after college—spoken from genuine care but causing me to question God's direction in my life. I majored in Women in Christian Ministries at Lancaster Bible College, but I didn't have a ministry job lined up. Instead, I worked where I had the past several summers, not planning to work there forever. I worked with women coworkers at the day care, many of whom were unsaved. I love children, and it prepared me for one of my dreams—motherhood. Still the questions came.

More than anything I missed the spiritual community at Lancaster Bible College. I longed to be back at the place that had been home to me for four years. God, however, had a better idea. Over the following three years, he drew me to Himself, causing me to cling to Him when I felt like I had no one else. I learned to depend more on His Word than on others' opinions and learned to run to Him when I seemed to be failing at life.

This past spring, He started putting the pieces together. A job opened at Lancaster Bible College. After several interviews, I took it. August marks a year that I have been living a dream. I am home again, at the place I love. This time, on the other side, positioned to minister to students—people in the same place I was—learning who they are in Christ, growing with other believers, and seeking God's direction. Now I can encourage them to discover the plan God has for them...in God's timing.

Jesus, thank You for having our lives under Your control, knowing us better than we know ourselves, and having our best in mind.

Mandi Wissler, financial aid and enrollment counselor at Lancaster Bible College, enjoys serving and mentoring students as well as the youth at her church.

On Patience

"You have need of patient endurance, so that, as a result of having done the will of God, you may receive the promised blessing."
Hebrews 10:36 (Weymouth New Testament)

From where I live, driving west on Airport Road, I need to cross Route 501, a busy highway between Lititz and Lancaster. During rush hour I need to sit at the traffic light for what seems like a long time until the light changes, sometimes trying my patience. I found a great definition for patience: "the ability to tolerate being hurt, provoked, or annoyed without complaint or loss of temper."

Christ and His disciples spoke a lot about patience and perseverance. Actually, patience belongs to the character of God. The patience of God with His people is shown frequently in the Old Testament. God was patient in redeeming the world, waiting several thousand years "until the fullness of time" came. Luke 15 illustrates the patience of God in the father and the prodigal son, the woman and the lost coin and the shepherd searching for a lost sheep. Jesus demonstrated patience with Peter and Judas.

Nature teaches us patience. It takes patience to sow seeds into the ground and wait for the harvest. We need patience to make solid achievements in life. A builder lays the bricks one at a time. The poet writes poems line by line. The teacher teaches the child precept by precept.

A patient man/woman does not run away from life; he does not give up. If a battle is lost he goes on to win the next; he waits for the help of God, aware that help will not be late; he knows that God will help him at the point of greatest need. I know that I need to accept the disciplines of life, aware that these develop this excellent, brilliant virtue of patience in me.

Lord, I need patience to be content to wait at the traffic lights of life until it is your time for me to move on. Amen.

H. Howard Witmer, retired bishop in the Mennonite Church, and his wife, Miriam, live at Landis Homes Retirement Community, Lititz.

The Seasons of Life

"There is a time for everything, and a season for every activity under heaven." *Ecclesiastes 3:1*

"This is just the season of life that I'm in." As a mother of a two-year-old and a newborn, I find myself saying this quite often these days. From late nights and early mornings to the piles of laundry that never end to the fact that a play set recently replaced my dream of a patio and garden in our small city yard, the responsibilities of motherhood have moved into my life, filling every crack and crevice, pushing other things that used to seem important out of the way.

While it is true that my children will not be young forever (this is the season that I am in), and someday I *might* sleep and conquer laundry and have my city garden, I need to remember that my true rest will not come in this world, but in the next. The sacrifices I am making for my children have eternal significance for them, as well as for those whose lives they will touch. This time is an investment that will not return void.

The reality is that other seasons will come, bringing unique interruptions and inconveniences. As a disciple of Christ, I need to be okay with that. I hope that whatever season of life I am in, I will learn to embrace it, pressing on, making the sacrifices God is calling me to for the sake of building His kingdom (see Philippians 3:12-15).

Father God, help me to be eternity minded as I labor for Your kingdom in each season of my life. Holy Spirit, strengthen me and guide me as I press on with my eyes focused on the heavenly prize, "well done good and faithful servant." In Jesus' name, amen.

Emily Yoder is the wife of Travis and mother of Hollyn and Lyrie. She is a member of In The Light Ministries in Lancaster City.

Night Songs

"…who gives songs in the night." *Job 35:10*

"…in the night His song shall be with me." *Psalm 42:8*

I laid my head on the pillow and a song began forming in my slumbering mind. "Jesus, Jesus Lord to me, Master, Savior, Prince of Peace…" My head sank deeper into the pillow, and I allowed myself to be enraptured by the soothing words of this song as it played in my mind. Soon I was asleep only to partially waken two or three times through the night, when I would again hear this song. This happens most nights, fortunately with different songs. Does this happen to you? Am I the only one?

God loves us and desires that we have deep restful sleep. Music soothes the soul. Songs of worship draw us closer to Him, and in Him is the peace that passes understanding. It is in the quiet of the nighttime hour, when the physical busyness of our day is done, that God wants to take us aside and revel in His presence. Life's distractions have faded with the setting sun and our verbal communication with others is over, so now He draws us gently into His embrace.

Why songs in the night? They keep us adjusted to the truth that God loves and cares for us. At times I almost think I'm hearing songs from God's side of heaven. Then there are times when He speaks, and I have to pour out words of repentance. At other times, His assurance wraps around my soul and all is well.

I'm learning, although it is not always possible, to complete the duties of the day, return emails, phone calls and formulate plans of action for the days ahead enabling me to sleep well at night. I want to hear His "songs in the night."

Dear Lord, Help us to release the cares of our lives into Your loving care so we hear the music of heaven through the night. Amen.

Richard Armstrong serves as assistant director of The Worship Center Global Ministries in Lancaster.

I'm Glad He Died at the Mission

"Blessed are the pure in heart, for they will see God." *Matthew 5:8*

Darrell recently died on our campus. A resident found him slumped over in a bathroom stall with a used needle on the floor and another half used still in his hand. We miss him greatly. He was a fixture on this campus, for at least a year, before leaving the men's program the prior summer. His recent relapse was devastating and hard to watch unfold.

Community members often ask about the "success rate" of our programs. And I sort of know what the questioners are asking. They want to know how many formerly homeless "are now in a home, are working, aren't using drugs any longer, have been restored with their families, etcetera?" And, most of the time, I am not sure how to answer them in a way that satisfies. You see, I believe Darrell is a "success story."

It was on this campus that Darrell realized that he was loved by God and others. It was here that he heard hard truth—about his addiction, about his willingness to embrace lies about himself, about how he allowed fear to trump what God says about true reality. It was here that he grappled mightily with addiction and his position as a child of God. And it was to here that he returned in the middle of a relapse with a bag of heroin and a few needles in his hand.

You won't read about Darrell in one of our newsletters, and his death won't provide one of our year-end statistics. Yet, his stepmother's statement at the memorial service was most revealing. Though she was devastated by the loss of her stepson, she was able to say, "I'm glad that Darrell overdosed and died at the mission, in this place where he knew he was loved, rather than having to be found dead in a back alley."

Lord, help me to trust You with the paradoxes of life.

Steve Brubaker is the director of Residential Programs at Water Street Rescue Mission, Lancaster.

Slow Me Down, Lord

"Be still, and know that I am God; I will be exalted among the nations, I will be exalted in the earth." *Psalm 46:10*

Racing down a country road to pick up my son, I found that my mind sped along with the car. *What should I fix for supper? What else do I have going on tonight? Why does my son's friend have to live so far away?* Suddenly, a small, brown fawn scampered across the road. I slammed on the brakes, barely missing it. My daughter cried, "It's 'Bambi' Mommy! Look, there's another one!" We watched in awe as the first one bleated to the other to come across. Waiting in the cornfield, afraid of our car, the second fawn hesitated. "Let's go, Mommy, we're scaring them," my daughter suggested.

As I slowly drove away, I sensed the Lord gently saying to me, *Slow down, you're missing the beauty I've created for you to enjoy.* On the way back, we passed the same spot and shared the exciting sight with my son. I drove home in joyful appreciation of all God has for us—if only we take the time.

Lord, I'm so busy all the time. There's so much to do! Yet I want to be like Mary, resting at Your feet. Not like Martha, rushing around and missing being with You or hearing what You say. Thank You, for loving me through these busy times. Keep my focus on loving You, Lord.

Shirley Ann Bivens serves at Christ Community Church as preschool teacher and is a Christian clown (Coco the Clown). She is also a full-time "Grammy."

The Brokenhearted

"The Lord is close to the brokenhearted and saves those who are crushed in spirit." *Psalm 34:18*

I work at the Water Street Rescue Mission, where I have served in one capacity or another for the better part of eleven years. I work with the brokenhearted, with those whose spirits are crushed whether by choices they've made, circumstances beyond their control or a lethal blend of both. I come to work every day expecting to see God at work, and I am never disappointed.

But the clients whom I counsel often are disappointed. They may not yet know God, or they may not yet trust that He is good. Coming from failed homes and families, they may have no earthly model for their heavenly Father, or they have only negative, punitive prototypes.

In this context, much of what passes for Christian counsel may seem trite, pat, superficial—or at the other extreme, cerebral and super-spiritual. The words one Christian uses to comfort another believer can sound clichéd and self-referential to Mission clients whose experience of Christian community may be limited or worse, negative. Again and again, sitting with a client who has just begun to share her pain, I am struck dumb. But I have come to recognize that in this reverential silence, God speaks.

I'm reminded that the essence of incarnation is presence, not words. Looking back at points of searing sadness and family tragedy in my own life, I do not remember what people said to me; I remember their healing, incarnational presence.

"You may be the only Bible some people ever read," goes the old saying. I am humbled by that truth but also set free. I do not need to know what to say.

Father, thank You that You are the healer of broken hearts. Thank You that You choose to use me to serve those who are crushed in spirit. May I be silent that You may speak.

Daral Boles attends Community Fellowship Church and is the director of the Women's and Family Ministries at Water Street Rescue Mission, Lancaster.

Unto You, Lord

"Let us not become weary in doing good, for at the proper time we will reap a harvest if we do not give up." *Galatians 6:9*

It was party time! The only problem was that I wasn't celebrating. I was having a major pity party! There were no other guests, just me alone in the kitchen, making supper at the end of another hectic day as a stay-at-home mom.

As I stirred the contents of supper on the stove, I was mentally stirring all the "ingredients" of why I thought I had it *so* rough. I wasn't getting the recognition I deserved. I had meals on the table, a clean house and children cared for. Does anyone thank me? Does anyone see all the hard work I do around here? Poor me.

At that moment, it was as if God entered my kitchen and stood right beside me. I sensed him saying, "I see Teresa. Will you do what you do for me?" I remember dropping to my knees and weeping. "Yes, Lord, that is my heart. Unto you."

That lesson has never left me. I can hear him like it was yesterday. In all the seasons of life—work, ministry, home—I want to do what I do unto the Lord. When that is my motivation, joy comes, expectations are laid down, I am strengthened, renewed, and a real party can begin!

Lord, forgive me when I become self-focused. Help me to be motivated to serve for You and You alone, no matter what season of life I am in! Amen.

Teresa Groff serves in various ways at The Door Christian Fellowship.

Is There Life or Death in My Words?

"The tongue has the power of life and death." *Proverbs 18:21*

I am learning the importance of my words. The Bible says the tongue has the power of life and death. What I speak is so important, so powerful. I suffered with severe back problems and stomach issues for over a year. I had an ultrasound and an MRI. When nothing showed up on either of the tests, the doctor said he didn't know what else to do for me. There was literally nothing wrong with me physically. I had been prayed for many times, but nothing seemed to change.

I was telling a coworker about it, and he prayed for me. He then suggested I talk to the head of the healing ministry that I am involved with. I called them and they readily agreed to pray with me. As Sue prayed for me, I could feel the sensation of water flowing through my veins and out my fingertips. I knew God's healing power was flowing through me. I went away from that prayer time with the knowledge that Jesus had healed me.

However, the devil doesn't play fair. Almost every morning for weeks I would start feeling like I was going to get sick again. I would remind Satan of the verse, James 4:7, "resist the devil and he will flee from you." I would speak it out loud. "Satan, I resist you in Jesus' name. You have to flee now!" I was speaking words that Jesus said to speak, and Satan has to listen to Jesus.

As a child of Jesus, I know he has to listen to me too. He finally got the message that I was not going to accept this sickness anymore. He has tried a couple of times since to put it back on me, but every time I say out loud, "Satan, I resist you. You have to flee now in Jesus' name." Satan will try every trick in the book, but you do not have to accept anything from him. Resist him and he will flee.

Jesus, thank you for those very powerful words that we can speak in Your name. Thank you that Satan has to listen and obey You.

Brenda Boll serves as an elder, along with her husband, Steve, at Newport DOVE. She is on staff at House to House Publications.

They Wrestle in Prayer for Us

"Epaphras, who is one of you and a servant of Christ Jesus, sends greetings. He is always wrestling in prayer for you, that you may stand firm in all the will of God, mature and fully assured."
Colossians 4:12

God is such a big God! He can take two people from the billions of people on earth and intersect their paths for His purposes.

About six years ago a young Kenyan family relocated from Ohio to Pennsylvania…one mile away from our church building. They began to worship regularly with our congregation and became members. One day I was introduced to their mothers who had traveled from Kenya to visit them. Mike's mother completed her visit and returned to Kenya. Lucy's mother remained…worshiping and serving in our church. Our people grew to love her and she grew to love our congregation. By the time Mary Thogo returned to Kenya, God had called her to become an intercessor for me and our congregation.

It has been a few years since Mary returned to Kenya, but she has continued to faithfully wrestle in prayer for me and the people of Towerville. Many times the Lord has given her insight and words to share with me and others in the congregation. Only heaven will reveal the countless hours that she has labored in prayer so that we might "stand firm in all the will of God, mature and fully assured." Even now we are grateful that God called Mary to pray for us. With the Psalmist, we agree that "the Lord has done this, and it is marvelous in our eyes" (Psalm 118:23). We serve such a big God!

Father, I thank You for intercessors like Mary Thogo who wrestle in prayer for people like me. Father, they have needs, too. Bless them! Provide for their needs. Give them strength. Protect them today. In Jesus' name, amen!

Daniel Wagner serves as senior pastor of Towerville Christian Church in Coatesville and as president of the Ministers Alliance of Coatesville and vicinity.

The Measure of Success

"Your works are wonderful, I know that full well." *Psalm 139:14*

Our adventure in church planting is proving to be quite exciting, and we are seeing God on the move in many ways. We are expecting the arrival of a new "member" to our fellowship in the next few weeks— a baby the doctors said had slim chances of being conceived without infertility treatments. Not a problem for the God who created the entire universe! We personally are experiencing the miracle of God's provision for our family as we stepped out in faith to pursue full time ministry. Our passion to advance the kingdom in the Pottstown, Pennsylvania, area has been fueled as we build relationships with other pastors, churches and ministries in the area whose desire is to come together and press in to receive the heart of God for our communities. We are gathering, not only as our own congregation, but with others in the community as well, in intercession to see salvation come to the lost.

People often ask how things are "going" with the new church. I would say things are going well, not because we have grown in numbers (although we have) or because we have a polished worship team (which we don't), but because we see God moving—in us and on our behalf. The pages of our newsletter are filled with articles written by people in our fellowship, sharing from their heart what God is doing in their lives. So are we being successful as a new church plant? The reason I can say yes is because, really, none of the elements of a successful church are dependent on us! It is about God, and what He is doing in our midst—and He never fails!

All praise and glory goes to You, Jesus, our Lord! We depend totally on You today and every day!

Jessi Clemmer is a church planter at Koinonia House, Pottstown.

We Need to Reach Our Neighbors

"If My people who are called by My name humble themselves and pray and seek My face and turn from their wicked ways, then I will hear from heaven, will forgive their sin and will heal their land."
2 Chronicles 7:14

I was meditating on this verse outside early one morning and my neighbor came to visit. We began discussing the depth of the Word and how we need to reach out to our neighbors. This was the beginning of an annual neighborhood picnic held the first weekend in August to share with one another about who Jesus is in each of our lives.

Families have had a great time of sharing and meeting each other, whether for the first time or to get reacquainted. We had several families move in recently from larger cities who could not believe this was being offered. We had a great response the first summer, and our gathering showed us the need for a home Bible study. This Bible study started the next month meeting monthly in my home.

The Bible study group volunteers quarterly in an outreach ministry. We truly have been blessed, and the Holy Spirit has fallen fresh on us. We serve an awesome God. He is faithful!

Lord, may the Holy Spirit continue to fall afresh on Your people. May we not be complacent in our work for You. May we not grow weary, and may we keep our eyes fixed on the author and finisher of our faith, Jesus Christ.

Julie Carroll serves as the local Nazarene Mission Director.

Too Good to Be True

"May he give you the desire of your heart and make all your plans succeed. He will shout for joy when you are victorious and will lift up our banners in the name of the Lord. May the Lord grant you all your requests." Psalm 20:4–6

My husband worked in automobile sales, a job that had long hours, working every Saturday and evenings during the week. For eighteen years this was our life. The long hours were starting to get to both him and me. I went to every church function by myself. Many people thought I was unmarried because I never had my spouse with me. At least we could attend church together.

I longed for him to be home more. I used to cry and ask the Father to give him another job. But, reasoning kicked in and I would waver with my questions. Who is going to hire a sixty-two-year-old man? I knew in my heart God wanted to bless my husband. I used to pray, "Lord, bless my husband. Bless him abundantly." I told my husband about my prayer time on the way home from church one winter Sunday. I said, "Tom, God wants to bless you, and you have to receive what he has for you." So, we prayed a prayer of agreement.

A few months went by and one night Tom came to me. He said, "How would you like for me to have a job in Commercial Leasing of autos and trucks, working Monday through Friday 8:00 a.m. to 5:00 p.m.? No nights or weekends, with a company car and insurance."

I thought it sounded too good to be true. Tom had sold a man a fleet of cars. This gentleman liked Tom very much and kept coming back each year. Tom displayed the fruit of the spirit while he worked and it paid off. He was offered the job and took it!

We are really enjoying spending more time together. Oh, and with the price of gas—well that's included too. Isn't God good? He really and truly hears the desires of our heart.

You are so wonderful, Father. Forgive me for bringing you down to my human understanding. Please increase my faith and help my unbelief that I will always trust You without question. Amen.

Cynthia Cotter is a Licensed Prayer Minister through DCFI and attends Reading Dove, in Reading.

Fruit in Every Season

"Those who are planted in the house of the Lord shall flourish in the courts of our God." *Psalms 92:13 (New King James Version)*

My friend began our prayer meeting with this note: "I'm thinking of selling my business." That would mean forsaking his source of income and completely trusting God for his family's needs. As we prayed, I heard in my spirit, "Hebrews 10:9." My friend looked it up and read, "God takes away the first that He may establish the second."

Suddenly, as he read I saw in a vision my friend crossing a bridge. I then realized that the bridge was burning away behind him as he walked over it! I said, "God burns our bridges while we're still on them!" We knew we had God's confirmation, and the sale of the business went through. But I was scared. I just told my friend to give up his source of income! How would he provide for his family?

I began to be worried, but God rebuked me. "Read Jeremiah 17." I read, "Blessed is the man who trusts in the Lord...He will be like a tree planted by the water that sends out its roots by the stream. It does not fear when heat comes; its leaves are always green. It has no worries in a year of drought and never fails to bear fruit."

I have watched my friends live deeply, abiding in God and knowing Him as their source of strength and supply. I see in them ones whose lives are a daily expression of God's goodness, truly bearing fruit in every season.

Father, may I, too, trust so securely in You that I hardly notice drought, trouble, and offenses, but always bear fruit worthy of Your name.

Lee Ritz is praying for kingdom fruitfulness as part of the Reading Regional Transformation Network.

Me Time

"The Lord said to him, "Who gives man his mouth?...It is I, the Lord. Now, go! I will help you to speak, and I will tell you what to say." *Exodus 4:11–12*

Getting on an airplane and away from my four young children for the first time in six years, I anticipated peace, tranquility and a whole lot of "me" time. I found my seat, made a little small talk with the stranger beside me and opened my book.

"What are you reading?"

Groooaaaan! Who is this person and why is he interrupting *my* time?!

As I showed him the cover of the Christian literature I was reading, I heard God gently speaking to me, nudging me, encouraging me to reach out.

"Are you a Christian?" I asked.

And thus began a most dynamic conversation regarding salvation, the gospel message, and our personal struggles and triumphs as we seek God's truth. I was able to share all the attempts I had made at trying to "save myself" from my sins, my guilt, my shame and my hurt. And that only when I fell to my knees and laid it all before Jesus, finally putting all my trust in Him, did I find the healing and restoration that made me whole.

It was a short flight, and our time soon came to an end. My new friend thanked me for giving him so much to think about and so much to believe in.

I am also thankful that I have such an exciting story to tell. That my gracious and Holy God is so alive in our everyday lives. And that He reminds me that rather than "me time," I can find abundant peace and tranquility in sharing "He time."

Lord, help me to keep Your truths always in my mind, on my tongue and in my heart. Open my eyes to see those that need to hear Your promises and know of Your love. Thank you for giving me the words to say to give You the glory You deserve.

Amy Domencic serves at Susquehanna Valley Pregnancy Services as a volunteer counselor.

My Prayers Were Answered

"Take the helmet of salvation and the sword of the Spirit, which is the word of God. And pray in the Spirit on all occasions with all kinds of prayers and requests...." *Ephesians 6:17–18*

In January of 2008, my son had a lower than normal temperature. I took him to the doctor, and we decided we should run some blood tests. They revealed a slightly elevated thyroid level. We were to retest in six months.

The July results came back almost three points higher. Our doctor then consulted a specialist and prepared a treatment plan. I was shocked by the news, and as I hung up the phone, I started to pray in tongues and declared healing over my son. I was healed of a thyroid goiter in 2004, and I knew the Lord could heal him as well. As I prayed, I asked the Lord for more time. I wanted to have him prayed for and to be healed before being placed on medication for the rest of his life.

My prayers were answered two days later when the doctor called and asked for another set of tests before treatment run at the lab of my choice, with results back in two weeks. That day, Wednesday, I called the church and asked everyone to pray and lay hands on my son. I felt that the Lord wanted me to wait until Monday to have the tests taken. While his blood was being drawn, the lady said, "Did you know your blood is blue? You are royalty!" I immediately knew that was a sign from the Lord. We are all royalty; we are sons and daughters of the Most High!

Ten days later the doctor reported that now the results showed no thyroid problems. He is in the normal range. Praise the Lord for healing my son!

Dear Lord, thank you for Your Word and Your promises to us. When doubt and fear try to overcome my mind, I give all my doubts and fears to You. I thank You for Your healing power available to us today.

Michele Apicella is a member of Christ Community Church in Camp Hill and serves on the ministry team and youth staff.

Let Me Help You

"I call on you, O God, for you will answer me, give ear to me and hear my prayer." *Psalm 17:6*

While driving fifty-five miles per hour east on the Pennsylvania Turnpike with two young children in the van, the rooftop carrier flew off. I quickly pulled over and praised God that no one was hurt. After picking up the empty carrier, I began the attempt to squeeze the carrier into the van. Trying several different maneuvers, I eventually gave up in defeat.

The year was 1992, before most people owned cell phones. I was relieved to see a turnpike call box only a few yards in front of the van. Walking the short distance to the phone, I kept a close eye on the van that held my youngest son and his friend. After making the call, I returned to the van and waited with the children.

Shortly, to my delight, a police officer pulled in behind us. My delight soon became fear as the officer yelled at me for calling him, stating that he had more important things to do with his time. As I fought back tears, I explained to him that I was alone with two small children and didn't have the strength to secure the carrier to the roof.

As the officer returned to his car to make radio contact with his supervisor, I prayed, "Dear Lord, please soften this man's heart toward us." A few minutes later the officer returned and said, "I'm sorry ma'am for the way I spoke to you earlier. I was wrong. Let me help you."

The officer and I worked together to secure the carrier. Soon the children and I were safely on our way in no time at all.

Thank you, Father, for giving ear to my prayer. I praise You.

Patty Eastep is director of PATH, serving families through life skill classes in Columbia, Ephrata and Lancaster.

Where Are You God?

"...Your Father in heaven is not willing that any of these little ones should be lost." *Matthew 18:14*

When my brother was twelve years old, he asked Jesus to come into his heart. He talked a lot about the beauty of heaven which created a curiosity within my heart. I was about eight when I came home from school one day and found my mother and sister gone. I was sure Jesus had come and taken my family to heaven, and because I was too bad, He left me behind. It was traumatic until my mother and sister came home from a delayed appointment.

One summer night our family went to a revival tent meeting, the one with the sawdust trail. I was very attentive to the pastor's message. When he gave the invitation to go to heaven when you die, I wanted to run up that trail. But when I asked permission, I was told I was too young to understand. I cried myself to sleep that night!

A few years later that same pastor who invited us to prepare for heaven committed suicide. My faith in God and His people was destroyed for a long time.

These childhood experiences crushed my tender, vulnerable heart, but God loved me too much to leave me in my bruised condition. He protected me as He carried me in His arms until I learned to trust Him completely with His everlasting love. He was there all the time.

I survived those trials and many more over the years. Now I can tell others of God's amazing grace. I have a passion for those who are lost and hurting and need healing. I find joy in leading them to the same Savior who is waiting with loving arms for anyone who receives Him.

God, thank you for being the healer of broken hearts.

Dona L. Fisher is chairman of the local National Day of Prayer, president of Change of Pace Bible Studies, and is a free-lance writer for Lancaster Sunday Newspaper.

Our Eternal Home

"For we know that if our earthly house, this tent, is destroyed, we have a building from God, a house not made with hands, eternal in the heavens." *2 Corinthians 5:6 (New King James Version)*

In my mind's eye, I lived an idyllic childhood until I was eight years old, when my father decided that he didn't want to be married to my mother anymore. Before my folks' divorce, my summer days consisted of playing among the Shasta daisies and the pollen-saturated buttercups. My winter days were comprised of Santa Claus, cookie-cutting and Barbie dolls. I was as happy as any child could be. After my folks' divorce and my dad's remarriage, I felt adrift at sea, not knowing where I belonged.

It wasn't until I was midway through college that I actually felt a strong pull to return to my childhood home. I tried to find my Garden of Eden, but to no avail. And I realized that I could never return to my childhood days. The door had been forever barred. No matter how much I wished it, my parents weren't going to magically remarry, and all the heartache of the past wasn't going to go away. I couldn't bring back that feeling of being at home ever again. At least not in this life.

I long to be home where I'll be whole again—a place where I'm safe, secure and loved. That longing is what's keeping me alive, pushing me along to my true home, where God lives. I've put my faith in that home. It's what my hope rests on. I trust that one day I'll be home again walking among the daisies and buttercups. And I'll never be asked to leave again.

Dear God, thank you for building a home for me in heaven, and thank you for Your promise to wipe away all of my tears. In Your name I pray, amen.

Wendy Komancheck free-lances from her home, writing about small business, agriculture and tea. You can reach her at wendykomancheck@yahoo.com.

He First Loved Us

"He will rejoice over you with singing." *Zephaniah 3:17*

For one to two weeks the brief song was on repeat mode in my head. Day after day, hour after hour, I heard, "I love You more, more than yesterday. I love You more, more than I can say. I love You more, more than anything. I love You more. I love You more." I seldom listened. But the message was always the same; "I love You more."

I knew the song was an expression of a child's love to his Father, a sinner's love to his Savior, and a slave's love for his Redeemer. While I wanted it to be my song, a sense of disappointment and personal failure were like a barrier preventing me from fully owning the message to the Lord. Yet the song played on, over and over and over again.

Finally, I felt compelled to intentionally listen to the whole thing despite my struggle with sincerity and integrity. As I listened, I dissolved into tears. The Holy Spirit was tenderly singing it *to* me. "I love you more, more than yesterday. I love you more, more than I can say. I love you more, more than anything. I love you more, I love you more." I don't know the theological defense of God's ability to love us more. But I do know the theological reality of God's love that is beyond comprehension. He had just demonstrated it to me in a very personal, intimate way.

Immediately, the response rose from my heart, "I love You more, more than yesterday...I love You more."

Thank you for Your perfect, faithful, consistent, tender and persistent love. Thank you for helping me to comprehend Your incomprehensible love. Thank you for loving me more than my pain and doubt, more than the sense of failure or not being good enough.

Ruth Ann Stauffer, wife, mother, grandmother and friend, is a prophetic intercessor who still has much to learn and grow in God's amazing love.

The Fred Box

"One generation will commend your works to another; they will tell of your mighty acts." *Psalm 145:4*

What will your legacy be? Almost twelve years after the boys' father passed away in an automobile accident, they wanted to learn more about him. Michael was nineteen months old and Freddie was due to be born within days when the accident occurred.

Their newfound interest was sparked by a writing assignment Michael had to complete for school. He had to write about a very sad time and a very happy time in his life. Thinking it would be a piece of cake, Michael jumped at the chance. He would write about when his dad died in the accident and when his current dad married me (his mom).

The more Michael thought about the accident, he realized he wanted to know more about his biological dad. Freddie shared his interest too, so we began to explore the contents of the "Fred Box" together. The boys gained a greater connection and appreciation for their dad and each one wanted to keep one of his belongings in memory of him.

As we were deciding who would get what, I came across a microcassette recorder with a tape inside. I turned it on, and we all fell silent as we listened to Fred practice a sermon about the thief on the cross.

Of the few sermons Fred had an opportunity to preach, this was one that really did represent his own life. He too had had an illicit past and was humbled by the awesome saving grace of God. Of all the "things" the boys could keep for themselves in the box, hearing their father's passionate presentation of the gospel was the one thing that could not be lost or taken away. He had left to them the legacy of his faith.

Thank You Jesus for Your awesome saving grace! May the lives we live today create a legacy of faith for our children tomorrow.

Chris McNamara works with Life Transforming Ministries in Coatesville and is a Woman of Hope leader at Hopewell Christian Fellowship in Elverson.

I'll Do It!

"I waited patiently for the Lord; and He inclined to me, and heard my cry. He also brought me up out of a horrible pit, out of the miry clay, and set my feet upon a rock, and established my steps."
Psalm 40:1–2 (New King James Version)

As she sat across from me, I was struck by the weight of shame that covered her like a shroud. The word *abortion* stuck on her tongue, but emblazoned itself on her soul, tainting her words, clouding her countenance and affecting every relationship in her life. Sadly, my words of comfort and God's truth seemed to fall on deaf ears.

Over the next four years, sporadic phone calls and notes kept us connected. Her argument was constant. "God can heal me! I don't need you or anyone else. Why does anyone need to know about my past?" How passionately and persistently the Lord pursued her, repeatedly inviting her to embark on a journey whose destination was healing and freedom. Not easily defeated, the enemy also incessantly threw obstacles in her path—lies, sickness, fear, distractions of many sizes and shapes.

One morning in desperation, she cried out to God, "Please help me! I can't forgive myself. I'm not going to call Carol, but if You want me to do this Post-Abortion Bible Study, You'll have to make her call me." And He did! That same morning as I was preparing to start another Bible study, the Holy Spirit prompted me to make one more phone call. A year had gone by since she and I had talked. As I began explaining why I was calling, she interrupted, "I will do it! I'll come to the Bible study." Once again, faithful, loving Papa Father calls one of His daughters out of captivity.

Thank You, Father, that You see the state of our hearts. Continue pursuing men and women caught in abortion's web of condemnation and shame. Open their hearts to hear and the courage to accept Your invitation to heal their wounds in the way You choose. Thank You, dear Papa.

Carol Weaver serves as the director of Post-Abortion Ministry with Susquehanna Valley Pregnancy Services.

Do You Have Ears?

"My sheep listen to my voice...." *John 10:27*

Recently a number of people from our church were planning to go on a short-term mission trip to Nicaragua. My husband and I felt the Lord wanted our sixteen-year-old son, Josiah, to participate, but we also believed it was important for him to hear God if, in fact, this was a divine directive.

So, Josiah prayed but continued to report he didn't have an answer. We were getting down to the wire. He had to make a commitment in the next few days, but was still hearing nothing. Then at his youth meeting he asked Jim, his youth leader, to specifically pray with him for an answer. When they finished praying, Jim told him, "I believe God is going to clearly speak to you on the way home tonight."

Now, our church is about seven minutes from our house, so if God was going to speak there would only be a small window of opportunity. But, about halfway home, Josiah happened to spot a landscaping truck parked by the road. Painted on its side was an acronym for its business, Y.E.S. in big bold letters. Josiah *knew* God had given him his answer. Some might call it a coincidence, but I believe God wanted to teach a young boy about the importance of expecting to hear His voice.

Hearing God is not reserved only for preachers and prophets. No less than fifteen times, the Scripture admonishes "those who have ears to hear."

If we have ears we qualify to have God speak to us. God is a communicating God. Let's confidently *expect* Him to speak to us. I believe He probably speaks more than we realize. But if we're not anticipating His voice, we're not positioning ourselves to hear.

Father, thank you for giving us ears to hear. Please help us become better listeners. May we learn to greet each day with the expectation of hearing Your voice.

Becky Toews leads the women's ministry at New Covenant Christian Church and is an adjunct professor at Lancaster Bible College.

In the Creator's Image

"So God created man in his own image, in the image of God he created him; male and female he created them." *Genesis 1:27*

What an amazing thought; we are created in the image of God. The Creator of the Universe paused to make man in His image and placed him in the Garden of Eden. The garden was a paradise—full of life and a place of fellowship between God and man.

Even though man and woman were later banished from the garden because of sin, God made a way for fellowship to be restored. Today we can enjoy a personal relationship with God, through Jesus, that is full of life and brings joy to His heart. As we grow in our relationship with Him, we become more like Him and reflect His glory to those around us.

We are called to be a light in the darkness, and bring hope to the hopeless. God has placed dreams, talents and abilities in our lives that he desires to use to touch people's lives. Remember we are created in the Creator's image, and He wants to release creativity in our lives in a greater way to reflect His glory to a world living in the darkness.

I encourage you to spend sometime contemplating God's creativity and ask how He wants to reveal His glory in and through your life. Maybe there was something He asked you to lay down for a season, because it was an idol in your life. Perhaps, now under His lordship and leading it will become an instrument for His glory.

Dear God, draw me closer to You today and make me more like You. Fill me with Your dreams and release Your creativity in my life to reflect Your glory to those around me.

Mark Van Scyoc is a programmer analyst, free-lance photographer and serves as Mission Director at DOVE Christian Fellowship, Westgate Celebration in Ephrata.

Tunnel Vision

"God has made a way of escape...therefore flee!"
1 Corinthians 10:13–14

Several years ago, I went with several people from our church on a mission trip to Bosnia. While in the city of Sarajevo, we visited a museum dedicated to a rescue tunnel that the people of the city constructed during the recent ethnic war in Bosnia. At that time, the Serbs and Croate forces camped on the mountains that surrounded the city of Sarajevo. The enemy guns picked off occupants of the city as easily as ducks in a small pond. So many Muslims died, bodies were interred on top of other bodies already in cemeteries or even buried in public parks. The siege cut off all food and medical supplies to the city. The city fought for survival. At last a secret tunnel was built that allowed aid to flow once again into the town.

As I walked through a portion of that rough-hewn tunnel I could easily imagine the desperation of those who had trudged its narrow corridor. It represented hope. It offered safety.

Back home safely in Pennsylvania, I again pondered how the tunnel had provided a way of escape for the citizens of Sarajevo, much like Hezekiah's tunnel provided hope for the people of Jerusalem during a siege by the Assyrians. Today, when you or I face temptations, we may feel like we too are under siege, but according to 1 Corinthians 10:13, no matter how difficult the situation, God promises that He has already provided us with a way to escape.

How foolish the people of Sarajevo would have been if they had access to the tunnel but didn't bother to use it. And how foolish we would be to ignore God's way of escape from our temptations. Let's not stand there wringing our hands when we can find our aid in God! That is why the next verse begins, "Therefore, flee!" He alone is able to bring us to safety.

Lord, when I face temptation, help me see the tunnel of escape and run through it to You.

Emily Parke Chase works with the Capital Area Pregnancy Centers of Camp Hill and is author of *Why Say No When My Hormones Say Go?* (Christian Publications, 2003).

Photo by Lisa Hildebrand

A Quiet Storm in the Office

"...Whoever slaps you on your right cheek, turn the other to him also. If anyone wants to sue you and take your shirt, let him have your coat also. Whoever forces you to go one mile, go with him two." *Matthew 5:39–41*

Little did Andrew know that all these past weeks, Steve had really been taking advantage of him at the office. Steve was always a nice man, smiling and friendly; he usually seemed to be right on top of the workload. However, one day, as Andrew was packing up his briefcase to leave, he happened to notice Steve replacing a document back into his own work folder, a photocopy of the same paper in Steve's other hand.

Shocked, Andrew approached him, "Steve, can I help you with something in my folder?"

Steve's face turned brick red, his eyes grew wide as he faced him, "N-no," he stammered, "I just had to check something. I'm heading home now. Good-bye!"

"Wait a moment, Steve!" Andrew called him back. "Listen, I know that's a copy of my paper...Can I help you figure something out with it? Really, I'm not angry. Can we try to work through this?"

Steve's face fell, "I've been under so much pressure lately...My wife just got diagnosed—I've been falling behind. I can't lose this job."

Andrew placed a hand on Steve's shoulder. Together, they sat down that evening, and after working through Steve's office work, Andrew gently took his opportunity to tell Steve all about the Savior who could give him peace in the middle of life's storms.

Jesus, thank you for giving me the patience and temperance to reflect Your gentle love to others. May You forgive me, as I have forgiven those who have injured me. Thank you for Your salvation!

Mandy Satta is a full-time student at Lancaster Bible College and Graduate School.

Get Out of the Boat!

"So Peter went over the side of the boat and walked on the water toward Jesus. But when he saw the strong wind and the waves, he was terrified and began to sink... You have so little faith; why did you doubt me?" *Matthew 14:29–31 (New Living Translation)*

I was facing a very difficult time in my marriage, and there was chaos in every situation. A friend of mine, who knew my struggles, called to see how things were going. For some reason out of my mouth came, "I'm doing well. I'm in the boat and feel safe."

Later on when I was visiting her mom, she showed me some books that she was interested in and wanted to share them with me. She plopped those books down on my lap, and when I looked down I almost fell out of my chair. The very first book's title was *If You Want to Walk on Water, Get Out of the Boat.* I couldn't believe it! I looked at my friend and said, "That's my problem. I need to get out of the boat."

As I read that book and reflected on the Scripture in Matthew 14:22-36, I realized that my sense of safety was really a lack of faith in the Lord. I have since gotten out of the boat, yet at times, find myself climbing back in for the very same reason that Peter did. I'm realizing that when I take my focus off Him, I sink. I want so desperately to walk on the water with the Lord, but I know I need to trust Him more to do that. Life is a journey and with each day I learn to walk on it a little longer.

Lord, help us to keep our focus on You and to trust You in all the storms of life. It is by Your strength alone that we can continue on. Help us to walk with You longer each day.

Eileen Christiansen is a leader/youth leader of Celebrate Recovery, a twelve-step Christ-centered program in Sadsburyville.

Wearing the Garments of the King

"...Behold those who wear soft clothes are in kings' palaces."
Matthew 11:8

Have you ever seen a little girl put on a dress that makes her feel like a princess? Have you ever seen a bride picking out her wedding dress?

One evening I dropped by my granddaughter's home with a shopping bag full of new "gently worn" dresses from the thrift shop. She and the bag disappeared into her roomy closet that doubles as her "back stage" dressing room.

One by one she appeared and I applauded how lovely she looked, and we imagined the occasions where she would wear the outfit. There would be picnics and parties and Bible school and preschool. About the third try-on, there emerged from back stage, not my granddaughter, but a princess of the King of Kings. Her countenance spoke her delight in this particular garment. She was instantly twirling and lifting her hands and then holding out her skirt to curtsy. That particular dress made her feel completely comfortable and "silky soft" as she said. She felt lovely and her countenance reflected the transformation.

I now remember the moment her mother stepped out of the bridal shop dressing room in just the right "silky soft" garment. Her face, too, was glowing, and she just knew her groom would welcome the sight of her coming down the aisle in this one.

There is a moment when the King dresses us in His garments of praise, His righteousness, and we are transformed into the likeness of a daughter or son of the Most High. It truly changes our countenance!

Do you remember the moment of the joy of your salvation? Be clothed in that moment today and go out with a joy-filled countenance and "silky soft" peace. Others may want to know where you got your outfit.

Emerge from your prayer closet clothed in garments of praise today! Smile like you've been with the King. Curtsy and twirl!

Lord, may we reflect the joy of Your salvation today!

Nancy Clegg is a worshiper and mobilizer in the regional church and the nations.

All Things Work Together

"... all things work together for good to those who love God, to those who are called according to His purpose." *Romans 8:28*
(New King James Version)

My mother was in critical condition in intensive care, having collapsed in my arms after an aneurysm burst in her brain. I experienced the privilege and trauma of keeping her alive, giving her mouth-to-mouth resuscitation while waiting for the ambulance. Having come to Christ a few years before, I wanted nothing more than for my anxious, cynical, Jewish mother to know Him as well. I knew God could use tragedy for good, and hoped He would do so as she fought for her life.

As she lay in the hospital room with a roommate who was in a coma from a head trauma, I prayed: "Father, please let this man wake up and please reveal Yourself to my mother."

I learned later that day that God had dramatically answered my prayer within hours. Her roommate spontaneously woke up and asked for his wife. My mother slipped into unconsciousness after experiencing a brain stem spasm. She later told me, "I was conscious of being unconscious and it was terrifying. But then, out of the darkness, the face of Jesus Christ appeared to me."

Despite this experience, she declined to place her faith in Christ, expressing concern that my father would divorce her if she became a Christian. Eighteen years later, I again asked God to reveal Himself to her "the same way You did in the intensive care unit." At that moment, miles away, the face of Jesus Christ appeared to her once again, just as He had years before. This time, she accepted my invitation to receive Christ and I had the privilege of leading her in prayer later that day as she finally asked Christ to come into her heart.

Father, give us the faith to trust You in the midst of tragedy, believing You will accomplish Your purposes.

Dave Wiedis is the executive director of Serving Leaders Ministries in West Chester, a ministry that provides pastoral care to pastors, ministry leaders and their families.

Just Like a Child

"Unless you are converted and become as a child you can not enter into the kingdom of heaven. Therefore whoever humbles himself as a little child is the greatest in the kingdom of heaven."
Matthew 18:3–4

Many years back I had the awesome privilege to travel the western part of the States with my husband. We did many things that stretched my ability to trust God, like rock climbing at Red Rock Park in Colorado and riding a tram over a highway in Utah. But the one thing during the trip that God kept revealing during these adventures was a fear of heights. I am not sure what state I was in, but I was on the stairs at a midway point at Seven Falls when my legs froze and fear overcame me. I quickly said to my husband, "Bill, I can't move or I will fall."

He replied, "Hon, you can't stand here in the middle of the stairs. There are people behind us."

With that a young boy said to me, "Lady, don't be afraid. Just do like this and follow me. You won't fall." Bill came alongside me and undergirded me as I followed the little boy to the top of the falls.

Just recently, I have looked back on that adventure and thought how life changing that experience has become. Just like a child, I was humbled to receive and able to surrender that fear of heights to the Lord, and it took a child to lead me. Approaching other challenges of life from this position has been some of my greatest experiences.

Father, thank you for the awesome blessing of allowing children to be the example to receiving Your kingdom. When fear comes at us big and scary, may we approach it just like a child and enter into Your kingdom without fear of falling, for You are always there to undergird us.

Debbie Davenport serves at Cornerstone Pregnancy Care Services and as an intercessor in various settings for the purpose of unity and regional transformation.

Behold, Our God

"The heavens are telling of the glory of God; and their expanse is declaring the work of His hands." *Psalms 19:1*

Many times I've been called outside by my precious family to witness the beauty of the sun going down. "Come quick!" is the command. "Ya gotta' see this!" is the cry. "Behold, our God!" is the unspoken decree, "…gaze at His Glory!"

And gaze, we do. Something in us says, "Soak this in." We breathe deeply and marvel at the fleeting beauty we are privileged to observe.

I have fond memories of times when our children were still young, and my husband would corral us all out onto the porch to witness the fury of a summertime lightening storm. Peering through the downpour, we'd be amazed by the awesome display of God's immeasurable power.

When the sky is an expanse of complete darkness and the God of thunder detonates lightening bolts across the heavens, it commands our respect and humbles our sense of self-importance. And when the Creator of the Universe splashes His unending canvas with incomparable color from His perpetual palette, causing the sky to appear as if it's been painted by hand, it fills us with wonder that He actually wants to share such magnificent splendor with us.

Replying to Job's complaints, the Maker of Heaven and Earth inquired, "Have you ever in your life commanded the morning, and caused the dawn to know its place," and "Can you send forth lightnings that they may go and say to you, 'Here we go?'"

Job's response says it all, "Behold, I am insignificant; what can I reply to Thee? I lay my hand on my mouth."

Amazing image, isn't it? Unwilling to take the risk of saying another word he covers his lips, ensuring his silence. There were no words left to say.

Lord, how grateful I am that You speak to me through Your creation so clearly and powerfully. You leave me speechless…

Kathi Wilson and her husband, Mark, co-authors of *Tired of Playing Church* and co-founders of Body Life Ministries, are members of Ephrata Community Church.

World View

"Then she called the name of the Lord who spoke to her, You-Are-the-God-Who-Sees; for she said, "Have I also here seen Him who sees me?" *Genesis 16:13 (King James Version)*

The visibility was great from my window seat as our flight began its long descent over central Pennsylvania. It seemed that our flight pattern over the mountains was similar to ones I had observed from the ground during childhood.I began to recognize the landscape. Could I see my childhood home?

From over two miles above I began to plot our location as if I were a human GPS (Global Positioning System). I traced the river, town, village, roads, and fields. There it was: the house we called home!

I reflected on how my perspective of life had changed since childhood. When I lived between those mountains, my worldview consisted of relationships, culture and life as I knew it there.

Since then I had established a new home in another community. I had traveled to many parts of the world and my worldview had expanded through my experiences.

More importantly, my world view had been shaped by seeing life more and more from God's point of view—recognizing Him at work in other cultures and locales.

My worldview was limited as a child. It has grown through life experience, but I recognize it is still very limited unless I learn to see things from God's point of view. When I ask the question, "How does God see this?" I begin to see my situation on the earth much more from His world view.

How good it is to have glimpses each day through His Word, His Spirit, His people of our world as He sees it.

Lord, Your view of my world is far greater than that of an astronaut or any one of the billions of galaxies beyond this solar system. Help me to see things from Your point of view today.

Keith Yoder is the chair of the Regional Council of the Regional Church of Lancaster County and president of Teaching The Word Ministries.

God Is My Refuge and Strength

"God is our refuge and strength, a very present help in trouble."
Psalm 46:1 (New American Standard Bible)

As the airplane accelerated down the runway-tears flowed down my face. After all, it was two months to the day of the terrorist attacks upon our nation, and the last place I wanted to be was on an airplane. Listening to worship songs on my portable headset helped me to stay focused on God, yielding my fears to Him. Since Jesus Christ is my Lord and Savior, I knew a warm welcome awaited me in heaven if the plane crashed. However, I feared a potential fiery ordeal. God was encouraging me to believe, "My times are in Thy hand" (Psalm 31:15a.).

One lesson that I have had to learn repeatedly, during times of testing, is that I can depend on God's love for me. During such testing I was convinced that my sanity would be lost, learning to exercise such trust. After all, my earthly father was not trustworthy; he abandoned me when his support was greatly needed. Thankfully, I can attest to the faithfulness of my heavenly Father!

As I have learned to trust that God is, indeed, my refuge and strength, I have had opportunities for joyful tears to flow, out of a sense of awe and gratitude. Recently, I graduated from college at the age of fifty-four, a testimony to God's love and grace operative in my life. Also, at a ministry where I volunteer my supervisor said, "You are an answer to prayer." Before becoming a Christian I could have been described many ways, but not as an answer to prayer. What a mighty God we love and serve!

All those difficult baby steps of believing have yielded undreamed of blessings. For example, I had long ago given up the desire to finish my bachelor's degree. "Taste and see that the Lord is good. Oh, the joys of those who take refuge in him" (Psalm 34:8 NLT).

Thank You, Father, for Your steadfast patience, faithful love and dependable character.

Susan Marie Davis is a member of Calvary Church in Lancaster.

The Perfect Place

"Nevertheless, each one should retain the place in life that the Lord assigned to him and to which God has called him...."
1 Corinthians 7:17

Trucks and cars roar by, only a few yards from my face, as I stab my spade into the clumps of weeds and gently pry them away from the indigo blue petunias in the front border of my house. A billow of truck exhaust reaches my nose, and I hold my breath for a moment, sigh and continue weeding. I hadn't wanted to buy this small fixer upper on the busy street near the college with the traffic and the student parties that rage all around. But my professor husband, who had always dreamed of walking to work as well as of renovating an old house, loved the place. So we moved in, and I planted a bright flower border to make the place mine.

Today as I look back over the freshly weeded strip of earth, I'm struck by the bright beauty of the fresh green and blue plants against the dark earth. In spite of weeds, car fumes and a frequent littering of empty beer cans, these trailing petunias have sent out green vines and bright blue trumpets over the ground. I'm reminded that in spite of my reluctance to be in this place, God has used me to send out the fresh green vines and brightness of His presence.

On this sidewalk as the cars zoomed past, I prayed with a neighbor girl. In my kitchen, I've prayed with professors. And after God enabled us to buy the student rental next door, one roomer started a Bible study. Because I'm in this place, willing to share the love of Christ, fresh vines have begun their progression over the landscape of lives.

Even when I don't like the place You've called me to, Father, bring me opportunities to make it the perfect place to share Your love with others.

Robin Mooneyham Archibald is a free-lance writer who attends Grace Baptist Church of Millersville.

Transformed

"The Lord will surely comfort Zion and will look with compassion on all her ruins, he will make her deserts like Eden, her wastelands like the garden of the Lord...." *Isaiah 51:3*

It was early spring and I was surveying my new yard. Our family of eight had moved into this beautiful, older home in the fall. However, the yard hadn't been touched in years and was overgrown. My husband, Chris, had just finished a week of "vacation" spent clearing bushes and brush from our corner lot. I was amazed at how much he had accomplished. Still, I lamented over the barren patches of earth the roots had left behind. I despised the remaining scrubby bushes that Chris didn't have time to dig out.

"How I wish he could have finished the job! How I long to see grass growing and flowers blooming! One of my favorite signs of spring is the delicious smell of lilacs in the air. Lord, how can I get ahold of a lilac bush and get rid of these awful ones?"

Days passed, leaves came forth in the warm sunlight, and I surveyed my yard again. I couldn't believe my eyes! Two of the ugly eyesores had been transformed into lilac bushes! The tiny lavender buds held the promise of that glorious scent.

"Thank you, God, that Chris wasn't overzealous in his yard work after all!" I prayed with overwhelming gratitude. God answered in His gentle way.

"You wish that I would remove all the ugly parts of your life. You even blame yourself that they still remain. But you don't judge as I judge. Under your barren ground there are seeds that will grow! I have allowed the thorns in your life to remain because I know that when the spring season comes, they will bloom and blossom. Then you will realize that the blessings you had prayed for have been with you all the while in disguise…as a trial."

God, help me to see my life as You do, full of Your promise and potential.

Anne Brandenburg is the wife of Chris, a pastor at Life Center Ministries and the mother of six.

Teach Me Lord

"All scripture is God-breathed and is useful for teaching, rebuking, correcting and training in righteousness." *2 Timothy 3:16*

My daughter, Alana, had struggled with Tourette's syndrome since she was four years old. On a family vacation, at the beach, we decided to go to the movies. If you know anything about Tourette's, you know the movie theater is not the best place to be. We mumbled a quick prayer, "*Lord, help Tourette's to be silent during the movie.*" As we watched the whole movie, Alana did not make a sound. When we came out, she announced to all of us, "God healed me."

Well, I wanted to believe what my twelve-year-old had just proclaimed was true, but I also wanted proof. Looking back, I was slow to recognize it as a healing because my heart was not ready to receive it. The next two years, Alana's Tourette's was dormant (now we know why). We slowly cut back on her medication and God started working on my relationship with Him.

He began fine-tuning all the truths in His Word I knew and gave me brand-new revelation about the ones I didn't. I spent time just pouring over the Word and letting it soak in. After a few months, my prayer life began to feel electric. As soon as my eyes popped open in the morning, I couldn't wait to read the Word and hear what God would say. God spoke to me about His glorious truths on healing, and, as I spent time with Him, He brought me to the place that I knew with all my heart my daughter was healed. Now the light-bulb was flashing like a neon sign and the truth she knew two years ago was my truth too.

Alana is now seventeen years old and was completely healed that day at the movie theatre from Tourette's syndrome, and, on the same journey, He taught me how to believe. God is so good and, for the slow learner, so patient!

Lord, thank you for Your perfect Word.

Robin Bingeman is an assistant cell leader at Newport DOVE, Elm.

Detour!

"Trust in the Lord with all your heart and lean not on your own understanding. In all *your* ways acknowledge Him and He will make your paths straight." *Proverbs 3:5–6*

That simple word *detour* on a yellow road sign instantly instills fear in my heart. Directionally challenged even on a good day, I dislike being unexpectedly forced into a new road pattern, hitting all my nerve endings. Now what?

Despite this gut reaction to detours, I have to admit that God continually shows me the beauty of these changes. My most recent detour took me through a tranquil, quaint "Mayberry" neighborhood that I never even knew existed, and yet it was only ten minutes off my beaten track. Now it has become an area of intrigue and lingers in my mind as one I want to explore.

God does this in my spiritual life too–throws up roadblocks so that He can direct me down a different path, one brimming with new ideas, new joys, new friends, and new ways of worship and prayer. My short-sightedness and routine patterns require Him to close doors with a "bang"! Otherwise, I would never grow. I would be content with status quo and never stretch or reach for more understanding of His word or of His plan for my life.

Why did it take me so long to learn this? "Too soon old, too late smart" certainly fits me to a tee. But it's never too late to pass these lessons on to my kids and grandkids. Getting older definitely has its advantages, and I thank Him daily for strengthening and brightening my spiritual walk even as my physical walk slows.

Dear Lord, thank you for loving me enough to throw up those roadblocks. Please continue to replace my fears with anticipation of getting to know You in a deeper and more loving and trusting way. Amen.

Janet Medrow works for the director of the National Christian Conference Center in Valley Forge. She serves as a deacon at Great Valley Presbyterian Church in Malvern.

Learn of Me

"Take my yoke upon you, and learn of me; for I am meek and lowly in heart: and ye shall find rest unto your souls. For my yoke is easy, and my burden is light." *Matthew 11:29–30*

I have learned, in my eighty-two years, that I need Jesus more today than ever before. I was on the tractor near Ephrata, Pennsylvania, over sixty years ago, when He called me to leave the farm and go into mission work. I realized then that I cannot do it on my own; I must have His help. He has been so faithful down through the years. One of the key principles I have learned is that His yoke is easy and His burden is light.

When we yoke up with Jesus, we learn from Him. Jesus is like the lead ox in a yoke of oxen. When the farmer puts together a team they put a strong ox with a weaker ox. So it is when we go through life walking with Jesus. The Scripture in 1 Corinthians 6:17 tells us "he that is joined unto the Lord is one spirit." We develop a new trust in Jesus to be always there to help us in everything we do. Jesus said that He will never leave us nor forsake us.

God has been speaking to me that I need to become sensitive to His Spirit each day. Then, when I obey Him as He tells me to share with someone I meet, He does some wonderful things through me. When we are going through some hard times, we need to remember, He is right by our side to help us in all He has called us to do.

Lord Jesus, I pray that You will impart to us the ability daily to see ourselves yoked up with You. Let us daily, yes, moment by moment, allow Your life to live out through us. During each challenge that I have today, may I realize that You are right there with me. In Jesus' name, amen.

Luke Weaver is the founding pastor of Grace Chapel, which he founded forty-eight years ago. He is an apostle and mentor to many leaders in this county and around the world. He is presently assisting his son, Mel Weaver, who is senior pastor of Grace Chapel.

Are We Called Heroes of the Faith Today?

"These were all commended for their faith, yet none of them received what had been promised. God had planned something better for us so that only together with us would they be made perfect."
Hebrews 11:39–40

These verses are a prophecy of our Lord (prophecy meaning "to boil")! It is a quickening of His Holy Spirit, the Holy Spirit of God!

Finally this verse hit my heart. I thought about all I read and I reread in verses 32 to 39 and the names of those including Gideon, Sampson, David and Samuel who through faith did greatest for our Lord, but the Word said they *gained* what was promised yet none of them *received* what had been promised. Wow!

What did these verses mean in my life as I believe I serve the Lord faithfully? Did it mean that I was not fully listening to His voice? How could these "men of God" do so much and they only gained but did not receive? What change or changes must I make in my life to know His plan for my life?

I realized again and again that He is only worthy. I realized that I should not be thinking of any earthly rewards. And I learned that the faith of chapter 11 of the book of Hebrews is the faith that is only finally revealed in its full glory in Christ.

The lesson to me was in simple words. It means holding fast to Jesus, and that holding means nothing less than salvation! I am saved and will live with Him forever!

Thank you, Lord, for Your plan for my life! Help me to reach others for You! Thank you for Your agape love!

Bob Burns is pastor of Spiritual Growth Ministries, a guiding ministry to church leaders in areas of spiritual growth, and serves on the advisory board of the Potter's House in Leola (an after-prison care ministry).

Adjusting My Time

"At the time of the banquet he sent his servant to tell those who had been invited, 'Come, for everything is now ready.'" *Luke 14:17*

It began as a rumor circulating around Lancaster County; President George Bush was possibly coming to our area for a visit. The local news began to pick up that story, using words such as "invitation only," and "intimate setting with a small number of people," "possible one-on-one time with the President." I remember thinking that it would be great to be a part of such a meeting, what an awesome opportunity.

It wasn't long before the rumors were confirmed: President George Bush was coming to Lancaster and the meeting would be all that they said it would be—invitation only in an intimate setting with a relatively small number of people.

You can imagine, then, that I was floored, when I received an invitation to attend the meeting, from the Lancaster Chamber, just five days before the visit. I was excited, but I also had to do a lot of rearranging my priorities and schedule.

At one point in this process I simply had to observe myself and my reaction to this invitation. Let's face it (and I say this with all due respect for our President and the Office itself) it is only the President. Every day I have an invitation from the Lord to spend personal one-on-one time with the King of Kings and Lord of Lords. If I am willing to adjust my schedule for a President, how much more should I be willing to adjust so that I can spend more time with my Lord?

Consider the invitation that you are receiving today, and every day, to spend time with the King! How will you respond?

Father, I pray that my heart would always be open to You in such a way that I'm constantly prepared and willing to make the necessary adjustments to respond to Your invitations to know You, love You and obey You, in Jesus' name, amen.

Kevin Eshleman serves as executive pastor with Ephrata Community Church.

Rivers of Living Water

"…Out of his belly shall flow rivers of living water." John 7:38

I was preparing to soak some very dirty clothes in the laundry tub when I was interrupted by a phone call. When the call ended, I discovered, to my horror, I had not turned off the faucet and there was water flowing out of the tub, over the countertop and onto the floor! It covered every inch of the laundry room floor.

After I turned off the faucet and began to clean up the mess, the Lord brought these words to my mind: "Just as the water was flowing from the faucet, my Spirit is flowing from you to cover those around you. The water from the faucet continued to flow everywhere until you turned off the flow! Do not turn off the Spirit in your life—let it flow! You can keep it flowing by getting into the Word, by praising Me, and by using your prayer language frequently. Don't turn off the flow. The Spirit will flow like the water into every space, crack or crevice if not cut off. It will quench a dry and thirsty soul. It is a mighty force! Allow it to flow."

The Lord sometimes speaks to me when I am in the middle of a mess. He uses everyday experiences to point me toward Him. He used my mistake to teach me about the Spirit working in my life. He didn't cause the mess, but He used it to show me how His Spirit can work through me if I don't turn off the flow of his living water.

Father, keep nudging me toward You as I allow Your Spirit to flow through me to those around me. Remind me to keep the water flowing by taking time for Your Word, praise and prayer. Thank you, Lord, for Your faithfulness.

Susan Brechbill is a wife, mother of four, grandmother of nine, and a nurse working at Landis Homes Retirement Community. She and her husband, Ray are small group and section leaders at The Worship Center.

The Eleventh Hour

"... I tell you the truth, no one can see the kingdom of God unless he is born again." John 3:3

As I approached John's hospital room, his children were huddled outside the door, grim and distressed. "Dad isn't doing well at all," the oldest daughter offered. Unaware of their dad's earlier request of me, I told John's children that a number of years earlier he had asked me to conduct his funeral. And knowing that he had never made his peace with God, I asked if I could speak with him.

Fortunately, John was still cognizant and was quite ready to discuss eternal matters. Among other passages, I read to him the words of Jesus from John 3:3: "I tell you the truth, no one can see the kingdom of God unless he is born again." As I explained to John the plan of salvation and prayed with him, his heart was soft as he accepted Christ into his heart by faith. A smile came across John's face as he said he now had peace, wasn't afraid to die and was ready to go anytime.

Within a day, John fell into a coma and remained in that state for the next two days. I wasn't with John when he passed into Eternity, but his children related to me that just moments before his passing , a dove came to the outside of his hospital window and hovered there. Undoubtedly God was reassuring John's family that all was well.

Funerals are wonderful opportunities to present the message of God's redeeming work of grace in Christ Jesus. Many of the attendees at John's funeral weren't believers, but as the gospel message was proclaimed, I knew the Holy Spirit would continue to do His work in bringing conviction to the hearts of those who have yet to experience what John did—in the eleventh hour!

Thank you, O Lord, for the overflowing heart of mercy and grace You extended to John and to each of us! Amen.

Paul Brubaker serves on the ministry team at the Middle Creek Church of the Brethren, Lititz.

Trouble Down on the Farm

"Love your enemies. Let them bring out the best in you, not the worst." *Matthew 5:44 (The Message)*

Intrigue enveloped our Elizabethtown, Pennsylvania, farm! Gasoline was missing from the tank used to refuel the farm machinery. I realized that Daddy was playing sleuth when I discovered string and wires exiting his bedroom window. With one end attached to an alarm clock and the other strung across the driveway, he hoped to be awakened when the would-be thieves arrived.

One night, shortly after going to bed, Daddy heard a suspicious noise outside. Hurrying downstairs, he crept cautiously past the garage until he spied the get-away car. Moving closer, he noticed that its license plate was bent in half. Darkness was their ally as the thieves drove stealthily out the lane.

Daddy suspected that the culprits were local teenagers, looking for excitement. One evening he drove into town and noticed a familiar-looking car with a creased license plate. Approaching the vehicle filled with teenage boys, he invited them to follow him to our house.

Surprisingly, they followed him home. He invited the young men to the kitchen table where he served them ice cream. In his kind, friendly manner, Daddy talked with the boys as they ate. He told them of his love for young people, his own and others, and his concern for those who do wrong things. After they had chatted awhile, the group left. As Mother cleared the table, she found money under one plate, enough to cover the cost of the ice cream.

We never had gas thieves again after "the evening of the ice cream!"

Jesus, thank you for the way You modeled love for Your enemies. Help me to love the hard-to-love today.

Leona Myer serves as a pastoral elder at Hosanna Christian Fellowship in Lititz.

Receiving My Life Back

"Father, if thou be willing, remove this cup from me; yet not my will but Thine be done." *Luke 22:42 (King James Version)*

When I started to have pain in my left leg, I went for an X-ray to make sure it was not fractured. The surgeon ordered a bone scan and wanted me to go to Baltimore regarding leg lengthening. However, I had already called my insurance company to find another orthopedic doctor and had set up an appointment. I just took the results to the new doctor.

More X-rays were taken, and it showed the femur was about to snap from pressure from the rod that was placed in my leg from my previous knee replacement revision, totally fusing it; the lower portion of the rod was about to break through the skin. I said, "If you need to amputate, God has already prepared me."

He said, "Amputation is the only way you will get your life back."

The weekend prior to this appointment, I saw myself skipping through a meadow, and I looked down and saw I had an artificial leg.

I was so angry for the next two days. Then, as clear as day, I heard the Lord say, "I am not taking anything away from you, I am giving you your life back."

I called the scheduling nurse and said I need to see the vascular surgeon. He confirmed the findings and said, "We will give you your life back." Isn't God so good! I am writing this three years later. I now have this unbelievable bionic leg and am learning to walk better and adapt more each day. I realize that even though I sometimes think I want to see the "big" picture as He does, I am so glad He knows best and does not allow me to see more than what He and I can handle.

Thank you, God, for Your goodness to us!

Darlene Adams is involved in Letters Of Victorious Encouragement and Celebrate Recovery at the Ephrata Church of the Nazarene as well as various prison ministries.

To God Be the Glory

"Is anyone among you suffering? Let him pray...."
James 5:13 (King James Version)

An unusual lump had developed. "You need to see a specialist," my doctor informed me back in 2002. With a great deal of concern, I made my way to the specialist for consultations, tests and a biopsy. When the results were in, my wife and I had the appropriate appointment with the specialist who gave us the straightforward answer, "Yes, the biopsy was malignant and you do have cancer."

You could have knocked me over with a feather. I was not overweight, had been a runner most of my life, watched my diet, took my vitamins and besides, I was a pastor. Certainly God wouldn't allow me to have cancer, would He? Although the shock of this dreaded announcement wiped us out, it also drove us to the heart of God in a fresh and life-changing way. That very night dear friends surrounded us with prayer and the comforting words of Psalm 112:6-8. Our hearts were firm, trusting in the Lord.

That event launched us on a spiritual, emotional and physical journey that continues to this day. We sought the finest medical treatment that could be found in this area and opted for surgery, radiation and hormone treatment. More importantly, we followed hard after God seeking His miraculous healing power. Church elders rallied around us with prayer, a special healing service in a neighboring church provided special prayer and the "healing rooms" ministry gave powerful support through intercessory investments on our behalf. God heard, God responded, God moved and God healed. Was it through the prayers? Was it the medical treatments? Perhaps it was a combination of both. But God did it and to Him goes all the glory!

Thank you, Lord, for Your healing and care for all of us!

David D. Allen is the associate pastor of Calvary Church.

Lord, You are Good

"You are good, and what You do is good; teach me Your decrees. It was good for me to be afflicted so that I might learn Your decrees."
Psalm 119:68, 71

It was a beautiful spring evening when I got the phone call. My twenty-year-old son was in a motorcycle accident with serious injuries. My heart dropped to my toes. Why would God allow this? What was the purpose? I remembered His Word promises that He uses all things for good for those who love Him. *I love You, Lord. What is the good You will bring through this "bad" situation?* I can't explain the calm I felt as we entered the hospital. I asked God to open my eyes to see the good that He was going to do. It kept me calm and thoughtful.

A few days later I came upon Psalm 119:68. It gave me courage as I declared that God is good even when I don't understand. What He does is good even when I am afflicted because it teaches me about His decrees. A decree means "to order or settle by authority. God decrees, man agrees." It is a foreordained event to bring about God's eternal purpose. So, I determined to agree with God's purpose for my son, myself and all those touched by his accident. I yielded my mind, will and emotions to Him. I chose to praise Him for His protection over my son, for sparing his life, providing skilled surgeons and medical staff, and for injuries from which he would recover. God is good.

I am a different person today because of what I walked through in the last year—more patient, more empathetic, more aware of people around me. My "affliction" drew me to the Father's waiting arms.

Lord, when I don't understand and life seems hard, remind me of Your goodness. Give me a grateful heart. Open my eyes to see You at work in my circumstances.

Charlotte Allgyer is a mother of four and serves as a volunteer counselor at Susquehanna Valley Pregnancy Services.

Walking Together

"Abraham took…his son Isaac…the two of them went on together."
Genesis 22:6

"He will turn the hearts of the fathers to their children, and the hearts of the children to their father…." *Malachi 4:6*

One of the many blessings God has given us as humans is parenthood. This role is not always easy, because no one is born knowing how to be a father or mother. This requires years, and during this process it is possible that we commit mistakes, as it was in my case.

When our children grow into the teenage years, the communication, trust, maturity, tolerance and the love for each other gets tested. It is during those times that we need the support of the family, church, true friends; but over all, we need the guidance, wisdom and fortress of God to be with us during this time of complex changes.

In the past few years we have had some difficult times as a family. I am grateful to the church, where I currently serve as a pastor, to my brother and sister-in-law, and overall to my precious Savior and God Jesus Christ, Who has always been with us.

God has truly blessed my wife, Jeanette, and me in 2008; we have seen our children accomplish important goals in their lives. In February our oldest daughter, Keyla, married Juan Carlos, and in May our son Mario graduated from Lancaster Mennonite High School. Now, I continue learning how to be a father God's way, while Katie, our youngest daughter, approaches the teenage stage as well.

I encourage all of the young parents that may be going through difficult times with their children to not give up. There is hope for you and your family in God's promises, and, through prayer, you will see results in the lives of your children.

Heavenly Father, I ask that You bless every parent who is going through tough times with their children, in the name of Jesus.

Mario E. Araya serves as a lead pastor of New Holland Spanish Mennonite Church.

Hidden Treasure

"But we have this treasure in earthen vessels that the surpassing greatness of the power may be of God and not from ourselves."
2 Corinthians 4:7 (New American Standard Bible)

My folks asked if I would drive them to visit my dad's brother and sister-in-law in New York. My aunt and uncle are elderly and she has been diagnosed with Alzheimer's disease. Because I do home care for the elderly, I am somewhat familiar with the symptoms and impact of Alzheimer's upon individuals and their loved ones.

I had not seen my aunt for many years and was not fully prepared for what I experienced in her presence. Or maybe I should say her *absence*, even while present. She had a sweet expression on her face, but would not engage in the dinner conversation, which is unlike her friendly and curious nature. I tried to ask safe, simple and familiar questions, but she would shake her head and not know the answers to questions like "How are you feeling? What is your favorite food? Can I pass you some more food?" She seemed to feel awkward and lost. I didn't want to embarrass her so I was quiet for a while until the others went out to the porch, leaving us alone.

Praying silently, I asked her if I could read some Scripture to her while we sat there in the kitchen. She nodded. I began reading some familiar Psalms. As I began Psalm 23, her face lit up and she became highly responsive, quoting the entire Psalm without faltering. She smiled at me with a look of such satisfaction and peace that tears stung my eyes. The hidden treasure was firmly there in her heart and her spirit responded and drew it out with passion!

Thank you, Lord, for the precious treasure and power of Your Word. Thank you that even though our bodies or minds may falter, our spirit is eternally alive and intact!

Cindy Riker, mother of four, is involved with her husband at Teaching the Word Ministries and also teaches at Change of Pace Bible Study.

Getting Along

"Now may the Lord of peace himself give you peace at all times and in every way. The Lord be with all of you." *2 Thessalonians 3:16*

The other day I stopped for lunch in a restaurant. It was almost 2:00 in the afternoon. I had eaten a bite about 11:30, but since I was rushing off to an appointment, I didn't eat enough. I thought it would be nice to catch some quiet time, reading and refueling. It was not to be.

The hostess seated me at a table next to two mothers who were trying to have lunch with their kids. I think the kids needed a nap because they where whiny and defiant. Every once in a while one of them would scream—one of the children, not one of the mothers. That, of course, frustrated and embarrassed the mother—who then tried to use me as a tool. "That man is probably trying to have a quiet lunch and get some work done and you are disturbing him!" (She got that right.) Actually the mother was being both firm and reasonable, but the child wanted to be disagreeable. He had no interest in getting along with anyone in the restaurant. Mercifully (for me), the mothers gathered their chicks and headed out for the next relational challenge.

Relationships, even with those you love, are sometimes a challenge. Being in right relationship requires work and it often requires help. I love the way *The Message* translates Paul's words: "May the Master of Peace himself give you the gift of getting along with each other at all times, in all ways. May the Master be truly among you."

I cannot have a right relationship with God without God's help. It is reasonable to assume that I cannot have a right relationship with my other loved ones without God's help. "Getting along" is a gift that God does give to those who belong to Him. It is the gift of His unconditional love. It is often said that the family that "prays together" (or the secular variation, "plays together") stays together. I would amend that. It's the family whose members stay close to God that stays together. Without knowing the Master of Peace, you cannot know peace.

Thank you, Lord, for Your peace in our hearts and in our families.

Dr. Steve Dunn is the lead (senior) pastor for the Church of God in Landisville and a sponsor of the Child Evangelism Fellowship's Good News Club at Landisville Elementary School.

The Journey of a Lifetime

"...Anyone united with the Messiah gets a fresh start, is created new.
The old life is gone; a new life burgeons!"
2 Corinthians 5:17 (The Message)

Becoming a disciple of Christ begins with a decision to take the journey and follow Him. It is a life of real adventure. We do not have a map and yet we are never lost when we follow Jesus. It is comforting to know that He is our guide and we do not need to know the way. The goal of the journey is our transformation. We become more like the people we hang out with. You'll know you are on the right road when your life looks more and more like Jesus in attitude and action, because He is "the radiance of God's glory" (Hebrews 1:3).

If you feel like your life is heading in the wrong direction, take up the challenge of Jesus Christ who is calling out to you, "Come, follow me." Jesus did for us what we could not do for ourselves. He paid the price of our sins by dying on the cross. He also defeated sin by rising again on the third day. Our part is accepting this free gift of salvation.

If you would like to ask Jesus Christ into your life, pray this prayer: *Lord Jesus, thank You for loving me. I know that I am a sinner and need Your forgiveness. I know that You died on the cross for my sins and rose from the dead. I want to turn from my sins and give You control of my life. Please come into my life right now, Lord. Help me to follow You always. Amen.* Read Acts 3:19 and 2 Corinthians 5:17.

Thank you, Lord, for new purpose and direction, for inviting us to the most wonderful journey of our lives...a journey that will transform the way we think, speak and act...a journey that will be more wonderful and fulfilling than any we can imagine. We praise You, Lord. Amen.

Dan Houck is the pastor at The Table Community Church, Lancaster.

Alone or Not Alone, That is the Question

"...Be strong and courageous. Do not be terrified; do not be discouraged, for the Lord your God will be with you wherever you go."
Joshua 1:9

Splashed across the pamphlet from the American Cancer Society were bold red letters: "You are not Alone." A war cry against an enemy! Indeed, the largest lie of *our* enemy, Satan, is: "You are alone, nobody cares." I praise God that Scripture is full of life giving ammunition to annihilate those lies—words like "Lo, I am with you always even to the ends of the earth" (Matthew 28:20).

When I was at my physical weakest I could only whisper "Jesus!" and I would hear, "I'm here." When my heart breaks, I hear "I'm here." I hear His voice in the majestic symphony of birds with the first light of morning. Even when the rooster crows during the night I am reminded that God never slumbers nor sleeps. All of nature cries, "Holy, Holy, Holy is the Lord. The Lord God Almighty come to earth."

We are not alone. We have a God who reaches out and embraces us through His body of believers, an intimate, loving God who touches earth with His splendor and who bends down and whispers, "I'm here." Stay connected to Him and the body.

Thank you, Lord, for Your presence. Today and every day, we can count on You to be near!

Christina Ricker is a cancer survivor, wife, mother and Nana. She is one of the warriors of Petra Christian Fellowship proclaiming Christ's love, faithfulness and victory in the midst of battle.

Pea Soup

"For we know in part and we prophesy in part, but when perfection comes, the imperfect disappears. When I was a child, I talked like a child, I thought like a child, I reasoned like a child. When I became a man, I put childish ways behind me. Now we see but a poor reflection as in a mirror; then we shall see face to face. Now I know in part; then I shall know fully, even as I am fully known." *1 Corinthians 13:9–12*

I slept in this morning: 4:30. I puttered around the house, watching the morning news and "Sports Center," and then headed to my office to read my email. Just before sunrise, I headed to breakfast. The trip was not easy. It was still dark, but getting up as I do at such an early hour, darkness does not inhibit my driving. It was the fog. Last night's heavy rains and the early morning temperatures produced a thick fog that was blanketing East Hempfield Township. I believe the proverbial cliché is "thick as pea soup." More like peas in a cream sauce this morning. By the time I emerged from breakfast, the fog was still present and the first sunlight only made vision more of a blur.

We all know what it is to live in a fog. So often our knowledge and our experience are insufficient for the challenges. Our ability to grasp the present is limited. We cannot roll along, merrily, with complete confidence. Our best efforts seem partial and our choices imperfect. It is not a situation that most of us like. It is a constant source of frustration to many, a trigger for anxieties. It's like the young parent who once told me, "Why do they give this job to amateurs?"

Yet two pieces of reality provide a beacon of reassurance to me. One is that this situation is only temporary. God subjects us for a time to a season of "knowing in part" as a way of shaping us, and requiring us to trust—not in our cleverness, our power—but His faithfulness. To learn that we are the junior partners *always*. The second is that even in the fog, I have His love. His love is *always there* even when I do not see it clearly. His love *never fails* even though I may get it wrong. And someday, His love will make the imperfect disappear. "Then I shall know fully, even as I am fully known."

Thank you, Lord for Your unfailing love.

Dr. Steve Dunn is one of the leaders of the Servant Church Conference offered annually through the Church of God of Landisville.

Photo by Joan Adams

March

Tune In!

"Then you will call upon me and come and pray to me, and I will listen to you...." *Jeremiah 29:12*

This summer LaVerne and I took a week away in Florida to just be together, talk to each other, listen to each other and relax together. Due to my intense travel schedule, we cherish these times.

One night over an evening meal at a beautiful spot next to the Atlantic Ocean, LaVerne decided that she was going to see how long I would go without talking. She is definitely the conversation initiator in our relationship. We had a wonderful meal together (at least from my perspective), and after the meal was finished she informed me that I had not talked at all during the entire time. I couldn't believe it! I guess I was focusing on other things, without even thinking about it.

The next meal I made up for it and talked nonstop. I overdid it, and she was ready for me to shut up. When I told my son-in-law this story, he said the greatest miracle was that LaVerne could go for a whole meal without talking!

In any relationship, communication is important, and it involves both speaking and listening. Our God wants us to have communion with him and relationship with him. This is a two-way relationship. Sometimes we express that relationship by being quiet and listening. Other times we talk or weep or sing. We've been created to praise and commune with our wonderful, heavenly Daddy, and no two days in our relationship will be alike! Let's tune in to the Lord today and communicate with Him!

Lord, I place myself in a position to hear from You today. Reveal Yourself to me as I acknowledge You in my life.

Larry Kreider is the International Director of DOVE Christian Fellowship International, Lititz.

Freedom

"The Spirit of the Sovereign Lord is on me, because the Lord has anointed me to preach good news to the poor. He has sent me to bind up the brokenhearted, to proclaim freedom for the captives and release from darkness for the prisoners...." *Isaiah 61:1*

From time to time I get asked to be involved in various activities and wonder, "How am I going to fit that into my schedule?" A while back our church was asked to help with the weekend of prayer in Lancaster, and one of our pastors was looking for volunteers to serve as intercessors. I immediately sensed this was a God thing, and that I needed to make some time for it in my schedule. I was really glad I did; it was a special time of worship and intercession.

During our assigned time slot, we focused on praying for unity in our region. It was good to join with believers from other churches, backgrounds and races to seek God's face for unity. I came away from that time with a deeper appreciation for my brothers and sisters in Christ, as well as a better understanding of our responsibility to walk in unity. As Christians we are the ones who need to proclaim freedom to those around us and break down dividing walls in the church and our communities.

I also sensed that God wants us to go places others are unwilling to go. It may just be to cross the street to reach out to someone who is different from us, or it may be something that requires greater sacrifice and risk. Either way, as we choose to obey God's leading, He will make us instruments of freedom and breakthrough.

Dear God, thank you for the body of Christ in our region and around the world. Please draw us closer to You and to one another.

Mark Van Scyoc is a programmer analyst, free-lance photographer and serves as mission director at DOVE Christian Fellowship Westgate Celebration in Ephrata.

Quieted Among Giant Bugs

"But I have stilled and quieted myself, just as a small child is quiet with its mother. Yes, like a small child is my soul within me."
Psalm 131:2

I like to think that the word *Nana* could be added to that scripture knowing full well that there is no one like mom.

The IMAX theatre was showing 3D *Bugs*. It was a great show and I had seen it with the special needs class I help with. So, when our grand-babies of two and one came to visit, we thought we'd take the family. Settling in and arranging squirming babies on laps, I had taken Stephen, the two-year-old. As I thought how overwhelming 3D could be for little ones, Stephen grabbed my finger, laid in my arms, rolled toward me, and fell asleep. All around him were giant bugs and noise, but he slept.

Just watch the evening news. There are matters too great or awesome for us to handle: tsunamis, global warming, terrorist attacks, inflation and bird flu. The list goes on; then add to that our personal storms.

The counsel of the psalmist is the way to peace. Turn your concerns over to the One who is able. Move close to the One who loves you. Be still as you press into Him, hold His finger, and be quieted.

Jesus, how often I need Your comforting arms about me. Help me to always remember that You are here. I don't need to immerse myself in the fear of the world. I need to sit close to You and be quieted. Amen.

Christina Ricker is a wife, mother and Nana, as well as an intercessor at Petra Christian Fellowship.

Fear-Splitting Voice

"The voice of the Lord echoes above the sea. The God of glory thunders. The Lord thunders over the mighty sea. The voice of the Lord is powerful; the voice of the Lord is majestic. The voice of the Lord splits the mighty cedars; the Lord shatters the cedars of Lebanon." *Psalm 29:3–5 (New Living Translation)*

Fifteen years ago, I hadn't flown much and always chose a window seat to make sure the earth was still safely far below. On this particular flight, though, we were landing in a storm and the clouds kept me from monitoring our descent. Yikes! We landed in Philly without incident, but you wouldn't know it from my heart rate.

The final leg of our flight was delayed because of the storm, and I tried to coax my friend into forgoing our flight and taking a taxi home. Four tires on macadam seemed pretty appealing to me. No go.

An hour later, they dragged us onto the water-logged tarmac to board a tiny commuter plane (with narrow steps that reminded me of the kind we folded down from our attic), with literal rope railings. Worst of all were the miniature engines perched on the front of the wings.

Fear ripped through me and I thought of the Scripture, "God hasn't given us a spirit of fear," to no avail.

Suddenly, and with no help from me because I was engulfed in fear, a voice thundered within me, "I'll take you home on My wings, Lisa."

I knew it was God, I knew He'd spoken directly to me, and my fear vanished. I thought to myself, "The wings of God. What could be safer than that?"

I sat back, enjoyed the bumpy flight home and haven't been afraid to fly since.

Father, thank you for the power of Your voice to cut through my human thinking and my wayward emotions. Please set me straight whenever I'm not lined up with You and Your Word.

Lisa Hosler serves at Susquehanna Valley Pregnancy Services and with teams uniting for regional transformation.

Leave Your Mark

"Join with others in following my example, brothers, and take note of those who live according to the pattern we gave to you."
Philippians 3:17

Holy Spirit-led divine appointments are certainly a favorite of mine. Traveling oversees recently, the stewardess removed the two people seated beside me and placed Anthony in the window seat of row 10, my row. For several hours, Anthony opened up and shared how he was separated from his wife and how they were involved in counseling. He told me he was not following God as his mother had raised him. He quit church attendance upon graduation of high school. Knowing we would return in one week on the same plane, I asked the Holy Spirit to seat us together so that Anthony and I could have opportunity to share together on the return to the USA.

One week later, same row, same seats, Anthony and I had four hours of uninterrupted time. Since then, we have been sending emails to one another. God loves Anthony and wants his marriage to make it. I am convinced that all of this was divinely inspired and I pray that in some small way a mark was left upon Anthony's life.

Who is watching you today, a child, a co-worker? The thing about leaving a mark is that it is left right now, yesterday, tomorrow…all the time, good or bad. What impression, impact, or fragrance will you leave on the life of those who you touch today?

Heavenly Father, give us Your fragrance so that those we come in contact with today will be encouraged, built up, and blessed by Your touch.

Steve Prokopchak helps provide oversight and direction for DOVE Christian Fellowship International's network of churches.

Fellow Workers

"I planted the seed, Apollos watered it, but God made it grow. So neither he who plants nor he who waters is anything, but only God, who makes things grow. The man who plants and the man who waters have one purpose, and each will be rewarded according to his own labor. For we are God's fellow workers; you are God's field, God's building." *1 Corinthians 3:6–9*

I grew up on a farm and it took teamwork to plant and harvest the crops. In addition to other crops, we grew up to seventy acres of tomatoes. There was no way we could do this with just one or two people. We needed a whole team. Our whole family got involved, our neighbors got involved, and we hired migrant workers to help. We had to learn to work together or the tomatoes would rot in the field. Over the harvest season we became one big family and were able to get the work accomplished.

If we are going to bring in the spiritual harvest, we, as the body of Christ, will need to work together. No one ministry or church or denomination is enough for the task.

I am encouraged with the new desire I sense among leaders to find ways to work together. Recently our church and a neighboring church decided to work together with an outreach program called Upward Sports. We can reach more people together and, at the same time, give a witness of Christian unity to our community.

We are fellow workers. We are partners, and together we will see the harvest.

Father in Heaven, remove the obstacles in our hearts and agendas that hinder us from uniting together for the sake of the harvest. Show us how to speak well of each other and how to effectively work together. In Jesus' name, amen.

Lester Zimmerman is pastor of Petra Christian Fellowship, apostolic leader of the Hopewell Network of Churches and council member of the Regional Church of Lancaster County.

Peace

"Then David got up from the ground, washed himself, put on lotions, and changed his clothes. Then he went to the Tabernacle and worshiped the Lord. After that he returned to the palace and ate."
2 Samuel 12:20

By the middle of December of 1999 my husband Joe's liver cancer was spreading rapidly. He had had three months of chemotherapy and the doctor said there was nothing else they could do.

Christmas had always been a special time for us since we met on Christmas Day of 1952, I spent most of the holidays crying and trying not to show Joe how upset I was. He would say this will be our last Christmas together, and I would have to leave the room to cry.

I knew how painful liver cancer could be, and I spent the next three months praying and asking the Lord to either heal Joe or take him to heaven. By the middle of March I could see Joe was in pain, though he never complained. We went to the doctor and he gave him oxycontin. After a few days I could see he was still in pain, so we went back to the doctor and he put him on morphine and suggested we contact Hospice. Hospice came to the house on Friday, March 31, and they increased his morphine dosage. They were to start regular visits on Monday.

My youngest daughter suggested it might be a good idea for her brother and sister to visit their father. The family got together on Saturday and Sunday. Joe died about 3:00 a.m., Monday, April 3, 2000. I remember being flooded with peace during the funeral preparations and the burial, though I did a good deal of crying. After the funeral I had this overwhelming sense of gratitude to God for the way He had orchestrated Joe's death. It didn't seem right to spend a lot of time in mourning. I decided I wanted to spend the rest of my life serving God and the next year was one of the most fruitful times in my life.

Dear Lord I will be forever grateful for the way You took the emptiness that Joe's death created and filled my life with meaningful and rewarding work for You.

Margaret McCaffrey is a member of Ephrata Community Church and a S.E.E.R. Intern at Gateway House of Prayer and prayer leader.

Is Anybody Out There?

"He who watches over you will not slumber; indeed he who watches over Israel will neither slumber nor sleep." *Psalm 121:3–4*

I'm sure if you're a mother, you can relate to this. You've just had a baby, and it's your first week home from the hospital. You're up every two hours in the middle of the night to feed your hungry, crying baby. You just want to yell, "Is anybody out there?" It's exhausting!

That's where I found myself after I had my first baby. As I was feeding him, it would be so dark outside I would look out the window to see if there were any lights on in the other houses. If there were, it brought me a little comfort to know I wasn't the only poor soul up at three in the morning.

But in the midst of being sleep deprived, I realized something. Even though it may have seemed like nobody else was awake, God was. God was looking down from heaven, and He saw me. He understood.

Isn't it great to know that God never sleeps! He doesn't need to. We can talk to Him any hour of the day or night. And He will hear us. We have such a loving and caring God.

Heavenly Father, in our darkest hours, may we remember that You are always near. You never slumber. You are right there with us to offer peace. Thank you, Lord, for Your omnipresence. Amen.

Jennifer Paules-Kanode is a DJ for WJTL Radio.

Lyle

"My times are in Your hands...." *Psalm 31:15*

Lyle was a young, seventeen-year old, hard-of-hearing man, who was put in a state institution for the mentally retarded. His parents were a very caring kind of folk but were overwhelmed with Lyle's behavior and communication problems. It grieved their hearts to have to send their son to an institution, but, at the time, it seemed like the only choice they had. Little did they know what a disastrous choice it really was. Little did they know that they would be "chosen" to pioneer changes for individuals housed in that institution.

Lyle's parents were different from most. Unlike some other parents who dropped off their kids and never returned to visit, they visited regularly (at least every week) even though it was a lengthy drive and a bit of a hardship for them. Lyle's parents became involved and tried to get the institution better funding, equipment and services.

Lyle began to get services in the Deaf Education Department, and his speech and language skills began to develop. However, the institution still did not even meet some of the most basic humane needs. Soap, personal clothing, deodorant and clean sheets were "luxury" items.

The final straw fell when all legislators and congressmen in the state were invited to an "Open House" at the institution. Only two bothered to come. The following week, there was an Open House two miles down the road, at a recently opened experimental agricultural center for animals. Over seventy legislators came for the ceremony.

Incensed, Lyle's parents, along with three other couples, formed a grassroots committee that began to lobby for better treatment for the approximately 1,500 mentally retarded residents of that institution. In addition to the pressure they applied on government officials, they also filed a class action suit—and won!

Sadly, Lyle died in his twenties. I learned much from Lyle and his love of life. I also learned something valuable from Lyle's parents—to never give up!

Lord, You put many people in our lives for a purpose. Thank you that nothing is "by chance."

Jim Schneck is a free-lance interpreter for the deaf.

Great Shall be Their Peace

"All your children shall be taught of the Lord, and great shall be the peace of your children." *Isaiah 54:13*

It was the custom for me, as a young mom, to make a special cake for each of our children on their birthdays. The one who was having the birthday had the privilege of choosing, from a "cut-up cake" book, the particular cake theme he or she desired. In the process of many birthdays, I became somewhat adept at making cakes and decorating them.

Once, I was asked to make a cake for a baby shower for some friends of ours, who were becoming new parents. I searched for a verse of Scripture that I could include on the cake that would be an encouragement to them. The verse that the Lord gave me is found in Isaiah 54:13: "All your children shall be taught of the Lord and great shall be the peace of your children."

I have often pondered this scripture, having tucked it into my memory as a mandate with a promise. The mandate is that we, as parents, have the awesome responsibility of making sure we teach our children in the ways of God. This means knowing God ourselves, obeying Him and showing, by example, how to live a life pleasing to the Lord.

This truth is spoken of in Deuteronomy 6:7, "teaching your children when you sit down, when you lie down, when you rise up and when you walk by the way."

We make many mistakes as parents; but when we recognize them and ask God for forgiveness, He is faithful to forgive, but then He urges us to continue in the fear of God. We do not have the luxury of giving up in this task of parenting. It is just that the type of parenting changes as our children grow up and are given more responsibility and show a kind of maturity indicative of their progress. All the while we are guiding them in the ways of God.

Heavenly Father, instruct us and teach us to be a good example to our children. Thank you for putting Your blessing on this important assignment as parents.

Naomi Sensenig and her husband, LaMarr, serve at Lancaster Evangelical Free Church in Lititz.

Let Me In! Let Me In!

"...For those who will believe in me...that all of them may be one, Father, just as you are in me and I am in you. May they also be in us...." *John 17:20–21*

How is it possible to join Jesus and the Father in such sacred intimacy? Jesus said we must receive the kingdom like a little child. Children loved to spend time with Jesus. In my mind's eye I can see Him now, down on His haunches, His eyes twinkling, motioning for the children to come. I see big grins on their faces as they totter, plod and scamper over to him. He embraces them into the warm, secure folds of his tunic. The big sleeves hanging from his arms wrap soothingly around them as they giggle and squeal with delight!

I have found that in order to receive Jesus' invitation to intimacy, I need to be willing to admit my need, and, as children do so instinctively, I must beg him to bless me. On one such occasion, while grieving my parents' deaths, I sat in my prayer chair and prayed repeatedly, "I am desperate for you, Lord Jesus" and "Hug me, Daddy God" and "I love you Holy Spirit of God." After about ten minutes a mental image came. Three robed figures stood with arms on each other's shoulders, enjoying a group hug. I saw myself as a thigh-high toddler, and begged "Let me in, let me in, let me in!"

They broke the circle and with outstretched arms looked at me and said "Welcome home, Evy!" I began to join the hug, holding onto their knees, but I became aware of other children looking on longingly. I said, "Can the rest come too?" They answered with hearty good humor, "Of course, the more the merrier!"

Dear Lord, thank you for this great gift of belonging to the coolest in-group ever!

Everett Myer serves as a pastoral elder at Hosanna Christian Fellowship in Lititz.

Jeep Accident

"For I know the thoughts that I think toward you, says the Lord, thoughts of peace and not of evil, to give you a future and a hope."
Jeremiah 29:11

How did I get here? Lying on my side, pinned against hard, packed snow by the jeep sitting on my head. Eight hours earlier I'd stepped off a plane excited because it was my first time in Germany. I was on temporary duty in Germany for the next 45 days. It was an eight-hour trip from Ft. Carson, CO, and I was running on adrenalin. With no sleep on the flight over, I was sleep deprived when I got behind the wheel of the jeep for late night maneuvers. Two feet of snow was on the ground, and I lost control of the jeep on a steep grade. After fishtailing several times, I ran into a rock formation on the side of the road. This flipped the jeep so that several smaller rocks propped it up.

I lay there praying for God to save me. I could move all of my limbs except my head, and I was trapped there for an hour. It wasn't until later that I realized God had already answered my prayer. Some things happened before the accident that prevented my death. I hadn't worn my helmet. If I'd been wearing it, my head would have been crushed beneath the weight of the jeep and helmet. Furthermore, the rocks along the side of the road propped up the vehicle enough to pin my head not crush it. There was not a scratch on me from this accident. He had saved me before I even asked.

Thank you, Lord, for protecting me from all unseen dangers. Lord, You provide my every need before I know that I need. Thank you for Your loving kindness, grace and mercy toward me. In the matchless name of Jesus, I pray, amen.

Carol Denson serves as a volunteer for the Parkesburg Point Youth Center in Parkesburg.

Stay

"So Isaac dwelt in Gerar...." *Genesis 26:6 (King James Version)*

There was famine in the land and Isaac was tempted to go back to Egypt. God spoke clearly that he was to stay where he was (in Gerar), sow his seed and wait for the harvest.

A well-known minister was proclaiming this word on sowing and reaping, but the Holy Spirit, in an instant, wrote on my heart: "Stay in Gerar." I didn't understand what it meant, but knew it was a God-word.

When I arrived home from that meeting, and researched the meaning of "Gerar," I found it meant *sojourning, journeying, a lodging place, to tarry.* Receiving this understanding, I rested in His directive that I was to *stay* where He positioned me.

Unaware of what was coming, I delighted that the Lord had anchored me in my "Gerar." Within a short time, there was an upheaval that in the past could have caused me to wonder if I was in the right place. Perhaps it could have even made me want to pack up and move on. However, in the midst of the emotional turmoil, I heard resonating in my heart: "Stay in Gerar." With expansion on the message I heard: "Sow your seed and wait for the harvest." His anchor holds! I was easily able to ride the dark waves on a stormy sea and watch His stabilizing love bring the whole event into submission to His heart.

Father, thank you for Your Holy Spirit who writes Your proceeding Word on our hearts so that we have an anchor with You in the spirit which holds the reins of our soul when we walk through uncertain, often uncharted waters. Thank you for telling us when to go and when to stay, according to Your purpose and plan today.

Diana Oliphant serves in prayer and ministry with a heart for the region and nations.

Whoops!

"Is there any such thing as Christians cheering each other up? Do you love me enough to want to help me? Does it mean anything to you that we are brothers in the Lord; sharing the same Spirit? Are you hearts tender and sympathetic at all? Then make me truly happy by loving each other—and working together with one heart and mind and purpose. Don't be selfish; don't live to make a good impression on others." *Philippians 2:1–3 (Living Bible)*

At age fourteen, I thought I was really strong and just a bit smarter than those around me. I was trying to lift a loaded trailer and hook it to a tractor hitch. I could lift it but did not have enough strength to pull it front a few inches to connect to the trailer.

So, very intelligent me, I blocked the trailer wheels, put the tractor in reverse and tied a string to the pull start handle. My plan was to lift the trailer, one tug on the starter, and the tractor would move back one or two inches, but *whoops*! I had forgotten to put the switch in "off" position. The tractor started and began to run up my leg! Believe me, at that point, I decided that God was smarter than I was, so I cried out to Him to save me! The tractor stalled, and I was shaken to the core!

I look back and ask, "Why didn't I just walk inside the building and ask someone to help me?" But no, with my pride, I was not asking for help, "I can do this job all by myself."

Dear Lord, help us today to humble ourselves and ask for help from a brother or a sister. Make us ready and willing to lend a helping hand to those who may need us. Amen.

LaMarr Sensenig serves with his wife, Naomi, at Lancaster Evangelical Free Church in Lititz.

Walnut Tree

"...But be transformed by the renewing of your mind, so that you may prove what the will of God is, that which is good and acceptable and perfect." *Romans 12:2 (New American Standard Bible)*

One of the most magnificent walnut trees I ever saw stood in the backyard of the home where I grew up. Under its deep, old boughs, many memories were made.

One day that great tree fell—thankfully, in the only direction without a building beneath it. We were all grown up at the time, and my children and I drove over to help clean up the rather humongous mess.

First, we were told to clear all the large limbs to one area of the yard to be worked on with the chain saw. When we were finished, we looked back at the yard and it was covered with medium-sized branches. I wondered aloud about where they had come from. We began dragging those branches to another area to make a second pile. Again, we turned around and even smaller branches remained. I was sure, at this point, that they were rising out of the ground. A third pile was created.

As we finished, we looked back to find a fine layer of tiny twigs. We thought we were done. Would this never end? With each layer that was removed, we were finding a smaller layer underneath. That's when it hit me—this is so like my own life.

When I first came to know Christ, He began a transforming work in my heart by dealing with the obvious. As each layer of the old self was removed, another layer was revealed. Each layer is more subtle than the one before it, yet needing to be conformed to His standards. God is forever working to bring me deeper into a relationship with Him and to transform me into His image.

Precious Father, thank you for sifting through the layers in my life to transform me into Your image.

Lisa Hildebrand works for Susquehanna Valley Pregnancy Services and ministers as a teacher and speaker in local churches.

Whose Body is It?
Which is the Right One?

"The body is a unit, though it is made up of many parts; and though all its parts are many, they form one body. So it is with Christ."
1 Corinthians 12:12

There was a time in my life when I became rather confused as to where or in which denomination God had placed His approval. I finally concluded that there must be more than one God, like a Methodist God, a Baptist God, a Catholic God, and so on.

Each denomination seemed to be in constant competition with each other. I watched groups in the church who were not able to get along and surely didn't mingle with other churches. For this reason, I found it easy to turn away from the Lord, which I did for twenty years.

But God is faithful to continue to draw us back to Himself, even in our wilderness. I not only returned to the church, but to Jesus Christ as my Lord and Savior and to His call to be a pastor. Just a few years ago, while on a sabbatical, the Lord answered those early questions for me. He brought this scripture to me and has kept it before me ever since.

He was showing me how our denominational structure has brought disunity into the body of Christ. Each boasts of its accomplishments in order to seem more significant or successful than others. We have made idols of our differences, and this has brought division and confusion wrapped in pride. *None* of us are the *only* part of the body. It's time we return the church to Whom it belongs and work at becoming a worthy Bride—not wearing any other labels than "The Bride of Christ."

Dear God, may we be part of the worthy Bride of Christ today.

John W. Shantz is the pastor of Spring City Fellowship Church, Spring City.

Together!

"Just as each of us has one body with many members, and these members do not all have the same function, so in Christ we who are many form one body, and each member belongs to all the others."
Romans 12:4

While in a meeting one day, a co-laborer asked me a very simple question, "In Chester County there are twenty plus pro-life ministries that all work independently. Why is it that they don't work together?"

My friend didn't realize the challenge he put before me that day. This simple question began a journey that would lead to much prayer and thought. I am an organizer by God's own hand. He made me, what some would call, a type "A" personality. I organize, simplify and stream-line everything I get my hands on. Even some things that I can't personally change I have already streamlined in my mind.

My friend's simple challenge caused me to say, "Why aren't we all working together since we are all working for the Lord for the same purpose?"

After approaching another ministry leader we began to put our efforts together and that became the beginning of the Chester County Pro-Life Leaders Network. Our group now understands the meaning of Romans 12:4 and recognizes some of us serve as the head, the legs, the arms...in fact; together we create a complete body.

Individually our prayers are heard; but corporately, as one body, there is greater strength in our prayers. This is when "not by might, nor by power but by my spirit says the Lord" becomes reality. We pray, He moves! Unexplainable in our mere humanness, but very exciting!

Thank you, Father, that You strategically place Your workers in various ministries and capacities to do Your will. Thank you that when we come together we can rejoice in Your bigger picture as we serve our community in Your name, amen.

Karen Pennell serves as CEO of CCWS Medical, a life affirming pregnancy care medical center ministry with two locations in Chester County (West Chester and Coatesville) and co-director of the Chester County Pro-Life Leaders Network. CCWS Medical has the awesome opportunity to introduce parents to the humanity of their pre-born babies through ultrasound technology.

You Need Not Fear

"I will never leave you nor forsake you...You need not fear."
Hebrews 13:5–6

We have a weekly ministry praying for patients in the chapel of the Med Center. One week a distressed nurse came to us asking for prayer for a doctor who himself had cancer. That morning his physicians had determined there was no further help from the medical community and his end was near. His medical scans showed that his body was "lit up with cancer cells." We prayed in the chapel for the ailing doctor and sensed a word from God on his behalf. "I will never leave you nor forsake you...You need not fear." What an encouraging word to one who had no further medical hope.

My husband and I went to the ailing doctor's hospital bedside with the word of the Lord as God's healing prescription. He shared with us that his body was no longer absorbing nutrients. He didn't know what to do next. We looked in his eyes and spoke the word of the Lord to him to encourage him and bless his spirit. After hearing those words, he said he had a deep reassured peace in his heart even with his poor prognosis. We reminded him of God's word in 3 John 1 that even as your soul prospers your body would be in health. We prayed, believing Psalm 103 that God heals all our diseases. We blessed his body, mind, and spirit. As we left, we knew he had peace and trust in his soul.

A week later his medical team noticed that he was thriving and getting stronger. They did another medical scan and were surprised to find no cancer cells in his body. He praised God knowing God heard his prayers and he received a miraculous healing by God.

God, thank you that we can be at peace, that You will never leave us or forsake us, and we need not fear.

Abby Abildness serves as director of Healing Tree International, a ministry focused on encouraging and equipping leaders to bring healing to the nations.

Daddy Makes a Difference

"Train a child in the way he should go, and when he is old he will not turn from it." *Proverbs 22:6*

After an especially tiring day at work, I sat watching the news and sipping hot tea while the January wind howled outside. "Dad, let's go sledding!" my eight-year-old son ran into the room yelling. "It will soon be dark and you told me we could go after supper."

I did promise him I'd go out, didn't I? But I have to catch this news story or I won't know if the blizzard conditions canceled work tomorrow, I thought. *Besides, Jesse has friends his age that he would have just as much fun sledding with, so he really doesn't need me, does he?* It was so tempting to give into my desire to stay indoors, but having promised, I knew I could not expect my son to keep promises if I did not keep mine.

As a parent, it's not always easy to make decisions based on what is best for our children. Sometimes the most difficult decision is to give our children time. No one can take the place of a parent in a child's life.

Nothing can replace time. From the perspective of children, how much adults care about them is measured by the quantity of time spent with them. It is important for parents to, enthusiastically, participate with their children in various activities and to initiate consistent and meaningful communication with young children, in order to provide a foundation for trust in later years.

So, that's what I have to tell myself each time I hear that begging voice query, "Daddy, would you ____ with me?" Just like on that cold winter's evening when sledding outside with my son seemed less desirable than snuggling up indoors, I remind myself that these years will soon be gone. Today's chance to influence my child's future will be gone tomorrow.

Lord, help me to lay down my life for others—for my children (natural or spiritual) and also those who do not know You as their Father. Thank you for being the true Father my heart desires.

Dr. Edward Hersh provides counseling and healing prayer ministry to individuals and families, trains lay counselors here and abroad and helps leaders receive spiritual renewal (http://retreat.bluerockbnb.com).

W.I.J.D.

"When he has brought out all his own, he goes on ahead of them, and his sheep follow him because they know his voice." *John 10:4*

Deep inside each of us is a need to feel appreciated and valued by those who want to be near us. At the depth of this need is a void that can only be filled by experiencing the ever closeness of the presence of the Lord.

Several months ago I was awakened during the night and sensed it was a nudge of God to spend some time with Him. As I opened my Bible, I heard an inner voice saying that I need no longer rely on WWJD (What Would Jesus Do?) as a premise for making decisions. I sensed the Lord saying, "I am giving you a new set of initials WIJD (What Is Jesus Doing?). The fact is that Jesus is not only a good teacher, but He is the Resurrected One who is the presence of the Living God that desires to be ever near us leading us through our day. He is committed to whoever honors him as Lord to walk beside as a personal friend, to walk behind as a protector, and to walk ahead as the One who knows the way.

As we approach situations that need answers in our day, the question of "What Would Jesus Do? (WWJD)" is not complete in itself. The real question for Christians is "What Is Jesus Dong? (WIJD)." He is the living Christ and we can trust Him to lead us always in the way that is right, and to the right conclusion.

Father God, I acknowledge my need for Your love and compassion for me as Your child. I value Your presence with me and choose to trust Your leading so I can find my way through the situations of life. With my love and thanks, Amen.

Lloyd Hoover is a bishop of Lancaster Mennonite Conference, on staff at The Potter's House, a leader of reconciliation ministries, and member of Regional Church of Lancaster County.

A Lesson from NASCAR

"...Long before he laid down earth's foundation, he had us in mind, had settled on us as the focus of his love...." *Ephesians 1:4 (The Message)*

On my journey, I have found God will use almost anything to reveal Himself to me. Since I'm an avid NASCAR fan, God used a race to do just that.

It was during a Dover, Delaware, race that God did His work. As a fan (and being "spiritual"), I naturally prayed for my favorite driver. I prayed for no mechanical issues, good pit stops, no accidents and so on. Well, not too far into the race another driver bumped my driver and knocked him out of the race. This bothered me—I prayed against that—so I questioned God.

He spoke to my spirit, "I am Sovereign, I rule and reign, but I do not control everything. I didn't control the driver's choice to bump him." That was an "aha" moment. God won't make our choices for us. He won't even make us love and obey Him. He gives us the freedom to reject Him and His love. This is an ultimate display of love—giving the freedom to reject that love.

God has invited us into the most unselfish love relationship. We are the focus of His love. He desires to foster that love. I realized in this process that sometimes I just want to see God's power—just give me the life *I* want; answer my prayers as *I* want. But, what *God* wants is to foster love. And He showed me that power does not equal love.

I am the focus of God's love—so are you. Do you live like you are the focus of God's love? Let's live, act and love like we are the focus of God's great love.

Eternal Love, may we truly comprehend the width, length, depth and height of Your love for us.

Kathy Nolt is an avid NASCAR fan and lives in Lititz with her husband, Gary.

Weeds

"But while everyone was sleeping, his enemy came and sowed weeds...." *Matthew 13:25*

We were driving home from a funeral, when my sister-in-law suggested we drive by the family farm. This had been the family home for eighty-nine years, where my husband's grandfather moved his family in 1919 and raised ten children. The uncle who had lived there had been in a nursing home for the past seven months.

As we drove up the lane, we could see that things were declining. The grass needed mowing. There were weeds in the flower beds. While the place was not in disrepair, there was an appearance of neglect. We continued to drive around, looking at homes that once were owned by various relatives. In some cases, we remarked on the changes and improvements. Someone would say, "That porch wasn't there before, doesn't it look nice?" Or they might remark, "Where did that big tree go?" At other places we commented, "Those new owners are really letting that place go," or "Look at the peeling paint." But in every case, nothing was the same as it was decades ago. The place either had improvements or it had gone downhill. Not one place was exactly the same as it was before.

So it is with our spiritual lives. We can't just coast. We cannot stay the same. We must grow and improve or we will "go downhill." We may think that we can coast along in our daily routines, but if we do, we will gradually let some weeds grow in our hearts. Eventually we may start to mistrust God and to trust in ourselves instead. We may let bitterness over hurts grow or even allow apathy to dampen our spirits. We fall into disrepair and the joy seeps away.

Lord, open my eyes to see where I have been coasting. Show me the weeds in my heart and help me to pull them out. Renew my spirit so that I may serve You with joy.

Karen Boyd is a contributing editor to *God Stories* and serves on the board of the Pennsylvania Homeschoolers Accreditation Agency.

Kingdom Power

"For the kingdom of God is not in word but in power."
1 Corinthians 4:20 (New King James Version)

While leaving a Friday night prayer meeting last May, I witnessed one of God's amazing kingdom power miracles! As I left the church building I was called over by my pastor, Craig, who was speaking with another couple.

A young man named Tony was walking by and came over to where we were talking. Tony was sharing with Craig about some near death experiences he has encountered.

Craig encouraged to me share the good news of Jesus Christ with Tony. As I shared with Tony the greatest news known to mankind, he shared with me that he had a cycle accident where he sustained a broken neck and nerve damage, which affected his right hand and left him with curled fingers.

I had an opportunity to pray with Tony for his hand and as I prayed I could feel the tension on his curled fingers between my hands. As I finished praying, I shared with Tony the account in Luke 6: 6-11 how this incredible man Jesus Christ healed the man with the withered right hand on the Sabbath.

As I shared this with Tony, he was now moving his hand and fingers in a way he said he had not done in a long time! I prayed a second time for Tony's hand and this time I could feel how relaxed his hand was between my hands! Hallelujah, Jesus! I praised God for what He had done as this night the same gospel power that healed the man's withered man on the Sabbath also did the same for Tony!

As we parted that night, I shook Tony's healed and very relaxed hand!

Amazed!

Thank you, Jesus, for Your loving healing and forgiving power that You want to release as a sign and a wonder for Your glory and honor in this latter time in which we live.

Mark Burns serves in the Prayer Station Outreach Ministry and Foundation Discipleship at Reading DOVE Christian Ministry Center.

Imperfect Parents

"For I was hungry and you gave Me food; I was thirsty and you gave Me drink; I was a stranger and you took Me in; I was naked and you clothed Me; I was sick and you visited Me." *Matthew 25:35–36*

"You f-for-got me-e!" wailed our four-year-old daughter, Bobbi. She was the very last child waiting anxiously for a parent to pick her up from day care.

"Yes, and we are *so* sorry!"

I felt very guilty. How could Bob and I have done this to our most precious possession? I could rationalize that after several long days during a military exercise, we were exhausted and not mentally alert. I could use the excuse that my administrative job didn't dovetail with Bob's schedule as a bomber pilot, and we just failed to communicate.

Twenty-five years later, Bobbi can still recall the details and the emotions of that moment in time. Yes, definitely one of those low points in our parental history—one that I wanted struck from the record.

Thankfully, we're not the only imperfect parents. Mary and Joseph, the parents of Jesus, traveled a full day before discovering that Jesus was missing! And it was three days before they found Him!

What encouraging, profound tidbit can I offer to parents who have fallen short during the child-raising years? You were there for them.

Children grow up quickly. Our oldest is twenty-nine years, and Bob and I can still recall Bobbi's wide eyes of amazement at the Pacific Ocean and her exclamation, "Big bath!"

Yet, children grow slowly. It's a long process to wipe runny noses, care for, teach and nurture, day after day after day after day. Not everyone is willing or capable of being faithful to such a long-term, and many times thankless, job. But somewhere in your journey you caught God's plan: "our children are messengers we send to a time we will not see." So...

You were there for them.

Dear Jesus, thank you for placing great value on feeding and clothing "strangers"—those unfamiliar infants we took into our homes and hearts. Help us to remain faithful to be there for them.

Tamalyn Jo Heim tries to be there for Bobbi and Steve, Joshua and Kari, Kendralyn and Rebekah.

We Serve a Big God

"Let us then approach the throne of grace with confidence, so that we may receive mercy and find grace to help us in our time of need."
Hebrews 4:16

As young parents, my wife and I were most anxious about a particularly difficult group of school peers our one child was continually exposed to, both in elementary school and into middle school. My wife continued to be actively involved in the school and observed the class dynamics and pressures that were indeed troubling. How do we help our child persevere in the midst of this? Should we assertively explore other options? Is simply committing this to prayer enough? We opted to pray and to continue being a visible and spiritual presence.

God was so very faithful as we committed this to prayer. In the years that followed, God moved in many beautiful ways that far exceeded our imagination. He orchestrated events and circumstances that were nothing short of miraculous. A circle of godly lifelong friendships were birthed in the midst of a seemingly godless setting. This child today, now a young adult, testifies that these were the most formative and shaping years and are today labeled as holding the most precious of memories.

Some practical lifelong lessons came out of this for me personally. It would have been easy to respond strictly in the flesh and assertively "make something happen." God delights in hearing our hearts. The reality is if God is concerned with numbering the hairs on our head, surely He is concerned with whatever our cares may be, no matter how big or trivial they may seem. There is no such thing as small miracles in the kingdom of God. We serve a big God. Let us approach the throne of grace in humility and boldness.

Today Lord, I will look for You in the seemingly small and insignificant places of my life knowing full well that there is nothing small and insignificant in Your eyes.

Brian E. Martin serves as lead pastor at Weaverland Mennonite Church in East Earl. He and his wife Shirley are the parents of four children.

Thirsty For God

"As the deer longs for streams of water, so I long for you, O God. I thirst for God, the living God...." *Psalm 42:1–2 (New Living Translation)*

David, the Psalmist, was feeling separated from God. He was desperate to find Him. He had a burning passion to draw close to Him.

When you got up this morning, were you thinking about all the things you needed to do today? Did you say, "Good God it's morning!" or "Good morning, God"? If you love the Lord with all your heart, your heart was panting for the streams of living water—panting for more of Jesus. Five times, in John 15, Jesus urges us to remain in Him. It's all about relationship. Jesus is the vine and we are the branches. If we are not remaining in Him we can do nothing—that amounts to anything. Remaining or abiding means we must make a conscious decision to keep our communication with Him open throughout the day. When we do this we will bear fruit, fruit that remains. In verse fifteen Jesus takes our relationship to a deeper level. He says we are not only servants, we are friends. He lets us in on what is going on.

He is the only one who can satisfy. He is the only one who can give us rest through a hectic day. Remain in him.

Ask God to give you a single-minded focus—a focus on pleasing Him. Practice spiritual breathing: exhale any thoughts or images that appear in your mind that would be displeasing to Him and inhale His love, forgiveness, grace and power. Notice the difference as you walk with Him today.

Lord, help me to keep focused on You today, to abide in You today. When the pressures of the day come upon me like a flood, help me to come running to You. Thank you. Amen.

David Eshleman is a church consultant for Eastern Mennonite Mission and Lancaster Mennonite Conference.

A New Parable: The Ferret and the Blender

"For I know the plans that I have for you," declares the Lord, "plans for welfare and not for calamity, to give you a future and a hope."
Jeremiah 29:11

I watched my daughter's ferret, Hunter, as he wriggled into my kitchen cupboard and laughed as the comedy played out before me.

"Oooweee! A treasure, Mamma's blender container. I must have this vessel." Determined to hide it in his "secret" stash, Hunter bit the plastic and raced across the floor. After extensive reconnoitering, he finally reached the entrance to his den.

"Wait a second!" he muttered to himself, amazed. "How can this be? It won't fit!" He crawled under the massive piece of furniture and pulled with all his might. Stubbornly, he crawled inside the container and pushed doggedly with his head.

"Curses! I had big plans for this vessel, if only it would cooperate." Bored, the curious creature quickly turned his attention to some other fascinating object. He was on to bigger and better things.

As I watched Hunter try to make that container fit into his plans, I thought of the Lord's plan for me. How often have I refused to allow Him to form me into a vessel that fits His purpose? Try as he might, Hunter couldn't reshape that hard piece of plastic to fit through the narrow opening. With remorse, I thought of God's attempts to mold me as a potter does the clay vessel he creates. Many times I don't cooperate. I harden my heart, and sometimes I even quarrel with my Maker. I thwart His plans for me when I hold onto my old ways and don't allow Him to transform me into Christ's image. With new resolution to follow God's plan for my life, I thanked Hunter and the Lord for this lesson.

Father, please forgive me for struggling against You. Thank you for not casting me aside. Have Your way with me that I may be a vessel that reflects Your glory.

Nancy Magargle is a member of Lancaster Christian Writers group.

God Heals in Unique and Marvelous Ways

"For the man [woman] was over forty years old on whom this miracle of healing had been performed." *Acts 4:22*
(New American Standard Bible)

One more test for bone density would let me know the damage that prescribed steroids had created throughout my spine. Osteoporosis was the presumed diagnosis. Twenty years earlier, after several serious car accidents resulting in chronic pain, I was diagnosed with degenerative arthritis in my spine.

Sitting in the doctor's office, I steeled myself for the results. "God is faithful," I thought, "His grace is sufficient. I will learn how to deal with this disagreeable setback."

Dr. Fisher entered the room and placed the test results on the table. "I want you to see this," she said. "The density of your spine is 104%." She went on to explain that bone density is measured against the bone density of a nineteen-year-old woman with the rating of 100% being optimum.

"How is that possible?" I said.

"Well, I believe the pounding that your spine has taken over the years riding your horse has strengthened your spine!" the doctor said.

That beautiful spirited horse of mine, with her fire and spring had become a catalyst of healing to my spine. Now I understood why I refused to part with her, even though everyone else thought she was "too much horse." Lord, only you could give me the spine of a nineteen year old!

Lord, thank you for working all things out for our good. Thank you that You are always with us even when we don't understand. May we learn to trust You above all else. We are grateful that Your grace is more than enough.

Mary J. Buch is a senior pastor of Breakout Ministries and serves the Regional Council of the Regional Church of Lancaster County.

Waiting for Pop

"Invite some people who never get invited out, the misfits from the wrong side of the tracks." *Luke 14:13 (The Message)*

Pop's abuse of alcohol was lifelong. His yellowish skin, creased and weather-worn, was the result of too many days and nights spent on the street. He was a man of great independence, yet I was very concerned about his health as his liver continued to deteriorate. So it was totally unexpected when Pop finally agreed to allow me to take him to the veterans' hospital.

At the end of the rehab he looked great, the benefit of a regular diet, sleep and medication. As I thought about his transition back into the community, I asked him, "Pop how about coming to church with me when you leave here?" Pop looked at me a bit quizzically before saying, "That sounds really good Stevie, but I couldn't go to church. I don't have a suit!"

It's been several years since Pop died of liver disease. He never did make it to church. I keep wondering what it would have been like if Pop had come. Would he have felt welcomed in his frayed and holey jeans and shoes? Would anyone look past the disheveled beard, the clothing that reeked of sweat and alcohol? Would anyone sit by his side, look him in the eyes, listen intently to his story and invite him home for Sunday dinner? Would Pop understand the protocol of church, from which book to read or sing? Would the words of the preacher make sense to him? Would the demons that drove him to drink be addressed? I'm not sure there is a seat for Pop in most of our churches, as it so often seems that a lot of our activity is pretty self-absorbed. Are we really expecting a guy like Pop to stop by? I'm not sure how to answer this question, but I do know this: I'm waiting for Pop. I'm going to be ready when he shows up. I'll be the one next to the empty seat, in jeans and sneakers.

Lord, help me to see others as You do.

Steve Brubaker is the director of Residential Programs at Water Street Rescue Mission, Lancaster.

God's Way Sure is Annoying!

"…feed me with the food that is my portion, that I not be full and deny You and say, "Who is the Lord?" Or that I not be in want and steal, and profane the name of my God." *Proverbs 30: 8–9 (New American Standard Bible)*

It would be so easy. Three strokes on the keyboard, and we had the largest order our business ever received. Not only that, it would meet a quota, providing extra earnings. Seconds ago, I was praising God. Now, I stared in disbelief as the system showed he was someone else's customer.

I knew a way I could enter his information as a new customer. I justified it in my head, *He must like us instead. This will make up for the two customers that were stolen from us last month. Isn't it really God's provision?*

I did do the right thing, but it was hard. Darryl and I prayed long and hard before our business launch two and a half years ago, and we had prophetic backup that we would be successful. We figured it would happen quickly and Darryl could come home from his current job and work from home. It hasn't been that way; we are just now in the black.

But, I have prayed with many customers. We have given out New Testaments through our "Free Bible" campaign. Those associates who joined us are devoted to God, and we encourage one another and build each other up. My life is richer, and my homeschooled children are receiving education in business management. And, when it comes down to it, my heart doesn't want to deny it is God who provides for us, nor to profane His name through dishonest action. Those three keystrokes would have cost more than I knew.

God, doing right things can be annoying. At least I know I can trust You and that it is for my best. As I walk through this day, help me remember that my richest possession is my relationship with You.

Carolyn Schlicher and her husband, Darryl, own and operate LiquidWholeFood.com out of their Elizabethtown home.

Cleanse the Inside

"For out of the abundance of the heart the mouth speaks."
Matthew 12:34 (New King James Version)

Discipline is hard, isn't it? Whether we're the parents trying to enforce consistent boundaries for precious souls placed in our care or we're on the receiving end of godly chastening, it's quite challenging. As parents, my husband and I make a point to consistently address our girls' hearts. We want them to contemplate and recognize the motives springing up from hearts gone astray.

I've been reading, *Instructing A Child's Heart,* by Tedd and Margy Tripp and by this time in my walk with the Lord, I'm not surprised how He has been speaking to my own heart as I diligently seek wisdom in raising my children. Lately, the slightest brush of irritation causes me to aim the spiritual flashlight towards the seat of my emotions.

Surface dwellers only see the foam on the surf, the color of the water, or the floating plant life that hints at the world beneath. Did you ever stop to think what lies beneath a scummy pond? How about one that displays vibrant lily pads and rippling currents? If we dared a dive, would we find the source causing the condition on the surface? God's Word answers a resounding yes!

I've been challenged to retrace the steps of my outward expressions or feelings to find the source no matter how justified I feel, because ultimately any ungodly behavior has a root. If I continue to surface dwell without diving to explore the depths within, the scum on the pond will persist. Even with repeated, consistent and faithful skimming, it will reappear. I'm reminded of Jesus' words to the Pharisees, "Blind Pharisee, first cleanse the inside of the cup and dish, that the outside of them may be clean also" (Matthew 23:26).

Father, continue to help us look beyond the surface of our own lives.

Amy Grumbling is a wife, mother of two beautiful daughters and a writer.

Photo by Jennifer Raff

April

The Cure for Procrastination

"He also that is slothful in his work is brother to him that is a great waster." *Proverbs 18:9 (King James Version)*

"Why should I finish that job now when I can wait until later?" "Why should I make that phone call now when I can do it tomorrow?" Such thoughts were once a common occurrence in my brain.

I used to suffer from that irritating problem called procrastination. I always intended to deal with the problem—later. But God wouldn't let me waste my life one day at a time.

Like most youth, I often lived as if life on earth would go on for many years. I found it easy to put things off because I took tomorrow for granted. It took a dose of reality to wake me up from my slumber. God repeatedly brought to my attention that people younger than I am are dying every day. I also remembered Christ's parable about a rich man who made big plans for his future (see Luke 12:16-20). Little did he know that he was about to die. God told him, "This night thy soul shall be required of thee."

Reality hit home.

We are not guaranteed any tomorrows. Once that fact settled in, I found it much harder to procrastinate. When I realized that death can come at any moment, I couldn't put off the things that must be done.

This really puts things in perspective. TV doesn't seem all that important anymore. Organized sports don't have as much appeal. Living with the knowledge of our mortality quickly straightens out our priorities! With right priorities, we are free to do more to advance the kingdom of God in our short time on earth.

We must not leave relationship conflicts unresolved. We must not neglect the work that God has called us to do. Today may be our last opportunity. We must make every moment count for the glory of God!

Father, please help me to make every moment count for Your kingdom!

Scott Eash, a longtime Lancaster County resident, is an author, filmmaker and the founder of Biblical Worldview Media.

Be Still and Know ...

"Be still, and know that I am God." *Psalm 46:10*

Many people can recite this verse from Psalm 46. At the beginning of this Psalm, comes one of my favorite Bible verses, in Psalm 46:1. That verse says, "God is our refuge and strength, an ever-present help in trouble." He surely is our refuge and strength—and many times it is not until we are still, in the presence of our Lord, that we sense His ever-present Spirit.

In the course of a day, it is amazing how full our schedules can be —meetings, appointments, phone calls, emails and many other things fill our time. How simple and easy it is to spend time in the study of God's word, and close communion with Him through prayer, but do we make it a daily habit to do so? Even in the midst of our busy tasks of the day, God is ready to go with us—all we need to do is ask for Him to guide us.

In times where I struggle giving daily time to God, I wonder what I may be missing Him telling me. Is He trying to tell me about my job, about the people I love most, about how I can serve him? However, what if I fail to quiet myself and give God the opportunity to speak to me?

That is one of the beautiful aspects of Jesus. He is always ready to speak. Always ready to give. Always ready to approach us. All that we have to do is quiet ourselves, our schedules, our minds and our hearts and know that He is God. He is ready to speak to me, to us, to you. Are you listening?

Lord, Your Word promises that we will find You when we seek You with all of our heart (Jeremiah 29:13). May You grant me the grace to humble myself and seek you daily as I quiet myself and be still and know that You are God."

Bryan Engle is currently employed at Messiah College as the head baseball coach.

Contentment

"For I have learned whatever state I am there within to be content."
Philippians 4:11

After college graduation, my roommate and I decided to write our life verses in calligraphy and hang them above our living room couch. Philippians 4:11 was my life verse. At the time, I was living in my home state of Kentucky. About a year later, I married and moved to Arizona, as my husband was serving at a local church. After a couple of years, we moved to Pennsylvania, his home state. The saying around our house soon became, "my life verse must have been geographical, since I am now in my third "state."

I would think of that verse from time to time, but it was only about two years ago that my life verse became very real to me. I lost my husband of almost thirty years and became a widow at fifty-one. As I dealt with the realization of living alone and all that comes with it, God became very real through that verse. He also placed it upon my heart to look at that verse differently. I had placed an emphasis on the content portion of that verse, and while it is so important, I am now focusing on what Paul says in the fourth word, *learned.*

Yes, contentment is learned. I think Paul is encouraging us to daily study and continue to learn, so that when life's journey has ended, we can say we learned contentment. I am learning that contentment through my daily walk with Him, through His word and spending time alone with Him. It has helped me focus on being content at home, at work, at church, in all steps of my daily life. Along this journey, God has sent blessings to provide that contentment: a daughter and family moved back to Pennsylvania (ironically from Arizona), and I watched my son's college baseball head coaching debut.

Lord, may I be a student of learning contentment through You and praise You for the blessings sent.

Mona Engle served as a pastor's wife for almost thirty years within the Brethren in Christ Church. Presently, she is employed as practice administrator for Drs. May Grant (Lancaster).

Lunchbox Notes

"Train up a child in the way he should go, and when he is old he will not depart from it." *Proverbs 22:6*

Have you ever felt that when you talk with your children what you say to them is "going in one ear and out the other?" I had an experience recently that caused me to think otherwise.

During this past school year, I got into the habit of writing a note of encouragement and putting it in my seven-year-old daughter's lunchbox. She never said much about it to me, so I didn't think she really cared whether I did it or not.

Then one day I was cleaning out her lunchbox, and I opened a pocket on the side of the box. In the pocket was every encouraging note I had written to her from the entire school year. She had saved them all! When I asked her about it, she told me that sometimes when she needs encouragement at school, she will just take a few of them out and read them. I was astounded that my daughter valued my words so much!

As parents, it is easy to forget that our words stick with our children, whether they are positive words or negative ones. Let's remember to speak encouragement and blessing to our children in faith, knowing that our words will have an impact on the next generation!

Dear Lord, please help me to speak words of encouragement to my children and to others today. I pray that these encouragements will positively impact the next generation. In Jesus' name, amen.

Sarah Erk serves the Lord with her husband, David, at New Covenant Christian Church in Washington Boro.

It Just Happened

"Pray in the Spirit at all times and on every occasion...."
Ephesians 6:18 (New Living Translation)

On a Palm Sunday morning a few years ago, my son Jacob and I walked into the church service. My wife was away at a women's retreat, so I asked Jacob where he wanted to sit. He picked a spot far from where we would normally sit.

I looked across the aisle and saw Justin, a young man I knew to be a new Christian. He was sitting with a woman I did not recognize who looked uneasy. I can't say I often get strong feelings to pray for someone, but at that moment I did. I said a quick prayer admitting that I didn't know who she was or what need she had in her life, but asking that God would touch her during the service.

A few days later, I received an email from a friend of Justin saying that his mother had trusted Christ in the service that weekend. A few months later, I watched as she was baptized and as she pointed to the seat where she had been sitting when she trusted Christ.

So my wife *happened* to be away that weekend and I *happened* to let Jacob pick our seat and Jacob *happened* to pick that seat and I *happened* to see Justin and his mom and I *happened* to think to pray for her and God touched her that day. I'm not smart enough to know what role my prayer played in her decision, but I do know that it was a privilege to feel a part of what God was doing in her life. In fact, I was overwhelmed at all the details that God orchestrated in order to give me the opportunity to be involved in even that small way.

Thank you, Lord, for allowing me to be a part of Your work in other people. Help me to be obedient when You are leading me to pray for someone.

Jim Whiteman is Next Steps for Adults pastor at Lancaster County Bible Church, Lancaster.

It's Gone

"Give thanks to the Lord, for He is good! His faithful love endures forever." *Psalm 136:1*

When a routine medical test showed "an area of concern," my heart felt peace. Through subsequent diagnostic tests and the surgeon's plans to remove the tiny mass, the peace remained. I recognized that the peace was partially based on previous experience…my husband's sudden death three years earlier took me to a deep understanding of how God's goodness can be revealed within intense pain. I felt in my spirit that, now, His goodness would come through an experience with cancer.

The day of surgery arrived and I was prepped for the procedure. A test was performed to pinpoint the questionable area for the surgeon. Oddly, the test was repeated. Minutes later the surgeon appeared and said, "The area of concern is no longer a concern. It's gone."

While I should have been elated at the news, I was perplexed. I expected that God's goodness would come in the midst of a cancer journey. But His goodness came to me through healing and wholeness. I didn't know how to receive goodness that actually looked "good."

As I took my questions to Abba, He reminded me of Paul's words in Philippians 4: "I have learned the secret of living in every situation, whether it is with a full stomach or empty, with plenty or little." Abba was teaching me more of His goodness—not just in the emptiness of emotional pain, but also in the fullness of physical wholeness.

Papa, thanks so much that my circumstances don't define Your goodness. You are good, Your love is always present and I thank You.

Kati French is a mother and grandmother. She serves as executive director for Susquehanna Valley Pregnancy Services and is on a regional transformation team for Lebanon.

Welcome to Old Age

"He who walks with the wise grows wise...." *Proverbs 13:20*

I officially became a senior. No, I did not have a birthday nor did AARP finally accept me. But I had a colonoscopy. Isn't that the gateway into senior-hood—the door we back into when we finally arrive to maturity?

It's been one of those things that I've been putting off, like thousands of my fellow baby boomers.

"So, how did it go?" you ask. Not bad. The preparation, noted as the worst part, was not bad at all. I did take a few books into the restroom. One such passage gave great meaning to the moment. In the Civil War book I was reading it read: "The Confederates, *flush* with victory after Second Manassas..."

The outcome—not bad either, but it needs to be redone, because my colon was too long for the instrument used. So, that means I have to go back for another one and, in the meantime, put up with the endless jokes like "you could cut it in half, Dan, and have a semicolon!" and "Have you thought of contacting Roto-Rooter?" "I knew you had a lot of guts."

Ah, the joys of getting older. But does wisdom come with age? In some ways it does. If we have surrounded ourselves with wise people, then it does. Solomon, the wisest man to live, wrote: "He who walks with the wise grows wise" (Proverbs 13:20).

And just being old gives us a natural wisdom, as Job 12:12 notes: "Wisdom is with the aged, and understanding in length of days. But true wisdom comes from God and is gained in fearing Him."

"The fear of the Lord is the beginning of wisdom and all who follow His precepts have good understanding" (Psalm 111:10).

Lord, give us Your wisdom as we mature in You!

Dr. Dan Allen is a pastor, writer, conference speaker, radio commentator and director of Pinebrook Bible Conference, East Stroudsburg.

The God I Don't Believe In

"Blessed be the Lord, the God of Israel, who alone does wondrous things. Blessed be his glorious name forever; may the whole earth be filled with his glory! Amen and Amen!" *Psalm 72:18–19*

In the past two years and through a fascinating set of "divine coincidences" my wife and I have become friends with a neighbor well known throughout our community as a champion of the "new atheism." A charming, intelligent, caring person committed to disabusing people of unscientific and irrational beliefs, our friend was once an active churchgoer and Sunday School teacher. With the help of friends, he has overcome serious life struggles and dealt with personal pain, without personal awareness of life-giving connection or belief in God.

One evening over dinner with out-of-town guests, our friend again took issue with the beliefs and behaviors of professed Christians and other religious people. While neither a scientist nor a philosopher, our friend is well-read and very committed to the worldview of people like Richard Dawkins and Sam Harris, two of the current apostles of atheism. As the conversation wound down, I felt moved to say, "I agree with you. The God you describe doesn't exist. So, as you define things, I guess I am also an atheist. But the God I do believe in is my life, my hope, and the One without whom there would be no meaning, joy and ultimate purpose to my life. I hope our friendship will someday see you also getting to know the God I am getting to know more intimately as my life goes on. In the meantime, I value you and our friendship."

Father, help me to go to the Mars Hill of today, as the apostle Paul did in his day, to meet people and examine their thinking for doors of opportunity to share Your gospel. May Your glory fill the hearts of people like my friend, even as it fills the whole earth.

Bruce Boydell and his wife, Joan, envision, equip and empower individuals and emerging leaders of businesses and ministry organizations for the advancement of Christ's kingdom through Lifespan Consulting and Coaching Services.

Extending Grace

"But to each one of us grace has been given as Christ apportioned it."
Ephesians 4:7

Life in the early 1900s did not have the modern conveniences we have now. Grandma spent long hours ironing heavily starched laundry with a flat iron heated on the cook stove. One day, I was playing in my grandparents' kitchen while she was ironing one of grandpa's starched, Sunday shirts. Grandma was called to the telephone in another room, and Grandpa turned to me and said, "Go ahead, finish ironing the shirt." I was much too young to know a great deal about maneuvering a flat iron, but I was flattered that he thought I could do it. I tackled that shirt with a vengeance.

I'll never forget the look on Grandma's face when she walked back into the room and saw the deep creases I had placed in that white, starched cotton shirt. Her expression was incredulous, but she knew immediately that grandpa had put me up to it. So, she didn't scold me or belittle my efforts, even though she knew that the only way to get those creases out was to rewash the shirt, and that meant expending a lot of energy again.

I'll never forget that incident because even though I had botched the ironing, grandma extended grace to me. Grace is a lesson I learned early. It helped me to understand God's character. God is full of grace and mercy, by not treating us as our sins deserve. He is slow to anger and quick to forgive. Our goal should be to become more like Him, and get a little bit better at extending grace to others each day.

Thank you Father for Your grace and love. Help us to extend Your grace and love to others today.

Charity Heller is 92 years old. She was a pastor's wife and recently widowed after 67 years of marriage.

He Hears Me!

"It shall come to pass that before they call, I will answer; and while they are still speaking, I will hear." *Isaiah 65:24*

One of the richest blessings we experience in women's ministry at Water Street Rescue Mission is, of course, having the privilege of praying with a client to receive Christ as their personal Savior. While this experience never ceases to excite us, there is another that fills our hearts with joy. That is, for a client's faith to become genuine and she realizes that "God is real and He hears me!"

Recently, one of our ladies prayed to receive Christ as her Savior in a chapel service. During our next counseling session, we discussed the gospel message to be certain she understood what she had done and its meaning for her life and future. She was assured that now the Holy Spirit inhabited her heart and mind, and God would reveal Himself to her in some amazing ways.

The next day in the shelter, a neighboring client came to her for help. "Please pray with me," was the neighbor's urgent plea. The new Christian attempted to decline, declaring, "I can't pray out loud! I wouldn't know what to say!" "Oh, but you must!" the neighbor pleaded even more urgently. And so my new sister prayed. She described her prayer as "a few stupid words strung together that barely made any sense." The ladies separated to their assigned rooms. Hardly more than ten minutes passed before the prayer of this new saint was answered. These two women marveled together at the "realness" of God. For this new believer, the miracle was "God *is* real and He actually heard *me*!" Wow!

God is in the business of changing hearts—beginning with my heart.

Lord Jesus, how marvelous to know that You, the almighty Creator and Keeper of the universe, reveal Yourself with clarity and truth to those who truly seek You. Help us never to lose the wonder of the realness of You.

Vicki Bollman attends Calvary Church and is a counselor in the women's shelter at Water Street Rescue Mission.

Home

"Surely goodness and love will follow me all the days of my life, and I will dwell in the house of the Lord forever." *Psalm 23:6*

Our toddler son will from time to time will say, "I home." That may not seem particularly interesting except for the fact that he has only arrived "home" a few months ago. My husband and I traveled to China and brought him home with us to be part of our family.

Some have said, "He doesn't know how blessed he is." But even at two years of age, he does truly seem to understand and appreciate his new forever family.

When he says, "I home," he will say it in a contented tone of voice. Of course, those words frequently bring tears to my eyes when I think of the things our son already has experienced in his little life. Not only was Bennett blessed by a family, but my husband and I are blessed by the joy that he brings to our home.

I am so grateful for our forever family God provides for us as believers. Sometimes I watch people in the world and wonder how they do it without the security God provides for His children. I, too, need to express thankfulness to the Lord for caring for me!

Lord, today may we count our many blessings including our eternal home with You. Thank you for embracing us with Your tender care. Amen.

Sarah Sauder enjoys being a mom as well as graphic designer with DOVE Christian Fellowship International.

Jesus Wanted My Heart

"But God demonstrates His own love toward us, in that while we were yet sinners, Christ died for us." *Romans 5:8*

Now I knew who Jesus was, and I truly believed He was a good man; I knew of the Easter celebration, and celebrated Christmas knowing it was the birth of Christ. I even took my children to Sunday school. I had head knowledge, but Jesus so wanted my heart. I wasn't sure I could give my heart to Him, because my heart was so guarded and protected with the lies I chose to believe. Jesus wanted Truth to break the lies.

Finally, a couple of years ago, I said yes to Jesus. This was the start of a personal walk with Christ! He showed me Jesus the Savior, the Son of God, the Provider and Healer. He showed me love and forgiveness I have never known before and has healed me and continues to heal me of the lies I chose to believe. His hand of mercy and grace and faithfulness has guided me on this journey.

I have been serving the Lord for twelve years. He is molding me, shaping me, pruning me, growing me. Jesus is knocking in your life. Are you willing to take action and be obedient to the Voice of Jesus, the Voice of Truth, love, grace, mercy and forgiveness? God wants to reveal Himself to you. The choice is yours. May all we do bring glory and honor to the kingdom of our Lord Jesus Christ.

Lord I praise Your name for those who have already said "yes" to You, and Lord I lift those who have not claimed You as their personal Lord and Savior to call upon You now. Amen.

Julie Carroll serves as the local Nazarene Mission Director.

In Our Weakness

"But [God] said to me, 'My grace is sufficient for you, for my power is made perfect in weakness.' Therefore I will boast all the more gladly about my weaknesses, so that Christ's power may rest on me."
2 Corinthians 12:9

I discovered an olive-sized sphere inside my arm in 2003. I ended up seeing several doctors, with no clear diagnosis. Finally, I had an MRI done, but unfortunately, it was inconclusive. The doctors were pretty sure it wasn't cancer, but it appeared to be growing in or through the main nerve in my right arm. I will never forget five or six experienced neurologists standing around my MRI photos saying, "Huh, that is interesting," and "I have never seen that before." I was not comforted.

Eventually, I learned that if the strands of the nerve were running through the mass, they would have to sever the nerve on either side and try to reattach it. I could possibly lose at *least* 70 percent of the strength and use of my arm. They hoped that it would just pop out of the nerve. Even in that case, my arm would be useless for weeks.

I began to struggle with fear, doubt and severe frustration. I asked God questions: "Why would You allow such a bizarre thing to happen to me when You know I need my arm to play the guitar so I can lead people in worship music. That is my calling, right?" Of course, whenever you enter a conversation with God where the basic premise is that somehow He desperately needs you, you are in trouble. I eventually came to a place of humility, and He gave me peace about the operation.

The procedure went smoothly, and the schwannoma (the benign tumor) was removed easily. Only minor pain and tingling remained in my hand, and my arm was placed in a sling. And then a mini-miracle happened. Guess what I was doing just a few days later? Leading my church in worship music...with my guitar. To God be the glory!

Father, in spite of our pride and struggles, You still choose to use us. In our weakness Your glory shines all the brighter. Be glorified in us. Amen.

Gary Buck is the worship pastor at Petra Christian Fellowship.

Lord, I Need to Know You're Real

"So Gideon said to Him, 'If now I have found favor in Your sight, then show me a sign that it is You who speak with me.'"
Judges 6:17 (New American Standard Bible)

I had been a Christian only one year when the president of Tufts Christian Fellowship (TCF) resigned. To fill that void, a staff member of Intervarsity called a special evening meeting. That afternoon, when praying specifically for God's will to be done, I sensed that He wanted me to pray about my filling that spot. "No," I told Him, "I'm too young in the Lord. Not me." Then I heard, almost audibly which surprised me, "If Harvey Gordon comes in at 12:50 and says, 'Does anyone want to go to lunch?' that means I want you to be president of TCF. Otherwise, you're not to be."

I told God that sounded silly and tried to ignore it. The impression remained and became stronger. At that time in my life, God was real, but not solidly established in my heart, my faith in the infant stage. I finally agreed to the conditions and prayed until the chapel bell rang at 12:50. Just as I breathed a big sigh of relief that the responsibility would be on another's shoulders, Harvey Gordon walked in and asked, "Does anyone want to go to lunch?"

He spoke the exact words that I had heard in my head. Harvey, who lived down the hall, had never done that before or even since then. I had needed a stake with which to firmly fix my faith tent. Thirty-eight years have passed. This event has kept me confident during times of self-doubt and uncertainty. Never have I wondered whether or not God existed, for I have always been able to look back and know: "No matter what I think or feel, God spoke clearly to me that day, and what He said came to pass."

God, the Father of our Lord Jesus Christ, and my Father, I thank You for specifically revealing Yourself to me in a way that I can understand, strengthening my often weak faith.

John Day is a co-owner of the Lancaster County Showcase and Amish Oak Direct.

Bigger than an Elephant?

"...O Lord, open the eyes of these men, that they may see." So the Lord opened their eyes and they saw...." *2 Kings 6:20*
(English Standard Version)

My six-year-old daughter had thought of an animal, and I was trying to guess what it was by asking her yes or no questions. "Would you have it as a pet?"

"No."

"Would you see it on a farm?"

"No."

"Is it bigger than me?"

"No."

So now I thought I had narrowed down the field to small animals that you would not have as a pet, perhaps a raccoon or a squirrel. I continued asking questions but could not figure it out. Finally, I had to simply ask my daughter what the animal was. Her reply? "An elephant." An elephant! An elephant is certainly bigger than me!

My wife suggested that perhaps in my daughter's eyes I was "bigger" than an elephant. After all, my daughter sees me every day, up close and personal, and I'm much bigger than her. How often has she seen an elephant? Once or twice, from a distance at the zoo?

This got me thinking. How often do I take the time to consider the world through the eyes of other people? If I did this more, would it not make me a more compassionate and empathetic person? And how about trying to see things from God's perspective? My vision is so limited. I can't see all that God is up to behind the scenes. It's so easy to get weighed down and discouraged by my circumstances and forget that our good and gracious sovereign God is working out everything in conformity with the purpose of His will, to the praise of His glory (Ephesians 1). Perhaps the more I look at God (through the lens of His Word), the better I can see.

Father, help me to see the world through Your eyes and to trust You at all times.

Troy De Bruin serves as associate pastor (Youth) at Westminster Presbyterian Church.

This is True!

"Ask, and it will be given to you; seek, and you will find; knock, and it will be opened to you." *Matthew 7:7 (New American Standard Bible)*

Wouldn't it be great to hear directly from God in such an unmistakable way that you couldn't help but believe? I have been blessed with such an experience.

In the early part of the year 2000, I was not a believer. But through what I now recognize as urgings of the Spirit, I was led to begin reading Scripture. I started with Matthew's gospel. When I got to chapter 7, verse 7, the verse quoted above, I heard, literally, a voice. It said, "This is true." And in that moment, I became a believer. I had no choice but to believe. There could be no doubt that Jesus had reached out to me and wanted me in His fold. It was a gesture that, like grace, was a pure gift. I did nothing to earn it or deserve it. Jesus became a real presence for me, and my relationship with Him and His Father was under way. Everything changed for me after that, and I started on the path of discipleship in Christ.

Since that evening in March 2000, as much as I've hoped for it, I have not experienced such a direct word from God. What that moment made clear to me is that God loves me and yearns for my love in return. I've tried to show my love by asking, seeking, knocking—and waiting on the Lord.

Heavenly Father, You showed Your love for us with the sacrifice of Your Son so that we could have a share of Your kingdom. May we respond with discipleship in Christ, through which we know You better.

Michael Degan is a book editor for Herald Press. He is a member of Forest Hills Mennonite Church, where he has taught Sunday school and served on the worship team. He lives in Ephrata with his wife, Becky, and son, Matthew.

Lightning Strikes and Faith Prevails!

"But they that wait upon the Lord shall renew their strength; they shall mount up with wings as eagles; they shall run, and not be weary; and they shall walk, and not faint." *Isaiah 40:31*

One day last year my friend Nicole called to ask, "Did you talk to your mother today?" "No, why?" I responded. "I heard everyone was evacuated, but there's been a fire at Laurel View." Laurel View is a retirement community in Davidsville, Pennsylvania. "I've got to try and call Mom." I abruptly hung up and dialed Mom's number, but there was no answer. Then, I tried Mom's cell; still no answer. I quickly called my siblings to see if they had heard anything. My brother Todd had just received a call about the fire and was headed to Davidsville.

I searched online for local news coverage and sat paralyzed watching flames shooting from my Mom's building. I played it over and over with disbelief, as my sister Tania and I sat by the phone praying to hear any word. Thankfully, Mom got a call through to my brother. We now knew that she was safe. Mom was manning an evacuation center and helping the two hundred evacuated residents.

That day, Mom had no idea that lightning would strike the building canopy and set fire to the attic. She and sixty residents evacuated the building with the clothes on their backs and lost all their earthly possessions.

Despite those times that she found it difficult to fathom that she had lost everything, Mom didn't complain. She was thankful to have made it out safely and was more concerned for those who had no family, insurance or faith. Her regret was losing thirty-five years of notes in her Bible.

She still had her heavenly Father who could not be taken away by any lightning strike. He would see her through this challenge as He had so many times before.

Thank you, Lord, for seeing us through life's challenges! Help us to focus on You and not on the things of this world!

Tasha Delaney is owner of Transfers of Learning and serves at Gateway Church and in her community.

Love That Transforms Lives

"Love is patient and kind. Love is not jealous or proud or rude. It does not demand its own way. It is not irritable, and it keeps no record of being wronged…love will last forever!"
1 Corinthians 13:4, 8 (Life Application Study Bible)

When I look back to my past agenda, I have to kneel down in His presence in awe. I see how the Lord took me to many places just to say to one person, "Jesus loves you," or simply to heal, to deliver, to supply his/her need, to hug a child, to bless a widow, to anoint a prisoner, to pick up a tired and beat-up woman from the street or to talk to a hopeless teen that is ready to commit suicide. I have seen that the love of the Lord is so great, so powerful, so healing that in the worst of the cases, the supernatural intervention of the Holy Spirit interrupts the natural, the psychological, the feelings, the emotions, the circumstances, the oppression, the attack of the evil one and the anxiety. That person who was dead in sin was brought to life in a split second. That woman was forgiven instantaneously, that kid found hope, that addict was set free.

I see how Jesus led me with great love—the kind of love that heals and does not keep record of my wrong, but the love that seduces me to do His will with passion and joy. I am aware of the many times when He touched me with His peace, that peace that surpasses my comprehension, and in that moment nothing matters but Him. I also recognized that in times when I was ready to quit, He gave me the strength I needed to stand firm. I know He has done the same or even more through you and for you. He is our God, Lord, King, Priest, Healer, Redeemer, Sanctifier, Husband, Friend, Prince of Peace—He is love.

Every person needs the love of Jesus to be healed and to be made whole; today is the day to share the love of Jesus with others.

Heavenly Father, we bless You because Your love has been poured out in our hearts through the Holy Spirit who has been given to us.

Marta Estrada is founder and director of Restoration of the Nations. She is part of the Lancaster Gang Outreach Initiative and author of the book *To the Mafia with Love.*

The Small Things

"And we know that in all things God works for the good of those who love him, who have been called according to his purpose."
Romans 8:28

Mark had been coming out to TNT Youth Ministry for almost a year, and I had slowly gotten to know him, but he was very shy. I invited him to join a friend and me for breakfast, and it went as most do: conversation about our jobs, family, school and interests shared over some coffee and home fries. Mark seemed open to share some things about his life, but he seemed uncomfortable, and when everything was over I assumed that we had scared him off for good.

A month or two went by and I was glad to see that Mark continued to come out to TNT, but it didn't seem like our efforts had made any impact. In fact as the days passed I had forgotten about our attempts to reach out to him.

One evening Mark showed up at Bible study at the youth center. Mark had never come to our Bible study and when I saw him my heart skipped a beat.

After it was over Mark took me aside to talk, but he was having difficulty sharing because of the tears he was choking back. I was excited and scared at the same time. I never saw Mark express any emotions, and I didn't know if he was happy or sad. He was thanking me and my friend Mike for taking him out to breakfast. It was almost half a year later, and I had all but forgotten about our breakfast, but he had not. He said no one had ever done something like that for him, and he appreciated it so much more than he could ever express. God showed me in that instance that he can use all things to His honor and glory, even home fries and coffee.

Father, thank you for revealing Your love for us, even in the small things.

Grant Gehman serves as the director of TNT Youth Ministry in Ephrata.

The Season of Waiting

"'Do I bring to the moment of birth and not give delivery?' says your God...." *Isaiah 66:9*

Every believer has to walk a similar path. God gives a promise. Then, there is a season of waiting, which ends in the joyful fulfillment. I have had the privilege of seeing this truth unfolding in my own body six times now! I conceived a child of promise in my womb. At first there was no evidence that the promise had come, but I knew that something was different. Then I would begin to feel sick, but it was not just indigestion, it was destiny! Excitement would fill me the first time I would feel the baby move. I would feed the unseen promise with lots of healthy food. But then I started to grow out of all my clothes. I felt awkward and uncomfortable and couldn't do the things that had once been so easy. I felt burdened and weary of waiting for the promise to arrive.

Once, a mother of eight told me to enjoy my pregnancy. I didn't understand how I could enjoy an experience that was so uncomfortable. I have since realized that it is in the waiting that I get to know God. It is in my times of total weakness that I learn to rely on His strength.

As I write this, I am waiting for the arrival of our sixth child. My husband and I are also waiting for many promises of God to be fulfilled. The waiting has been so long and some days I fight to hold onto a shred of hope. Have we gone off the path? Have we somehow nullified God's promises? Will we *ever* see the fulfillment?

Yet God keeps telling me, "No woman remains pregnant forever! This baby will come forth. All of my promises will come forth. Though they tarry, wait for them. As surely as the sun rises each morning, all of my words will be fulfilled!"

Thank you, God for Your great faithfulness!

Anne Brandenburg is the wife of Chris, a pastor at Life Center Ministries, and the mother of six.

Restrain Your Voice

"Restrain your voice from weeping…there is hope for your future."
Jeremiah 31:16–17 (Amplified Bible)

I was perched in my rocking chair in the predawn hours, cup of tea in hand. My regular date with God was about to commence. With barely a "good morning" spoken, I went right to the heart of the matter. After all, it was Monday and a very long week lay ahead. At the foot of God's throne I unleashed my voice. A torrent of concerns, anxieties, requests and worries came pouring forth. That's when God interrupted me.

Mid-flow, He stopped me and said, "Restrain your voice, daughter!" Actually, it came across more like, "Excuse me, Jen, but you sound like you don't think I can handle this! Listen to yourself. I am big enough for these concerns. I am up for the task! Now, would you care to rewind your prayer and try again? This time remember faith."

Oops. Yes. God was right in His correction. I had to chuckle to myself. How often had I stopped my own son—mid-torrent—to give *him* the opportunity to rephrase his requests of *me*? And now my heavenly Father was doing the same. "Would you care to rephrase that?" He was asking.

And so I began again. However, instead of presenting my panic list, I followed the advice of Philippians 4:6 and brought each request before Him with thanksgiving. God and I had a great time together as I praised Him, declaring that He was indeed able to handle each and every one of the situations.

That week was one of the best weeks of my life. God outdid Himself. I almost thought He might be saying, "I told you so!" as I watched the impossible happen over and over again.

God, help me to restrain *my voice from unbelief and* retrain *it to be one of faith, confidence, and thanksgiving. You are more than able to tend Your sheep!*

Jenny Gehman lives in Millersville with her husband and son, where she continues to enjoy her morning voice lessons with God.

Walk Like a Ferret

"Whether you turn to the left or to the right, you will hear a voice behind you saying, 'This is the way; walk in it.'" *Isaiah 30:21*

My daughter's ferret, Hunter, scampered around his "pet" octopus excitedly. His comedic antics provide great entertainment. "Maybe I should go this way. No! That way looks more exciting." Choosing one of the five tentacles of his favorite toy, he disappeared into the belly of the creature, blazing trails with sweet abandon.

A few seconds later, his furry little head popped happily out one of the portals. "What an adventure!" he exclaimed grinning from ear to ear.

Whew! If only I were more like that ferret. I sometimes get muddled in the middle of decisions. Tangled in my tentacles, I become stuck in a maze of choices, not knowing which way to turn. Why do I struggle so? Fear. Fear sometimes paralyzes me. Momentarily, I may not see, feel or hear God. At those times I need to hold on with bare white knuckles to my faith in who God is and the truth of what He says. I call it stubborn faith.

As I focus on the truth of God's Word to guide me, I gain the courage to step out in faith, faith in who He is. God is love.

As I focus on His great love for me, fear loosens its grip. I see that His love stretches wider than the chasm created by sin, lasts longer than life on this earth, reaches deeper than the depths of depression, and is higher than my understanding.

Equipped with this knowledge, I know that "nothing can separate me from the love of God that is in Christ Jesus" and I can walk victorious into His plan for my life.

Dear Lord, forgive me for listening to any voice other than Yours. Thank you for Your great love that guides me from my fears to peace and rest, and gives me joy that I, too, may grin from ear to ear.

Nancy Magargle is a member of Lancaster Christian Writers group.

Pools of Rest

"Blessed are those whose strength is in You, who have set their hearts on pilgrimage. As they pass through the Valley of Baca, they make it a place of springs; the autumn rains also cover it with pools. They go from strength to strength till each appears before God in Zion."
Psalm 84:5–7

I always know God wants me to pay special attention when a scripture stands out. I had been thinking about and asking about the part about springs and rains. I had been meditating and researching this for months letting it rest, then looking at it again, trusting God to open this up for me. I had learned a while ago that *baca* meant weeping. The Revised Version says "passing through the Valley of Weeping they make it a place of springs, yea, early rains cover it with blessings." I waited.

A series of sorrows happened quite close together, in the span of a week our daughter announced a far away move, and then two people I loved died. I was walking through the Valley of Baca.

On my way to work one morning I passed a field with large rain puddles. It had rained the night before and there were geese plopped down in the puddles. Out loud I said, "You stupid geese there's a large pond just over there." If they had just flown a little farther they would have had a much more appropriate stop.

Immediately, I heard the Lord gently speak, "That's what I mean." He showed me they were resting from their travels. They had gone so far and the puddles were there to rest and refresh in. He had provided a place for them. Tomorrow the puddles would be gone. He had provided what they needed today. They were still traveling with purpose but they had stopped to gather strength.

Are you weary? Rest in His strength. He has provided the rain ahead of time. He has gone before you. Rest, and then you can continue knowing that He'll provide another puddle when you need to rest again. He knows what you need to be strengthened.

Lord, in Your tender love You provide for us, comfort us. Your Word feeds and strengthens us. Thank you for Your intimate care in the midst of sorrow.

Christina Ricker is a wife, Mom, Nana and a fellow traveler from Petra Christian Fellowship, New Holland.

Where are You?

"Then the Lord God called to the man, 'Where are you?'"
Genesis 3:9 (New Living Translation)

Soon after God created the perfect helpmate for him to magnificently complement the perfect conditions in the Garden of Eden, Adam was ducking God and nowhere to be found. The serpent's temptation worked like a charm, and sin entered into God's perfect creation, causing Adam to evade God. Not until Jesus came to pay the price of redemption on the cross at Calvary did the creation once again see perfection—and someday soon His redemption will be complete and those who have trusted Him will enjoy it and worship Him forever. Until then, the shame Adam and Eve experienced as a result of their sin is something we all must struggle with.

Until God used the discomfort of my doomed efforts to avoid my own sin and shame, in order to make me submit to His will for my life, I was not ready to hear His call. I thank the Lord that He allowed this Prodigal Son to not die, but return home.

Make an inventory today of those close to you who are "clothing" the shame of their sin with rebellious acts of deception, or even a cloak of religiosity. Let your heart be touched by the pain you know these individuals feel and pray for them by name.

Now examine yourself. If you know you are forgiven by God because of your faith in Jesus, stop and praise Him now. If you are experiencing shame because of something sinful you have done or because of something sinful *someone else* committed but that affected you (and there are so many in pain right now because of the inability to deal with the consequences of destructive actions perpetrated within broken relationships), receive His forgiveness. Pray this prayer:

Father, You have created me with a purpose far beyond my complete understanding. I recognize Your ability to authentically walk with me by Your living and Holy Spirit, and Your ability to forever remove anything sinful and its consequences in me. "Create in me a clean heart, O Lord, and renew a right spirit within me."

Bill Shaw is executive director of Life Transforming Ministries in Coatesville, a sinner saved by the grace of God, and reminds himself each day that this fact is not going to change and he needs to tell somebody about it!

Confidence

"And we know that in all things God works for the good of those who love him, who have been called according to his purpose."
Romans 8:28

My dear friend, Jesse Owens, was scheduled for triple by-pass surgery early Thursday morning. Renee, another dear friend, prayed with me confidently declaring, "No complications, Lord! We pray in Jesus' name for no complications!" She was very specific in her request.

Later that same day, Jesse's daughter, Laurie said to me, "Isn't it amazing how God put extra veins in our legs, and then gave wisdom to doctors to connect them to our hearts!" We marveled together at God's creative handy-work.

A short time later Laurie was rushing to the hospital. Her dad was having complications.

"Complications?" I said to the Lord. "But, we prayed for "no complications!" As my question hung in the air and I pondered God's goodness, He reminded me that we had brought the request to Him!

My questioning tone became a confident tone, as I realized God had heard our prayer. Peace came over me and I knew I could trust God was at work.

Finally, the news came, "Jesse is doing much, much better."

Heavenly Father, thank you for creating us so purposefully. Thank you for hearing our prayers and answering our prayers according to Your will. Thank you for giving us promises to hold onto in times of crisis, and thank you for healing my dear friend, Jesse.

Lisa Dorr is a wife, mother, public speaker, writer and editor.

I Still Believe

"...If you open your eyes wide in wonder and belief, your body fills up with light." *Matthew 6:22 (The Message)*

I first bought into the reality of God because of a lawn mower. I remember listening to my mother's thirteenth attempt to start it and then going into the chicken house to pray. I heard the sound of the mower immediately after I said "Amen."

I understand, on an intellectual level, the arguments made about prayer versus coincidence. Even at a young age, I kept God's answers to myself because I intuitively knew that most adults would doubt His interest in small things. I have close friends and colleagues who challenge the existence of God. Years of education have sharpened my analytical thinking to the extent that I could argue against the signs of God as well as any atheist. Above all else, my training and understanding of psychological needs and brain neurology make me aware that a belief in God can be argued as resulting from existential angst and a need for security.

Although I understand I may appear naive, I still believe. I believe that God is in me, around me and that He moves through me. I believe that He can provide sunshine, just for one friend's wedding. I believe He guided the young man (angel?) who helped me in a Dallas airport. I believe that He can heal my car, wake me up on time, give me wisdom in a therapy session and heal my clients. I really don't understand the process of all this, but the consistent confirmation of it makes me aware that it is so. I used to be worried that time or challenge might cause me to lose my faith. To the contrary, growth and questioning have increased my faith until it has become as strong, supple and simple as it was in the chicken house long ago.

Thank you, Jesus, for showing Yourself to me. Help me to remain soft and vulnerable as I continue to choose You.

Tricia S. Groff, M.S., has been a therapist in Lancaster for the last seven years.

The Appointment

"Do two walk together unless they have agreed to do so?" *Amos 3:3*

Some people think it odd that a preacher chooses to go to church even when on vacation. I don't, but then again, I am the preacher.

Going to church on Sundays when I don't have to lead worship is one of the ways I have of honoring the Sabbath day and keeping it holy.

A friend of mine helped me with this concept several years ago by challenging me to think of God as one who is waiting for us. The Amos text reads: "Do two walk together, unless they have made an appointment?" The word-picture is of two people who have agreed to meet at a certain place at a certain time. Of course, its application has been extended to other things in terms of continuing in a way of life.

In terms of keeping the Sabbath, it means if one wants to be in God's presence, no other day will do. God has an appointment with His people to meet with Him at a special time, a set time. Moreover, it is different from other times—even as one's appointment with a professional (like a doctor, dentist or lawyer) is different from another. In everyday life, we make agreements to meet with certain people at a certain time. Unless we make an appointment and both parties agree on it, there would be no meeting at any time.

So going to church on Sunday, even when I am on vacation, is simply a way of keeping an appointment with God and the people God has promised to love. I don't have to do it, but if I don't, I am the one who misses something, not God.

Thank you, Lord, for keeping Your appointment with us every week as we gather to offer You what You deserve. You didn't have to do it, but you gave us Your time and paid attention to our every need, and for this we are grateful.

The Rev. Dr. Randolph T. Riggs is pastor of First Presbyterian Church in Lancaster and president of the Lancaster County Council of Churches.

God Must Have Made a Mistake

"And God is able to make all grace abound to you, so that in all things at all times, having all that you need, you will abound in every good work." *2 Corinthians 9:8*

A few years back out of desperation to be in ministry, I applied at Water Street Rescue Mission as a chaplain, never thinking I could actually get the job. I knew that God would lead me to the place where I was *strong* and *knew* how to do the ministry. A suburban boy like me could *never* thrive in the city. Was I ever surprised when it all came together; they offered me the job and I found myself accepting, unable to deny God's hand in the matter.

However, as the job approached, I pictured life at the Mission: men fighting, knives flashing, crazy people looking off into space, tough guys in my face and smelly, dirty drunks slouched on the sidewalk. I had never pictured myself in such a place; it was far away from where I had dreamed of serving God, in a nice clean church with finely dressed people who also wanted to serve God. As my first day drew nearer, my stress level rose through the roof. Half of it was the job, but the other half was the fear of a world where God could make such a mistake with a life like he had mine. This job was totally alien to my experience and job interest. I felt doomed!

The mission people took my hand and walked me through those first few shaky days. Quickly I saw through the tough exteriors and the tragic circumstances, to men who were not that different than me, people who simply needed the care and concern of Jesus. Amazingly they were affected by our counseling times, and they made steps toward the Lord through the classes I taught. The fear quickly disappeared and in a short time, the stress was gone. I was the one who had made a mistake. God could indeed use me in such a place.

God, you never make mistakes. Thank you for giving us all that we need to "abound in every good work."

Craig Hickey attends Calvary Church and is a counselor in the Men's Ministry at Water Street Rescue Mission, Lancaster.

Consider the Lily

"So why do you worry about clothing? Consider the lilies of the field, how they grow: they neither toil nor spin; and yet I say to you that even Solomon in all his glory was not arrayed like one of these."
Matthew 6:28–39 (New King James Version)

It was my day off, and as usual I had more on my "to do" list than I could accomplish in three days. Stop here. Stop there. Drop this off. Talk to that person. Go to the bank. Rush in. Rush out. As I worked my way down the list, one of my stops was at a local greenhouse to buy spring flowers to plant around our house. I stopped and rushed into the greenhouse.

At first I slowed down because there were so many different kinds of flowers from which to choose. Wow…so many different colors and sizes. Then someone behind me said, "Hi, Brian." It was a friend I hadn't seen for years. She asked me about my children. After giving her an update I asked her about hers. As we went on our ways and I focused back on the flowers I realized I was enjoying the beauty of the flowers and the quiet stillness of the greenhouse with fans circulating air in the background. Then I thought about taking the flowers home and planting them with my six-year-old daughter when she got home from school. All of the sudden I didn't want to rush the planting of the flowers. It seemed like I should just relax, slow down, enjoy the beauty of the flowers, and enjoy planting them with my daughter. I went home and did just that.

So what about beauty? Our lives should both embrace and radiate the beauty of the Lord. God was the first artist, and we are His master-piece. Beauty feeds your spirit and causes worry to dissipate. You have heard people say, "Stop and smell the roses, but let's take it straight from Jesus when He said, "Consider the lily…."

Lord, we ask that today our hearts would be full of appreciation for Your attention to the smallest detail of creation around us. You, who hold the balance of nature in Your hands, certainly have a firm grip on our lives and the challenges we face. Thank you. Amen.

Brian Sauder helps provide oversight and direction for DOVE Christian Fellowship International's network of churches.

I Press On

"I press on to reach the end of the race and receive the heavenly prize for which God, through Christ Jesus, is calling us."
Philippians 3:14 (New Living Translation)

I may not be the fastest kid on the block, or even the most improved. But since I started tying on my shoes and hitting the pavement one year ago, I've kept up a more or less consistent pace, i.e. I haven't quit! Sometimes my runs get a bit sporadic, especially in cold weather, and many times I become tired and feel like giving up halfway through a run, but I've learned that the only way to get from one point to the next is to take another step.

Yes, I've had setbacks, like pain in my Achilles heel and sore knees, but I try to set realistic goals so I am not tempted to give up. And I don't beat myself up if I occasionally fail to meet those goals. I've learned that at times the best part is just being able to finish.

As Christians, we run a spiritual pace as we live consistent, purpose-driven lives. The Holy Spirit living within supplies us with all the power and strength to run the race.

So, we "press toward the goal" and keep the pace going, because Paul, the apostle, isn't talking about running just for the sake of running. He is intent on the goal line. To reach the goal line, a runner in a race doesn't keep looking back at who is behind him. Instead, he is intent on the goal up ahead. We can't live our lives looking backward, counting our regrets or failures.

The goal for each one of us is to complete God's purpose for our lives. The goal for each one of us is to become all that God created us to be. And so we press on.

Father, help me keep my single focus on You and pursue You only as I press on to the end of the race.

Karen Ruiz is editor of House to House Publications, Lititz, and is content to call herself a runner who presses on.

May

Really Free

"Trust in the Lord with all your heart and lean not on your own understanding; in all your ways acknowledge him, and he will make your paths straight." *Proverbs 3:5–6*

Before I was a full-time pastor, I worked in the excavating business. Occasionally we were hired to dig ditches through wet areas to drain the water out. On one such occasion I was digging a ditch about three feet deep. A frog that was disoriented by the disturbance I was causing jumped into the ditch. I felt bad for him and decided to get him out. I hopped off my backhoe and into the ditch.

The frog, unaware that my intentions were good, began to leap away from what he perceived as danger. I ended up chasing the frog partway down the ditch before I was able to catch him and set him free.

Partway through the chase, the Spirit of God began to speak to me, "Kevin, you can be just like that frog. Sometimes I want to lift you out of ditches of bondage and set you free, but you keep hopping away."

God desires to set us free from bondages. Sometimes He wants to redirect our course, but we hop away from Him because what we see causes fear. Our circumstances may seem overwhelming, but He may use them to bring us greater freedom. We can resist His firm grip as He picks us up to get us out of the ditches we have fallen into. His intentions for us are always good. We must trust Him and allow Him full reign in our lives.

Lord, help me to trust You and not allow fear to control my life, robbing me of Your very best. Amen.

Kevin Horning is the pastor of New Life Fellowship in Ephrata.

The Glowing Report is that I've Clung to You

"How great is the love the Father has lavished on us, that we should be called children of God! And that is what we are!" *1 John 3:1*

The virus raged on. It had been two weeks with no sign of abating. I'd missed eight of the last ten days of work and was beginning to wonder if I'd ever get well.

When I first became sick, God cautioned me not to succumb to the doldrums of TV watching. But I didn't listen. I vegged in front of the TV, ate junk food, couldn't connect with God and became discouraged.

What was going on? How did I slide so low physically, spiritually and emotionally?

Finally, I was well enough to process things with the Lord. I said to Him, "I'm not proud of the way I've gone through this. I have no glowing reports of how I've clung to You." He responded, "The glowing report is that I've clung to you."

As I recounted the downward spiral I'd been in—unproductive at work, unable to connect with God, sinful behavior, bad attitudes—God broke through with these words:

"Your daughterhood is always intact with Me. My love for you never changes. Even in these weeks when you've slid to a low place, My Father's heart of love for you as My daughter has remained intact. It's immovable, unchangeable, undeterred. That's part of why I allowed you to go so low, so you could experience My love more deeply. You hit the skids, and My love remains the same."

God had lavished His love on me in many different ways over the years, but this time He wanted me to experience it in the midst of sickness and sin.

Thank You, Abba Father, for relentlessly filling every area of my heart with Your amazing, unchanging love.

Lisa Hosler serves at Susquehanna Valley Pregnancy Services and with regional teams seeking God for transformation.

Who Is My Source?

"My help comes from the Lord, the Maker of heaven and earth."
Psalm 121:2

My wife and I had just moved to Illinois from Indiana in 1975. I was a teaching candidate working at a grocery store, and my wife was pregnant with our second child.

Our daughter Rachel was born about six weeks early. Everything seemed fine at first, but she developed breathing problems the next morning and died eleven hours after her midnight birth.

We had a strong faith in God and were comforted by the presence of our two-year-old son, James, but still it was devastating, emotionally and financially. We didn't know how all the bills would be paid. We had attended a great church in Indiana, and I expected financial help from the church and our friends there.

Although we got cards from friends in the Indiana church, we did not receive money. Money and provision did come from family and friends in Illinois and even unexpected sources.

I learned a valuable lesson through the tragic loss of our infant daughter and God's blessed provision. I had my faith in people, and while God does work through people, He was my source. I needed to redirect my focus to the One who has everything under His control.

God, I thank You that You choose to work through people. But people are not my source. Only You are, God. I look to You in all things, and trust You to be the One to meet my needs. In Jesus' name, amen.

Mike Ingold is on the prayer leadership team at Petra Christian Fellowship and teaches fifth grade at Living Word Academy.

Rest

"I sought the Lord, and He answered me, and delivered me from all my fears...Oh taste and see that the Lord is good; how blessed is the man who takes refuge in Him." *Psalm 34:4, 8*

"The Lord is giving you this gift," my friend spoke as she challenged me to rest for a season. As I agreed to lay down everything I could for the next three months and just rest in the Lord's presence, allowing Him to bring refreshing and healing to my body and soul, an overwhelming sense of peace and protection came over me.

Shortly after I arrived home, there was a knock on my door. A co-worker was reporting an emergency situation which required me to work double time the next week and then time and a half the following two weeks. While I was in the midst of my three-month rest, it became clear that the circumstances were a Divine setup. The Lord wanted to teach me to rest in the midst of the storms of life. I need to be centered in Him, so that I don't get caught up and spun around in the whirlwinds where confusion and fear take over.

He wants to hide me in His presence and let His light shine into the circumstances of life. Will you join me in trusting Him to do that for each of us today?

Lord, I will not fear for You are with me. Thank you, that I don't need to look anxiously about me, for You are my God. You strengthen me and You help me. You hold me up with Your righteous right hand. I rest in You today for You are my refuge and strength. Amen. (From Isaiah 41:10).

Liz Ingold works for Friendship Community and is involved with prayer ministry at Petra Christian Fellowship.

Really Seeing

"Open my eyes that I may see wonderful things in your law."
Psalm 119:18

Walking one morning on one of my normal routes, I suddenly noticed a house sitting back on a lot in plain sight. Attractive. Interesting architecture. Something that raised a bit of curiosity and appreciation for whoever had designed it.

Although I had walked by that same property many times in the past, I had never noticed this structure. It wasn't due to a new viewpoint, or any apparent change in landscaping or a new paint job. I had even approached it in the past from both directions.

It reminded me of life. Oftentimes we become so absorbed in what we are doing or focus only from a viewpoint we always have had that we miss the blessings or the bits of knowledge the Lord places all around us.

This same situation occurs in study of His Word. Each time we read it, although it may involve a familiar passage, His Word can take on a whole new meaning if we are open to it.

Lord, help me see from a fresh perspective the many blessings that You put in my path each day, whether they be people, other designs of Your creation or new applications of Your Word. Amen.

Casey Jones, who resides in Parkesburg, is an advocate for development of comprehensive marriage and family ministries, including ministries to the hurting, in churches. He is developer of a Transformation Initiative for Building Healthy Communities Through Healthy Families.

Toads Aren't Ugly, They Are Just Toads

"And God said, 'Let the land produce living creatures according to their kinds…God made the wild animals according to their kinds, the livestock according to their kinds, and all the creatures that move along the ground according to their kinds. And God saw that it was good." *Genesis 1:24–25*

My daughter Breanna, age seven, and I love all aspects of nature and one of our great joys is finding nature's treasures together. Last fall as we were looking at what God created just for us to find, we came across an American Toad. When we picked it up, it startled us as it became vocal and chirped like a baby bird.

Since then "Toad" has become a part of our family and has given us great delight as we talk and play with it. Some might ask, "How can a lumpy, bumpy toad—something so unattractive—bring joy to our heart?" I think it can be summed up in a road sign we saw last year as we were traveling to the ocean. It said, "Toads aren't ugly, they are just toads." The Word of God challenges me to believe that all creatures were made good.

Our family has found great joy in the creatures of this world because in some way or another they characterize their "Good Creator." We have found God's fingerprints all over this world, in creatures that we find extraordinarily beautiful and in those that we tend to overlook.

I am constantly challenged to look at creation with the ambition of finding God's reproducible characteristics. You see, the view from the Creator's eyes shows me that beyond doubt *toads aren't ugly, they are just toads* and they are made good. Is creation perfect? Not since the fall of mankind. Is it good? Unquestionably so.

Praise God for His Creation!

Dear God, the creator of all things past, present and future, give me eyes to see Your fingerprints, Your characteristics that draw me closer to You.

Curtiss Kanagy serves as pastor of the New Danville Mennonite congregation.

Live by Faith

"The faithful love of the Lord never ends. His mercies never cease. Great is his faithfulness; his mercies begin afresh each morning. The Lord is good to those who depend on him, to those who search for him." *Lamentations 3:22–23, 25 (New Living Translation)*

Dogs have always been a special part of my life since I was a child. Years after I was married, I wanted the company of a dog again. I got a Pit Bull puppy and named him Buddy.

At a routine visit, when Buddy was ten, the vet found lymphatic cancer. He gave him three, maybe six months, to live. When I got into the car I cried out to God. When my husband got home, I told him the news.

We agreed we weren't going to tolerate the enemy stealing Buddy, so we prayed for healing.

The fight began! The Bible says the "just will live by faith," and God never allows anything to come upon us, unless He has made a way of escape. Whenever I'd look at Buddy and see his swollen lymph nodes, it was challenging to keep my words in agreement with God. The Lord would remind me, "You can't go by what you see, you have to go by what you know," and He would add, "Trust Me." I found in my weakness, God's strength was there.

God never saw fit to shrink Buddy's lymph glands. It was more important to teach me to walk by faith, not by sight. Buddy died at the age of thirteen and a half, of old age.

Father, thank you for Your covenant of love and grace You have given to us by the blood of Your precious Son, Jesus. You are faithful to be Daddy to us as we cast our cares on You, because You care for us. You are good and Your mercies endure forever. Amen.

Dorinda Kaylor is a regional intercessor at Gateway House of Prayer and minister at Lancaster County Prison.

God's Care for Us

"Look at the birds of the air, for they neither sow nor reap nor gather into barns, yet your heavenly Father feeds them. Are you not of more value than they?" *Matthew 6:26*

While driving through Lancaster City, suddenly four lanes of traffic came to a screeching stop. I could feel frustration starting to rise up within me, and then I looked and saw something amazing. Approximately twenty-five ducks and ducklings began their waddling journey through four traffic lines, and the motorists graciously demonstrated respect to these furry creatures by stopping. As I viewed this, tears started to flow, and the Lord was reminding me of His love and care over these ducks and ducklings.

Then I remembered the passage in Matthew 6 of how He took loving care of the birds, and why should we worry, because we are more valuable than the birds. I also remembered an earlier event that day that demonstrated the Father's care.

One hour earlier, a family dropped by our church's outreach center on East King Street in Lancaster after a Bible study. Not knowing that they had no food, our church fed them and supplied them with meat. The wife then expressed appreciation and said they had no food. I don't believe this woman would have asked for food; however, our heavenly Father knew their condition and sent help.

I was touched and teary for about an hour over the Father's love and care for these ducks and this family. Why give over to worry and anxiety about food and provisions when our Father takes such care over the birds of the air, the waddling ducks and ducklings, and how much more does He take care of us?

Lord, thank you for Your love, care, and daily provisions in my life, and that I don't have to worry or be anxious. You so take care of the birds and ducks, how much more is Your care for me. Amen.

Brenda Keller is associate pastor at Breakout Ministries.

A Portrait of a Mother

"He does not want any one to perish, but every one to come to repentance." *2 Peter 2:9*

My mom and I were always close. She taught me many things, especially about our Lord and life. She helped me to find my identity in Christ, so that I could focus my life on serving Him, not worrying about what others thought about me or my family.

Even when mom and I lived apart, we always shared scripture with each other. Mom instilled in me a desire not only to serve Him, but to live with an attitude of gratitude. Because of the example my mom set for me, I learned to appreciate and recognize all that God has done for me, including the little things.

Mom is gone now, but the most important thing that she taught me was that I needed to be "born again." I needed to turn from sinful, worldly things, ask Jesus to forgive me, put my trust in Him and then begin on a path of building a relationship with Him.

When I asked Jesus to forgive me, His Holy Spirit entered my life and I've never been the same. I'm now more concerned with what I can do for Him, not what He can do for me.

If you haven't before, I encourage you to put your trust in God. Ask Him to forgive you for all the things that you've done that hurt Him and begin a new, fresh relationship with the One who can and will love you more than anyone you will ever encounter on earth.

Please invite Him to share in your life this day! Pray this prayer:

Lord, I know my sins have separated me from You. I am sorry and turn away from my wrongdoing and turn to You. I believe that Your Son, Jesus Christ, died for my sins and paid the penalty and took my shame so I can be free. I invite You, Jesus, to become the Lord of my life and live in my heart from this day forward.

Pastor Carolyn Sites is an associate pastor in Glenvale Church of God, married 57 years, and has one son, who is blind and the church organist.

Dedicated to the Lord

"For we are God's workmanship, created in Christ Jesus to do good works, which God prepared in advance for us to do." *Ephesians 2:10*

I woke up one morning at age fourteen, and heard my father telling someone my mother had been killed by a drunk driver the night before. The person who had loved and advocated for me unconditionally was gone, without warning or good-bye!

My mother had always taken us to church, so I knew and loved God, but I hadn't yet learned how to "trust in the Lord with all my heart and lean not on my own understanding" (Proverbs 3:5). Her death was both a personal tragedy and a crisis of faith. Emotionally, I felt abandoned by God and my mother. Overwhelmed with anger and grief, for many years I ran from my emotions and God. In my late twenties, following marriage and the birth of our first child, I was drawn back to church and found God's amazing grace and unconditional love that had never let me go. Healing and purpose flowed into my life. Most surprisingly, the Lord then called me to ministry as clearly as He had Samuel in the Old Testament.

When I later preached in my mother's church, my grandmother shared a secret. When my mother almost died birthing my older sisters, she (like Hannah in 1 Samuel) had promised God if she ever bore a son, she would dedicate him to serve the Lord. My mother first gave me life, but her prayers and God's faithfulness, gave me new life—joy and purpose in following Jesus.

Sovereign and loving God, help us when we fail to recognize Your faithful and steadfast love for us. Give us grace to trust You in all circumstances. Help us see how all things work together for good, when we love You and seek to follow Christ's purpose for our lives. Amen.

Rev. Scott Fischer is the executive director of the Lancaster County Council of Churches and sits on the Regional Church Leadership Council. Ordained in 1985, he has pastored churches in Massachusetts, Michigan, Indiana, Oklahoma and Pennsylvania.

The Singer

"He will take great delight in you, he will quiet you with his love, he will rejoice over you with singing." *Zephaniah 3:17*

There once was a man who loved to sing. He woke early and walked among the fields, his voice mingling with the dawn and rolling down the hills of Father's farm. And in the echo he could hear Father smile.

One day a traveling Salesman heard the song. The music was so full, so rich. It touched the Salesman and he worshiped.

The Salesman decided that others must be touched, so he arranged a concert.

Singer, flattered and humbled, came to the theatre. He had been told that his music could touch the heart and bring others to worship. Singer tuned up his voice and began to feel nervous.

He entered the stage and pierced the silence with his song. The music was beautiful, and it stirred the hearts of the people around him. He sang with greater effort than ever before.

The Audience was moved. The Salesman was pleased. And Singer's ears were full of applause.

The Audience wanted more. The Salesman needed more. So Singer sang for them again. He needed to share his gift.

Singer practiced regularly. He would wake early and go into the fields alone. But when he sang, he was blinded by the lights of the stage and deafened by the clapping of men. But in the morning mists he could not hear Father smiling. Maybe he needed to sing more.

Finally Singer stopped and listened to the silence. He covered his ears and tears ran down his face. He heard a voice that sounded like Father.

It said, "Lie down and rest. Let me sing to you."

But he dismissed the temptation and recommitted himself to a rigorous routine of singing.

Father, grant me the grace to know Your delight, to rest in Your love, and to receive Your joy over me.

Dwight Kopp was born in Zambia where his parents were missionaries until his high school years. Dwight and his wife, Doe, have four children, one dog, two cats and nine chickens! Dwight teaches eighth grade writing at the Milton Hershey School.

Trust in the Lord!

"He has heard the voice of my supplications. My heart trusted in Him, and I am helped; therefore my heart greatly rejoices…."
Psalm 28:6–7

How often do we just charge into our vacations, forgetting to seek first His kingdom and righteousness, even taking a vacation from Him? Last fall, my family embarked on a vacation with a burden that my wife's son and his family would experience God in a powerful way. This time we chose to put our trust in Him.

A good distance from our destination, cruising along the turnpike late at night, we were jolted by the loud bang from an object getting run over by my wife's son's vehicle. Pulling to the side of the highway, inspection of the tire revealed that the outer tread was completely destroyed, leaving only the fragile inner tube. Instead of falling into grumbling and depression, we cried out to the Lord and asked for His help! Only as we finally exited the turnpike ramp did the tire blow, allowing us to safely park near the toll booth.

It was clear that this place was nearly deserted, except for the tollbooth and service station attendants nearby. We were struggling to change the tire with poor lighting and the wrong tools when along came a man, out of nowhere and without a vehicle, inquiring as to what our problem was. He explained that he was just passing through. In response to our plea for help, he briefly left us but returned to hand us a flashlight and an old wrench as he declared, "That's why I'm here!" As we were finishing the task, he took the flashlight and then simply disappeared. Needless to say, we were in awe, sensing that we probably were just ministered to by one of His angels! Hallelujah!

Heavenly Father, we thank You that when we call upon You and trust in You, we can count on Your help, sometimes in unexpected ways that make our hearts rejoice!

Doug Kramer is a project architect and attends Reading DOVE Christian Ministry Center with his wife and son.

God's Constant Protection

"For He will command His angels concerning you to guard you in all your ways; they will lift you up in their hands so that you will not strike your foot against a stone." *Psalm 91:11–12*

Four-year-old Katie was so excited that we were going to Sturgis Pretzel. As I released her baby brother David from his car seat, I mentioned that Katie would be allowed to get out of the car without climbing over the car seat because no cars were coming down that side of the street. I noticed the old green station wagon coming down the opposite side of Main Street but was sure Katie would wait to take my hand to cross the street.

She surprised me and the elderly man driving the green station wagon, when she bolted across the street directly into his path. I yelled her name, my heart seemed to stop and time suddenly slowed down as I watched helplessly, holding a baby, seeing the terror on the driver's face as he braked as quickly as he could. I watched my precious four-year-old run right in front of his car. In that miraculous moment Katie was suddenly and inexplicably standing twelve feet down the road, exactly where the driver's braking took full hold. His car stopped there and almost gently knocked Katie down.

This (then) young Christian Mom gathered up her daughter with shaking hands, amazed at what I had just witnessed. Within days, God led me in His Word to the confirmation scripture in Psalm 91. He was there watching over us, as always.

All-knowing, all-powerful God, I thank You for Your loving involvement in every detail of our lives. Thank you for hearing the "cries of our heart," our prayers to You, and for the ways that You answer with all wisdom. Help me to recognize and remember the wonders You have done and continue to do. You are worthy of constant praise!

Gail Larkin has had eighteen years involvement with Moms In Touch International, an interdenominational ministry of prayer for our children and their schools.

MAY 14

Spared from Being Crunched!

"Cast all your anxiety on him, because he cares for you." *1 Peter 5:7*

I stopped at a turnpike rest area, parked, took a short break and returned to my car. I went to the trunk to retrieve some cassette tapes and then hopped into the driver's seat. I had just gotten into the car when it was jolted from the back. I looked to the rear of the car and saw, to my amazement, a large truck smack against the back bumper.

The driver of the truck had perhaps forgotten to set the parking brake, and the truck had slowly rolled forward until it came to a stop against my Chevy Cavalier. I found the driver, and we waited for a police officer to arrive on the scene. We exchanged information and gave our report to the policeman.

I wondered afterwards what would have happened to me if I had stayed at the rear of the car for a few more moments, and the truck had pinned me between the two vehicles. Would I have sustained two fractured legs, or worse?

I heard the Lord speak gently to my spirit, "I do care for you, Jim, and I love you." I had been feeling despair and was skeptical of the Lord's love and care for me. But God had spared me from injury in a freak accident, and I sensed the Spirit softly whispering (or was it a loud whisper?), "Yes, Jim, although you may not have been sensing it, I love you, and this incident of my watching over you was simply a gentle reminder of that."

I have often thought about that intervention by the Lord or His angels. I remember it still, years later, as a reminder of God's continuing care for me as one of His children and as an affirmation of His steadfast love.

Loving Lord, thank you for Your constant care and Your continuing love, and that You are with me in my journey today. In the name of the Good Shepherd, amen.

Jim Leaman has been a pastor of Groffdale Mennonite Church in Leola, and along with his wife, Beth, enjoys being a grandparent to five (soon to be six) wonderful grandkids.

Watching Over Me

"...for he guards the course of the just and protects the way of his faithful ones." *Proverbs 2:8*

Recently, friends of ours were visiting from Oregon. We decided to take them into Philadelphia for a day of sight-seeing. We took the Amtrak train from Lancaster into 30th Street Station. Then we crossed the street to the subway. The train pulled in, and as we were waiting for the people to get off, I saw our three-year-old son dart into the car. Just as he did, the doors started to close and the announcement was made that the train was leaving. My heart dropped to my toes, and I began to panic.

Caleb was the only one of our group who was on the train. Everyone else was still standing on the platform. I pushed forward and wedged myself in between the closing door and the train. I shoved on that door as hard as I could, determined that that train and my baby weren't going anywhere without me. Finally, a gentleman already on the train realized what was happening and helped me open the door. He held the door open for the rest of our party and we continued on our way.

As I thought through that incident at home, profusely thanking the Lord for sparing us the anguish of a lost child, it made me wonder how many times the Lord has guarded me without me even knowing about it. I felt the Lord speaking to my spirit, telling me that, just as I had pursued and fought to protect my son, He pursues and fights for me. Even though Caleb was blissfully unaware of what was happening, I knew and was watching over him. The Lord reminded me that He watches over me the same way.

Father, thank you for Your love and protection even when I don't know that I need it. Thank you for seeing what I don't and working every situation out for my eternal good.

Nancy Lenhardt is a member DOVE Westgate Celebration in Ephrata.

A Lesson on Sovereignty

"'For My thoughts are not your thoughts, nor are your ways My ways,' says the Lord." *Isaiah 55:8*

Life was good!

Our latest drama: we were moving from California to Washington in three months. And the Lord was rapidly orchestrating events for us to begin the next act of our lives. We had been warmly welcomed into a new body of believers. Our Christian realtor put a bid on an absolutely incredible house; the owner was Bob's air force academy classmate—a "shoe-in" deal! And Bob successfully interviewed for his air force dream job: second-in-command of a bomber squadron. Our various auditions complete, we looked forward to this new theater.

Our realtor called. "We didn't get the house. A 'contingent' couple placed a higher bid, and it was accepted."

The curtain flew down. In the dark, we were confused.

But the Lord is good. Because Congress cut back military funding two months later, the base in Washington would eventually lose all its bombers. So, instead, the air force sent us to a base in Louisiana. Thank you, Lord, that we weren't stuck with selling an empty house in Washington!

And the Author is sovereign! Several months after settling in Louisiana, we received news that a B-52 from Washington had crashed, killing all the crew members on board. We learned that Bob knew one of them well—another academy classmate who had actually commanded the bomber squadron. The deputy commander died in the crash as well, and that job originally had been earmarked for Bob. And had we moved to Washington, Bob would most likely have been on that aircraft that went down.

To the Author of life's events, thank you for being in control of all the acts of our lives! Even when we don't understand some circumstances, remind us that You have been faithful to us in the past and will continue to be faithful to us in the future.

Tamalyn Jo Heim, a former executive officer in the air force, still relies on the sovereign Lord to protect her husband, Bob, a former B-52 pilot and now a Southwest Airlines captain.

All of Your Ways

"For he will command his angels concerning you, to guard you in all your ways." *Psalm 91:11*

I have lived in Pennsylvania my whole life. Most of my traveling has been in the United States, plus a bit in Canada and Mexico. Never an adventurous person, I was surprised that a trip to Haiti with Compassion International even got my attention. But after sponsoring two children in Haiti, I was hopeful that I could meet them face-to-face.

I prepared for my trip by packing essentials, including gifts for the children. I would fly by myself to Miami, stay overnight and meet the rest of the group at the airport for a flight to Haiti the next day.

Prior to leaving, the staff at SVPS prayed for me. One Scripture passage that was shared and was very meaningful to me was Psalm 91. As I flew from Miami to Haiti and throughout my trip, I was reminded of the verses from Psalm 91 because they were included in the devotional pieces that we were given for the days we were traveling.

A common concern when traveling to other countries is illness from food or drinking water or from disease. We were encouraged to be careful with eating and drinking and were also encouraged to take malaria medicine. I struggle with anxiety and the possibility of being sick and away from home was a cause for me to be anxious. When several of my traveling companions became ill, I was really starting to worry. Then the Lord spoke directly to me from Psalm 91: "Even though others succumb all around...no harm will even graze you. You'll stand untouched, watch it all from a distance..." (Psalm 91:7-8 The Message).

Those were the exact words I needed, and I held on to that promise for me throughout the remaining days of traveling. My trip was not without concerns—losing most of my belongings with still two days of travel remaining, delayed flights home—but I never got sick. And I had a great time learning about Haiti, getting to know other Compassion sponsors and being able to meet my sponsored children.

Thank you Lord, for speaking to me through Scripture just when I needed it! Your faithfulness to me is unending.

Dani Longenecker serves at Susquehanna Valley Pregnancy Services and is a member of Mount Joy Mennonite Church.

His List

"I glorified You on the earth, having accomplished the work which You have given Me to do." *John 17:4*

Last summer I mentioned to a friend that God wanted me to focus more intensely on relationships. Being task oriented, that would be no easy change for me. Two weeks later, my husband and I went camping at the lake—an annual tradition all about relaxing, reading, praying and meditating, quilting, some exercise and family fun. It was all part of my mental "Vacation To-Do" list. Our grown children joined us some days, and we invited a few friends for picnicking and boat rides. This year we entertained sixteen *additional* people in eight days. I enjoyed those times, but in the back of my mind was "maybe tomorrow I'll get to read in the hammock" and "I hope I have some alone time today." I came home feeling like I needed a vacation, having spent just thirty minutes in the hammock. My "To-Do" list did not get finished. And I really missed the extended time alone with the Lord that I'm accustomed to on vacation. In seeming juxtaposition to my longings was the shift God had spoken to my heart previously. I told a co-worker later concerning our relationship-full vacation and the changes in my life, "I know this is what God wants, but I don't *like* it; I was happy with the way I was before."

Okay, so I know outward obedience and conscious cooperative thoughts aren't enough. The absorption of the John 17:4 perspective— accomplishing what *He* has on my list—is slow. I need a willing heart. Experience reminds me that the rewards will be peace and blessing over the entire panorama of life!

Do as You wish with my time, Lord. But I want to come joyously rather than reluctantly. Fulfill in Your time and Your way my deep desire for time with You. Infuse into my relationships Your compassion and loving kindness.

Cynthia Clark mentors women at New Hope Bible Church, Loganville, and teaches at Moms Morning Out at Jonestown Bible Church.

Rock Me, Nana?

"Find rest, O my soul, in God alone: my hope comes from Him."
Psalm 62:5

September, 2007, our fourth grandchild, Lucas, was born. He joined his brother Stephen and sister, Tillie. A few weeks after he was born we flew out to Seattle to meet him. Staying there allows us to have precious chunks of time with them all. One day as I was walking into the living room, Tillie looked up and said, "Nana, rock me like a baby."

Now Miss Matilda Grace is a very active and independent two year old. But, hearing those words as a heart need, I scooped her up, held her close as a baby and rocked her gently. She stayed that way quiet and relaxed for longer than I expected. Then, her need filled, she jumped off my lap to play again.

This was so profound to me—the honesty of a child who knew she needed a fill of comfort and safety. Is that what the psalmist meant by, "rest in God"?

Do you need to be held today? Do you need to be close enough to hear your Father's heartbeat and be enveloped by the love of our Creator? Then run to Him and ask Him—even the strong and independent need to be "rocked" sometimes.

Abba Father, sometimes life is too much. I don't have the strength. Please Father, scoop me up and hold me close. I release my independent "I can do it myself" attitude. Let me rest in Your arms awhile then I'll go about life again.

Christina Ricker is a child of God, wife, mother and Nana.

A Life Lesson with Pears

"For judgment is without mercy to one who has shown no mercy. Mercy triumphs over judgment. *James 2:13*

When I gave my life to Jesus Christ at twenty-seven, I told Him that I wanted Him to teach me to glorify Him in all my ways. Having worked in the secular world for the first six years of my Christian life, I was thrilled to be hired by an organization with a Christ-centered mission. My expectation was that because those whom I worked with were also Christians, it would be a taste of heaven on earth. It did not take long to realize that Christians are all under construction. I was so disillusioned with the gossip and competitiveness that I chose to eat my lunch alone one day.

My lunch included a pear, one of my favorite fruits. I was thinking, as I bit into it, how wonderfully soft and juicy it was. Imagine my surprise when I discovered that the inside was rotten! I did not have much time to lament about it though, as I heard the Lord's still, small voice saying, "You are as close to Me as you want to be. This pear is an example of someone who appears soft on the outside, but is rotten inside. If you do not stop judging these people, you will become just like them. Instead of judging them, stand in the gap and intercede on their behalf."

I have never forgotten this pear word picture. Whenever I am tempted to judge another's behavior, I am prompted by the Holy Spirit to immediately intercede as soon as I am tempted to judge. After all, there but for the grace of God go I.

Thank you, Abba, for shining Your holy light on us and exposing the darkness within. Help us to be so attuned to Your voice that we are able to take captive every thought before it becomes an unholy action. Empower us to turn our judgments into intercession.

Denise Colvin has served in several life-affirming ministries, directed a deaf and hard of hearing agency, and worked in various secular settings. She is blessed with four daughters and ten grandchildren. She and her husband, Rich, a volunteer pastor, minister to older seniors in a residential setting at The Villa St. Elizabeth in West Reading.

So Much

"Let us then approach the throne of grace with confidence, so that we may receive mercy and find grace to help us in our time of need."
Hebrews 4:16

It was our one-year wedding anniversary and we were with a friend touring the shops around Niagara Falls. We weren't looking to buy anything, just looking around. One store caught our attention so we went inside. There were rows of barrels full of candy! The clerk immediately asked us what flavor candy we liked. I got uncomfortable because I knew we weren't there to buy anything, but we answered his question.

With the passion of an archaeologist discovering lost artifacts, he proceeded to show us the location of candy in each of our favorite flavors. "Take as many samples as you'd like!" he said when the tour was complete. Instead of being "a kid in a candy shop," I was feeling more like a kid in a dentist chair.

I wanted to leave but took some to be polite. How many was the "right" amount to take? Taking too many would be greedy, but too few would appear ungrateful. I would have preferred he said how many we were allowed to take. I would have *really* preferred if I could have done something to deserve the candy.

He wanted to see what we found before we left. My wife and friend each had two handfuls of candy. They were given bags. Embarrassed, I had only three pieces of candy.

I was praying before going to sleep that night and I sensed God speaking to me, "Jeff, the way you were in that candy shop is how you approach my throne of grace. I have so much for you, but you feel guilty receiving what I have for you because you do not deserve it."

Father, I'm humbled by Your grace. Today I want to boldly approach Your throne of grace with confidence and with open hands receive from You.

Jeff Comeaux is the associate pastor at The Door Christian Fellowship, Lancaster.

A Steadfast Faith

"Though He slay me, yet will I trust Him...." *Job 13:15*

Having wrestled for years with difficulty in trusting God the Father, I prayed with a sense of frustration, "Lord Jesus, please help me to trust the Father as You do." It is obvious that the gospels, for example, portray this foundational trust in many portions. Some of the most selfless and compassionate words ever spoken reveal this. While dying for us as our sin-bearer on the cross, our beloved Savior prayed for His crucifiers, "Father, forgive them; for they do not know what they are doing" (Luke 23:34). In the garden of Gethsemane submission to His Father's plan of redemption also illustrates this attitude.

I do not recall the length of time between my prayer and its answer. However, I will not be able to forget the answer. One evening, while I was vacuuming, the distinct, inaudible voice stated, "Though He slay me, yet will I trust Him." In that instant I knew that the Lord was revealing to me the depth of His trust in His Father. Our Lord's love for and commitment to God the Father empowered this reliance that led Him to the cross for the salvation of our souls. What an example the Lord has set for us! By relying on our heavenly Father, even when it is difficult to do so, we will develop a steadfast faith.

God has given me opportunities to apply those confident words of Job. One of the most challenging happened when I experienced great physical distress due to herbicide chemical toxicity. One night, as I was trying to fall asleep, my eyes, nose, mouth, throat and esophagus were burning. Worse yet, I could barely breathe. Adopting my Lord's attitude, I prayed Job's words, and I was able to rest in the will of my Father.

I am thankful to have a faithful Shepherd who watches over my soul!

Heavenly Father, thank you for showing me great patience as I learn to trust You more fully.

Susan Marie Davis is a member of Calvary Church in Lancaster.

Ask Questions

"Call to Me, and I will answer you, and I will tell you great and mighty things, which you do not know." *Jeremiah 33:3*

I walked into the office the other day and stopped to ask Evie a question. She laughed as she turned to her co-worker and explained, "Liz is always asking a question."

I responded that my youngest granddaughter is the same way. Four-month-old Kylie is always stretching and raising her hand as if to say, "I have a question."

Many times I've heard her daddy say, "Yes, I see that hand. What is your question?"

But with all this talk about questions, I had to stop and ask myself, "Why do I ask so many questions? Do I *need* an answer? Am I *afraid* I'll do something wrong? Could it be that I'm just *curious*? Am I *over-protective*? Have I buried my head in the sand or am I just *uninformed*? Might I be too *lazy* or too *busy* to find out for myself? Is it *genetic*?"

My questions didn't stop there. I asked the Lord, "Do I ask too many questions?" He reminded me of Jeremiah 33:3. Yes, even more than Kylie's daddy wants to hear those questions, the Lord welcomes my questions. But more than that, He longs for me to just wait in His presence and listen for the answers.

Oh, Lord, help me to wait patiently for Your answers. I want to linger in Your presence and really hear Your heartbeat today. I will listen for Your voice and wait for You to guide me. Be the filter through which my life flows today. May I bring glory and honor to You today. In the precious name of Jesus, amen.

Liz Ingold works for Friendship Community and is involved with prayer ministry at Petra Christian Fellowship.

Greater Love

"Greater love has no man, than that he lay down his life for a friend."
John 15:13

May 22, 2007, just two days before his forty-seventh birthday, my son Bob, flying for the US Customs Service, had just directed the arrest of three illegal immigrants crossing our border from Mexico, when a shot, or rock or mechanical failure hit the tail of his helicopter, and it began to spin out of control.

At an altitude of two hundred feet, he could have set down safely in a yard below him, but he saw three small children playing there. He made an instant life decision and forced his craft over the roof of an adjacent building and crashed into a truck parked in a lot. At the last second he flipped so that he hit first, while his copilot was hanging in his straps above him. The copilot survived, but Bob died instantly. The children's mother saw it all, and she thought her children were goners. She told me later that when the media rushed in for pictures, she forbade their entrance to her property saying, "This is holy ground. A man gave his life here for my children."

Bob was a strong believer and soul winner, so I know he is with Jesus, and that is what keeps me going through it all. He was my hero and my closest friend. In a speech President Bush referred to him by name, calling him "an American hero."

Lord Jesus, I thank You for the great blessing my son was to me and to all those who met him. Thank you for taking him to his reward with You.

Bob Smith Sr. served as the international director of Full Gospel Businessmen's Fellowship and is a member of Grace Chapel.

A Paradigm of Patriotism

"As you have therefore received Christ Jesus the Lord, so walk in Him." *Colossians 2:6*

I have to admit that I don't like going to bed without my husband. We just celebrated our thirtieth wedding anniversary. That's many nights of "playing spoons" with him, where our bodies nestle together just like spoons in the drawer. I get used to his warmth, hearing him breathe, having his arm around me to hold me. So when Bob is away, it's much harder to fall asleep.

Having served in the air force for twenty-three years as a B-52 pilot, Bob "pulled alert" during the cold war. That's when he and twenty other six-member crews slept in bunk beds seconds away from nuclear-loaded planes, ready to take off within minutes. His goal: get safely airborne before an incoming enemy missile would obliterate our base.

An "alert tour" was when Bob slept with his plane for one week out of every three weeks. He did this for nine years. That means my husband didn't sleep at home for three years. Bob also had "short" deployments that took him away for days, weeks or months at a time.

My children would ask, "Why is Daddy willing to be away so much?" I answered, "There are a few things in life that are worth fighting for and perhaps some worth dying for. One of them is our Christian faith. Another might be to protect a family member. And a third area is our country and all the ideals, freedoms and faith it represents."

In our morally shifting environment people ask, "How can I support our troops?" Prayer, gifts and encouragement to the families are great examples. May I suggest one more, a less-chosen pathway: be willing to give up *your* life. Genuinely strive to become imitators of God, die to self and put on more of Jesus Christ, so that our troops may continue to defend our one nation, *under God.*

Dear heavenly Father, open our eyes to not only the physical wars around us but also to the spiritual war in which we are engaged. Protect all soldiers as we engage in battle and encourage us to persevere in our walk with You.

Tamalyn Jo Heim, a former executive officer in the air force, moved twelve times and lived in eight states, to support her military husband, Bob.

Our Tupperware

"...Cleanse me from my hidden faults." *Psalms 19:12*

We all put things off in life, until we get to the point that we are telling ourselves—"Just do it." For instance, washing the car. It's pretty bad when the kids write "wash me" all over your vehicle, or when you open your closet door and an avalanche happens. Or how about the good old cleaning out the refrigerator.

I recently had this chore to do myself. I gathered my cleaning materials and grabbed a trash can. Knowing I was going to throw out stuff, I got myself ready to do battle. As I got farther into the refrigerator, I saw a Tupperware container that was buried in the back. The container looked good on the outside but when I opened it up, I realized I had just created a new color scheme for the Crayola Crayon Company. It might have looked good on the outside but inside, whoa! It was very unhealthy. The Tupperware was my mother's, or I might have just tossed it. So I scrubbed it clean and ran it through the dishwasher.

How often does this happen in our own lives with our hidden "stuff" that is old and pushed way back, or stuffed down deep in our hearts? Sometimes we don't realize the hidden stuff we carry around in us, like anger, pride, unforgiveness, bitterness, jealousy. These things hinder our relationship with God and with those around us.

In Psalms, King David understood this and asked God to show him any hidden faults. Hidden sins. He wanted to be blameless before God. Ask God to show you the Tupperwares in your life. And Mom if you are reading this, I still have your container.

Thank you God for Your mercy and patience with us. Show us Lord, any thing that we carry in us that is hidden, so that we may be forgiven and not hinder ourselves from You. Give us Your strength to acknowledge these sins and the courage to ask for forgiveness.

Lisa M. Garvey serves with the Hosanna Christian Fellowship Prayer Team Ministry.

His Love is Unconditional

"...Not by might, not by power, but by my spirit says the Lord of hosts." *Zechariah 4:6*

Do you believe that God through His Holy Spirit can save souls and transform lives? I know that He is able. He saved my soul from the utter darkness and He is transforming my life. I grew up in a dysfunctional home. My father was abusive, often cursing me and telling me he would cut me up into a thousand pieces. One day as I was walking home from school, I felt a strong oppression. I felt hopeless thinking, "What's the use, I'll never be good enough to enter the gates of Heaven! I'll never amount to anything!" It seemed that I had one foot inside Hell.

I heard the enemy speak those things to me until I was 12 years old. Up to this point I had heard the Truth only indirectly. I knew there was a God but I didn't know how to reach him.

One night while I lay in bed, I cried out to God, "God if you are real, then show up! Come, because I can't live this way anymore." I don't remember how I asked for His forgiveness, but He came in spite of my inadequate prayer. Once the Holy Spirit entered my heart, I sensed a great peace. He poured His love deep into my innermost being. The only voice I could hear was, "I care about you deeply." He very gently, picked up the broken pieces and through His love, gradually transformed me. He's a gentlemen; He does not push, shove or pull. He only walks alongside of us, holding us close to His heart. He doesn't love us for what we do or do not accomplish. Through his Holy Spirit, His love is revealed to us unconditionally. His Holy Spirit will save our friends and transform them. What the enemy means for evil; God turns into good.

Thank you Father for saving my soul, for loving me just the way I am. You are faithful and Your is love is everlasting.

Lydia Miller is married to James Miller. They have five girls and two boys. Lydia has served the body of Christ through intercession and prophetic gifting for fifteen years.

Soul Cancer

"Get rid of all bitterness...along with every form of malice. Be kind and compassionate to one another, forgiving each other, just as in Christ God forgave you." *Ephesians 4:31–32*

Cancer is a villain and it does not play fair. What family has not had their lives turned upside down traveling an emotional and physical roller coaster after hearing a diagnosis of physical cancer? Webster's dictionary also defines cancer as a pernicious, spreading evil. I believe many in the human race suffer from both types of cancer. Unforgiveness is the cancer of the soul. It is a prison. It slams the door on new beginnings and entrenches you in your present pain. Unforgiveness suffocates joy and paralyzes your ability to move on. It slowly eats away the marrow of your existence and impairs your judgment, your personality and your ability to love again. Thanks to Christ, there is a 100% cure rate from soul cancer.

The truth is, forgiveness has nothing to do with who is right or wrong. Forgiveness is a free agent. It is not attached to reason or understanding. It is, however, attached to wholeness, healing and liberation. If you can't forgive for your own sake, forgive for *God's* sake. He needs your hands open in order to bless and use you. Cooperate. Forgive because you need to be forgiven. How can you expect what you are unable to give yourself? Forgive, you are not alone. We have all been there. Come and join us on the other side. Travel the road to forgiveness and healing of your heart and soul.

Father, the words don't come easily. Help me to choose to forgive from my heart and not just from my head. Free me from the anger, the pain, and all the questions that assault my mind. Lead me to a better place. I want to find freedom through forgiveness. And though I may never forget what has happened, help me to forgive, even as You have forgiven me, in Jesus' name. Amen.

Coleen Gehman is a wife, mother and a soul cancer survivor. She serves with her husband, Bryan, at Lancaster Evangelical Free Church.

Filled to Overflowing

"They drink their fill of the abundance of Thy house; and Thou dost give them to drink of the river of Thy delights." *Psalms 36:8*

One cannot read this verse and maintain an image of a stingy God. The whole idea of us drinking our "fill" illustrates how genuinely generous God is. "No good thing does He withhold from those who walk uprightly" (Psalms 84:11). What a relief.

Perhaps you've heard the phrase, "soaking in the Lord," another way of explaining that someone has been spending special time alone with God. It makes sense in light of this verse. The idea of drinking our fill expresses the sense of being completely saturated or deliberately drenched. It's not a drizzle, we're talking a deluge!

As a matter of fact, the original language renders the word *river* in this verse as a "torrent." We don't use that word to describe a gently flowing stream. This is an overwhelming overflow! This "drink" is not a polite sip. It's a gulping, chugging, brimming mouthful of His goodness!

Which demonstrates the relentless kindness of our God. He so delights in you and me that He gives us "far more abundantly beyond all that we ask or think" (Ephesians 3:20).

Because I happen to be in a time of dry desperation, this verse is a fountain of life to me. I will trust Him for what I cannot see and allow Him to fill me in my seeming emptiness. I open wide my heart and drink deeply. May "rivers of living water" flow from my innermost being as a result!

Oh, how I need You, Lord Jesus! Teach me how to drink deeply of You. I want to know the abundance of Your house and I long to taste the river of Your delights. Fill me, Father, fill me with Your love...amen.

Kathi Wilson and her husband Mark, co-authors of *Tired of Playing Church* and co-founders of Body life Ministries, are members of Ephrata Community Church.

Witchcraft at Water Street

"...to another the word of knowledge...." *1 Corinthians 12:8*

Pastor Brenda, of Breakout Ministries, and I teach at Water Street Rescue Mission most every Tuesday. In October of 2007 while praying before the teaching, I felt the Holy Spirit urging me to "bind up the spirit of witchcraft." I was familiar with binding and loosing, as the Holy Spirit had directed me in the past. So, I silently bound up witchcraft. Then the Holy Spirit directed me to "say it out loud." "But Lord," I protested, "I don't want to scare anyone." "Just say it out loud," I heard again in my spirit. So of course I obeyed. When I obey, it always produces good fruit, even if it is not immediate.

After I obeyed, I noticed one of the women getting very uncomfortable. The next week, the same woman was hiding, a spiritual darkness hovered around her, and I knew she was the one the Holy Spirit had in mind. The third week she wasn't there, and she did not resurface until April of 2008.

For months I had a burden to pray for her. In April a woman that resembled the woman with witchcraft sat with us, but I wasn't sure because she seemed bright! Halfway through the teaching, she cried, "May I please give my testimony." "Please do," we said. She said, "I was here last fall and you (pointing to me) bound up a spirit of witchcraft. I was a practicing white witch. I was a high priestess. I trained others in Lancaster City for the past five years to chant, cast spells, and do séances. When you bound up the spirit of witchcraft, I just wanted to run and hide. I left the mission and started living with a man who physically abused me. Every Sunday morning I would return to the chapel here at the mission. Last week I gave my heart to Jesus! I renounced witchcraft, left the abusive relationship, and I'm back here to get my life together."

Thank You, God for caring enough to pull our feet out of the miry clay!

Donna Brown attends Wayside Presbyterian in Landisville, where she has been ordained as an Evangelist. She is a deacon at Wayside and has been for six years. She is involved in Street Ministry with Breakout Ministries in downtown Lancaster. She is a muralist, plays guitar, sings, and works with elderly part time.

Word and Spirit

"When the Day of Pentecost had fully come, they were all with one accord in one place." *Acts 2:1 (New King James Version)*

It had been ten days since Jesus had ascended into heaven. The disciples waited for the Promise of the Father just as Jesus had instructed them. Meanwhile they appointed Matthias to take the place that Judas had vacated. There was harmony.

Men and women, disciples and relatives—worshiped and asked for the Promise. They prayed according to *the* prayer (Acts 1:14) that Jesus had taught them. They called forth the kingdom, His will to be done; they entreated for the Promise to come from heaven to earth.

On this holy day, Pentecost, or fifty days after Passover, they prepared to celebrate the Feast of Weeks, the Feast of Harvest. On their exodus from Egypt, their ancestors had come to Mt. Sinai fifty days after the Passover night. At this mountain God spoke His Word to His people (Exodus 19 and 20) accompanied by great shaking, lightening, thunder, smoke, clouds and loud trumpet sounds. It was noisy. They trembled in the fear of the Lord.

As faithful Jews who now knew that Jesus is the Christ, as they waited they read the lectionary (scripture) assigned for each day. Their reading for Pentecost was Ezekiel 1. The prophet's vision of spirit beings is punctuated with torches of fire, lightening, and noise of wind, water and tumult in war.

Just as the Spirit entered Ezekiel (2:1-3) when God spoke, so the Spirit entered into the waiting disciples in accord with the Scripture. The Holy Spirit acted in one accord with the law and the prophets to which they were giving attention. With noise and tongues of fire, again God was glorified in holy amazement.

Father, I know that Your Spirit faithfully manifests Your Word. Enter my life today by Your Spirit according to the truth of the Word to which I attend.

Keith Yoder, founder and president of Teaching The Word Ministries, serves as chair of the Regional Council of the Regional Church of Lancaster County.

June

Dealing with Fears

"Remember I am with you always, even until the end of the age."
Matthew 28:20

My nine year old granddaughter loves to draw and is quite a talented artist. One day she sat on our patio sketching for quite a while. She rolled up her papers but forgot to take them with her when she went home. Later, I unrolled them to she what she had done.

Across the top of one, written in block letters, was her memory verse, "Remember I am with you always, even until the end of the age." In the center of the page was a drawing of Jesus standing next to her. They were looking at each other and smiling, his arm around her shoulder and her hand resting on his arm. Surrounding them was a series of drawings. They identified things that usually cause fear in both adults and children. The last drawing brought the whole picture into clearer focus, because it was a representation of something about which she has expressed a strong fear. I realized then that these were not generalized fears, but a particular portrayal of those things for which she was looking to Jesus for protection.

Through the influence of a child, I was reminded that I need to recognize and name my own particular fears—fears of loss and change, of aging and poor health, of being ineffective. These, just as surely as fears of monsters and bombs, need to be brought to Jesus so that *this* child can rest in His love and protection

Lord, help me to come to You with those specific fears that cripple and challenge my faith. You are faithful to Your promise to be with us always, through all of our ages and until the end of the age.

Joan Boydell is credentialed through Teaching the Word Ministries. She has been active in pregnancy center leadership for twenty years. Her delight is being a wife, mother and grandmother.

What Can't God Do?

"Behold I am the Lord, the God of all flesh. Is there anything too hard for me?" *Jeremiah 32:27*

Recently an associate of mine and I were booked to visit an orphans' home in India that we support. Nobody told me that I needed a visa. On Friday, the day before departure, I was informed that a visa is mandatory for travel to India. A frantic phone call to the Indian embassy got me the director, who told me that although highly irregular, he would grant me two visas if I could make it to his office in downtown Washington, D.C., by 5:00 p.m. It was around noon in Coatesville, Pennsylvania. This was nigh unto impossible. My wife and I hopped in the car, hurriedly got the required two passport pictures, and prayed that I-95 would be open. It was. But as we approached the train station, it was already around four o'clock. Finding the correct train was challenging for two rookies like us, but the Lord provided a sympathetic gentleman who saw our perplexity and guided us.

By the time we emerged from the underground tunnel in downtown Washington, it was 4:45 p.m. We raced to the embassy and found the visa window, only to realize that we had forgotten the forms. The embassy was on the verge of closing. They allowed us to fill out new forms, but my traveling associate was not physically present to sign his. In the sight of the hostile clerks, my wife forged his name as they rolled their eyes in an exaggerated gesture of contempt. Then they took the money and paperwork to the back of the office and disappeared. By this time the embassy was closed. We figured we were doomed and the visit to the orphans' home was up in flames. To our delight, they returned with two visas and promptly kicked us out. Praise God! The trip was salvaged.

Lord, help me never to doubt Your capability.

Dr. Rick McGovern is pastor of Brandywine Christian Fellowship in Coatesville.

School of Faith

"Trust in the Lord with all your heart, And lean not on your own understanding; In all your ways acknowledge Him and He shall direct your paths." *Proverbs 3:5–6 (New King James Version)*

In early 2002, I had two surgeries at the Reading Hospital for thyroid cancer. In January, while traveling for my first surgery, I found myself not able to find a parking space nearby the Surgery Center.

In April, traveling for my second surgery, God impressed on me to pray for a parking space this time! This time there was an open space nearby. Thank You, Lord! It was neat to see that while praying for what would appear to be something small like a parking space, God showed me He wants me to involve Him in all aspects of my life and in doing so would provide for my needs as well as those of my family.

Many times in the small steps in God in His School of Faith He shows Himself true in our lives. In this our faith increases each step of our walk with Him. We will have memorial stone testimonies of how the Lord is not some far out there creator that has wound up his creation and stepped away; but the Lord of Heaven and earth is very intimate with us and wants us to seek Him first and involve Him in everything we do!

It's truly the Great Adventure living for Jesus as He has a parking lot of spaces available for each one of us as we follow, serve and live for Him; He also has many mansions already prepared for us in eternity, too!

Heavenly Father, I praise You that You want us to involve You in every part of our lives! It's an exciting and amazing harvest time hour You have us living in as we make your wonderful Son Jesus Christ known. Hallelujah!

Mark Burns serves in the Prayer Station Outreach Ministry and Foundation Discipleship at Reading DOVE Christian Ministry Center.

Long Month

"But I will restore you to health and heal your wounds, declares the Lord." *Jeremiah 30:17*

Are you facing major trouble in your life? If so, I want to give you a word of encouragement. The first thing to do is to see what God says in His Word.

I went to the doctor for a regular check up. He looked at the results of my blood studies and noticed that my prostate level was a bit high. He sent me to a specialist in this area who wanted to run some tests. To make a long story short, I continued to have blood work done and after a couple of months the blood levels kept going up.

The specialist was concerned; he wanted to do a biopsy because 75% of men with blood levels this high end up with prostate cancer.

I looked at him and said, "I do not receive that!" He just looked at me kind of funny.

He scheduled the biopsy and I had to wait almost a month to get the results. During the month of waiting, I got into the Word of God to see what He had to say. I set my faith on His Word and chose to believe every word that I was reading. I chose not to believe what the specialist was saying. I received prayer from the believers in our small group. I read every healing scripture in God's Word and received it into my spirit. Matthew 21:22 says, "If you believe, you will receive whatever you ask for in prayer."

I won't lie to you, this was really a long month. The only thing to do was to put all my faith and trust into the Word of God.

I went to the specialist to get the results. He said, "I don't know what happened. I never had a case like this. Your prostate levels are normal and you do not have cancer."

The specialist may not know what happened, but I do! We serve a good God and a mighty God who wants to restore us to good health.

Father, I thank You for healing me. There's nothing too big or small for You. Thank you for Your faithfulness to heal Your people. You are the source of all good things

Andy Parsons works part time as a pastor at Wernersville State Hospital.

Rise and Shine,
Give God the Glory, Glory!

"O Lord, in the morning you hear my voice; in the morning I prepare a sacrifice for you and watch." *Psalm 5:3*

I remember singing that old children's song "Rise and Shine" in front of our church congregation with my wife, Denise, and her four adult brothers. They were remembering that their mother would often wake them up by singing this song. The occasion was a combination birthday party and family reunion. What a pleasure it was to extend this memory and blessing to our church family! It is certainly a song that just seems to get locked into your mind, causing you to sing the words to yourself day after day.

I have always been a morning person. There is nothing better than getting out of bed before the sun rises, and giving God the glory in the stillness of the morning, as the birds sing in the dawn. When we start each new day with the Lord, before that day's hustle and bustle, we are reminded of His faithfulness. "Because of the Lord's great love we are not consumed, for his compassions never fail. They are new every *morning;* great is His faithfulness" (Lamentations 3:22-23).

If you are not normally an early riser, set your clock an hour or so before your normal waking time. Rise and shine and give God the glory, glory! Rejoice, for this is the day the Lord has made!

Thank you, Lord, for every new day. Thank you, Father God, that Your Son shines on us all the days of our lives.

Rich Colvin is the volunteer pastor at the Villa Chapel in Reading.

When Life Does Not Make Sense

"My God in His lovingkindness will meet me...." *Psalm 59:10*
(New American Standard Bible)

This precious verse offers comfort when life does not make sense from our perspective. We struggle for answers; we try to connect the dots. Our questions remain unanswered, sometimes for years. Our circumstances seem chaotic, lacking the unity we desire as disciples of Jesus Christ, since He is the Master of a universe that displays orderly purpose. Yet when we examine the path of our lives, we feel smothered by the fear that we are going to walk right off the edge of a cliff. This fear is trying to overtake me today. Why?

Before answering, I will briefly look back to other periods in my life that were perplexing. I had experienced several lay-offs, followed by a car accident that only increased my employment woes. *Does God care? Does it matter to Him that my heart is breaking?* I eventually realized that He had used those adverse circumstances to develop in me character and perseverance.

The Lord eventually led me to an employment situation where my skills were utilized, and I was able to minister to my coworkers with a more stable faith. Then after five years, the Lord made it clear that it was time to leave. *Why, Lord?* He alone knew that within the year I would be moving to Pennsylvania. However, having my employment situation come to an abrupt end was puzzling. In due time, God graciously opened the door for me to attend Lancaster Bible College. I marveled at His stunning faithfulness in enabling me to return to college at the age of 52. Those deep, crushing trials prepared me for the rigors of writing countless term paper pages!

I am facing perplexing circumstances *again*. Still unemployed more than eight months after graduation, I am struggling with feelings of worthlessness. Bringing my aching heart to the throne of grace is an important step. God is giving me the opportunity to discover afresh that regardless of my circumstances, He is my all in all!

Abba Father, thank you for Your matchless wisdom and guidance!

Susan Marie Davis is a member of Calvary Church in Lancaster.

Scarring

"But He was wounded for our transgressions, He was bruised for our iniquities; the chastisement of our peace was upon Him; and by His stripes we are healed." *Isaiah 53:5*

On the back of my right hand I have a scar that will not disappear. The scar occurred when I was five years old, and I would get angry because it would not fade. Most scars disappear after some years, but I've had this one for decades. The pain I suffered has faded to nothing, but the reason why I have it is still clear to me.

As I reflect on the scar now, I think of the pain and suffering that Jesus went through on the cross. His hands and feet marked forever for my sins; His body pierced and flayed, but never broken, for my misdeeds and His head scarred for my peace of mind. This little scar is nothing compared to what my Lord and Savior bears. Jesus bore all sin, hurt and sickness on the cross for me. It's humbling to know that the blood of Christ covers my sins.

Dear Jesus, thank you for the price You paid on dark Calvary. The scars that You bear are an everlasting reminder of the love You have for me. Thank you for my own scar that reminds me of the pain and suffering that You endured. It is in Your precious name that I pray, amen.

Carol Denson serves on the praise team at Church of the Open Bible in Parkesburg.

Honestly Speaking

"If my people, who are called by my name, will humble themselves and pray and seek my face and turn from their wicked ways, then will I hear from heaven and will forgive their sin and will heal their land." *2 Chronicles 7:14*

This may be a very familiar verse, but if we rush to the promise at the end and skip the conditional "if" at the beginning, we miss what God is speaking to His people. Contextually, this verse is found in ceremonies led by Solomon to dedicate the Temple. Why, during this act of worship, would God remind His chosen people of the wicked ways at the core of their hearts?

God desires a radical commitment to heart transformation. Genuine change begins with an honest assessment of man's desperate need. While one part of a person's heart may be seeking after God, other parts still need to be turned over to God.

Those parts not yet turned over to God are often held captive to the mind seeking to protect the heart from hurtful situations. Repression is a protective mechanism created by the gradual forgetting of conscious material. For example, a person who has abandonment-related experiences connected to a parent may use repression to help convince himself that the feelings of abandonment were not so bad. The mind works very hard to shape feelings, to make life a little more livable.

Rationalization serves that purpose as well. The hurt gradually turns into bitterness and resentment, but efforts to live a good Christian life camouflage this. Honestly facing the emotional pain is the only hope for genuine repentance, release and forgiveness.

Perhaps verse 14 could be summed up as "if humility, then healing." I find this true in my own life. When I discover emotion attached to negative feelings, I need to honestly admit the painful memory (experience) attached to it, and humbly take it to the cross for healing.

Lord, help me to honestly assess my true condition before You. There is still stuff in my heart I need to release control of and need Your help to be honest about what those things are. I trust You to accomplish Your work of redemption.

Dr. Edward Hersh provides counseling and healing prayer ministry to individuals and families.

Treasures

"You turned my wailing into dancing...." *Psalm 30:11*

In the mid to late 1990's, my husband owned a videography business. He was a talented videographer, but as we discovered, not a good business person. He would reduce his price for a client or allow extra time for a client to pay his bill. Consequently, he could not keep the business afloat, and we had to sell our home to pay off the business expenses. I had always taken pride in paying our bills on time, so this was particularly humiliating to me.

The apartment we moved into was so tiny we could not unpack most of our belongings, and cooking meals in the galley kitchen was a real feat. As most often happens to committed Christians, I learned a powerful lesson during that dark time, one of treasures and loss. The Lord taught me that nothing is guaranteed in this life. We can lose everything—our possessions, our health, our livelihood and our loved ones. But, there is one thing we cannot lose—it is our relationship with God! My relationship with Him was the only thing that genuinely belonged to me, and it became my pearl of great price! I have learned to hold everything with an open hand—everything, that is, except my relationship with God—that I treasure above all else.

Lord, thank You for the tough lessons of life and turning my wailing into dancing!

Ellen Dooley is assistant pastor at Crossroads Wesleyan Church.

Tree of Life

"Hope deferred makes the heart sick, but a longing fulfilled is a tree of life." *Proverbs 13:12*

For a time I thought "waiting is just part of the process" was the lesson God was teaching me as He built our family, but I have come to see He was teaching a much deeper lesson.

Waiting is indeed part of the process of God's building a family. When my wife and I were first married we had a shared picture of what our family would look like and by what schedule it would unfold. God had a different plan that involved much waiting. We waited through many long months, a miscarriage, a long battle with secondary infertility, several adoption processes and many periods of painful uncertainty. Our journey took many unexpected turns, and we waited. Our family turned out differently than our initial picture and certainly according to a different schedule. But what a marvelous outcome and great source of joy! Our three wonderful children are truly a "tree of life" for us.

Proverbs 13:12 tells us that a tree of life springs up after a longing is fulfilled. A longing can only be fulfilled if a hope is, at least for some time, deferred. That hope deferred does require a time of the "heart sickness" of waiting. This means that waiting is a necessary part of having a tree of life.

There is, however, a deeper lesson. As we wait, we are not just waiting for the desired outcome, which is sometimes all we focus on. As we endure the heart sickness of a hope deferred, we are waiting *for God* to come and deliver the fulfillment of our longing. And He does. It may not be exactly according to our picture, vision or schedule, but God always brings the "tree of life" after we have waited for Him.

Dear Lord, please strengthen my faith to see You at work in my waiting and keep my hope firmly fixed on You and Your plan.

Rev. Kirk R. Marks is the pastor of St. Paul's Evangelical Congregational Church in Reamstown.

God Began a Good Work in You!

"Being confident of this, that he who began a good work in you will carry it on to completion until the day of Christ Jesus."
Philippians 1:6

For many years, this promise from Paul's letter to the Philippians has been special to me. In fact, this verse was prayed over me early in my ministry. I have made mistakes in life and didn't always carry out my commitments, but praise God, He continues to do a work in me and through me. Over the years, I have also used this verse to bless and encourage others who are on the journey of life.

Recently I was impressed with how the same Scripture can speak in such different situations. One evening I used Philippians 1:6 to challenge a group of pastors and church leaders, both to know who they are in Christ and to call others to Christian maturity. Just a few days later, I used the same Scripture as I talked to a number of people who were just getting out of prison. The message was the same. If God did indeed start a new life in us when we came to Jesus, then we are all special persons for Him. God loves us and has a plan for our lives. Each one of us is created to honor God and serve others.

You might not be a pastor or have a specific leadership assignment. You might not be an ex-inmate or a recovering addict. But wherever you are in life, you can claim this wonderful promise.

God, thank you for providing Jesus as our Saviour. Thank you that the Holy Spirit is at work in our lives today. Continue to lead my life, and may Your plans and purposes be worked out in each day's experiences.

Nelson W. Martin serves as a bishop in Lititz area Mennonite Churches and directs Support for Prison Ministries. He and his wife Anna Mae live near Lititz.

We Have the Fire!

"That all of them may be one, Father, just as you are in me and I am in you. May they also be in us so that the world may believe that you have sent me." *John 17:21*

A few years ago, I was invited to speak in Manaus, Brazil, a city of two million people in the Amazon region. This city has no roads coming into the city. To get to Manaus you either travel by boat up the Amazon River or you fly in by plane. I was expecting to see thousands of mud huts, but I was shocked to find Burger King, Pizza Hut and Shell stations, right in the middle of the Amazon jungle.

The conference was held at an Assembly of God Church. There are close to 100,000 Assembly of God believers in the Manaus area meeting in 700 churches in the city. They baptized 10,000 new believers at one time a few months before I came. However, I noticed that the people who came to the conference came from many different denominations. I sensed there was something very special going on in this city.

I ministered on Sunday at the Church of God Pentecostal Church in the morning and at the Presbyterian church in the evening. As I sat with the minister on the platform of the Presbyterian church Sunday evening, I noticed that the worship style was lively, almost like the Pentecostal church. I leaned over to the gray-haired Presbyterian minister and said, "I feel like I am in a Pentecostal church, not a Presbyterian church." He smiled and quipped, "Brother, we have the fire!"

It dawned on me: they were not concerned primarily about their denomination, they were in love with Jesus, united in their city and "on the same team" to reach their city and nation for Christ. There is amazing unity in this city. Perhaps this is what Jesus was talking to the Father about in John 17.

Lord, bring us into a place of oneness in Christ in our region so that You will be glorified.

Larry Kreider serves on the executive team of the Regional Church of Lancaster County and as the International Director of DOVE Christian Fellowship International, Lititz.

Who Will Build a Wall of Protection?

"I looked for a man among them who would build up the wall and stand before me in the gap on behalf of the land...." *Ezekiel 22:30*

A couple years ago I felt a tug in my heart to take a team to offer prayer to a legislator. He was used to people coming to tell him to fight for their issues. But he wasn't used to people offering prayer support for him in government.

We were welcomed into his office and gathered around him to encircle him in prayer. He looked at us and said how much it meant to him to have this support. While praying, we heard over his television monitor that he was being summoned to a meeting. He didn't move because he said prayer was more important. He said it was lonely as a Christian in government and where were the Christians to offer support.

That day I determined I would be more faithful in praying for government leaders. I set up a legislative prayer team to be a prayer shield for every week they are in session. It has opened opportunities to offer strategic prayer and godly counsel to legislative leaders making critical decisions. It opened an opportunity to help bring forth the seed of a nation, the godly covenant established by William Penn in the government of our land. I want to be one person who God can count on to build a wall of protection around the leaders of the land and pray for God's blessings over our state and nation.

God bless America and support her rich Christian heritage to bring healing and justice for all. I pray as Your eyes search the earth for ones You can count on to stand in the gap on behalf of the land, that we will be counted in that number to help restore healing to our land.

Abby Abildness is the director of Healing Tree International, a ministry focused on encouraging and equipping leaders to bring healing to the nations.

Being a Disciple of Jesus

"And these signs will accompany those who believe: In my name they will drive out demons; they will speak in new tongues; they will pick up snakes with their hands; and when they drink deadly poison, it will not hurt them at all; they will place their hands on sick people, and they will get well." *Mark 16:17–18*

Uncle Bob came back to his hometown the summer of 2007 to tell his mother and brothers that his battle with cancer was not over; there was nothing more the doctors could do. He would not speak to anyone else. One year later, he was still alive but the condition had worsened.

My pastor was healed of a similar type of cancer, and my sister-in-law felt led to send our pastor's testimony. Bob called us and asked if our pastor would call him. We all felt Uncle Bob had never accepted Jesus as Savior.

As the weeks passed, we had an opportunity to share the gospel with him. My husband and I felt that we needed to speak with him in person, to pray with him and lay hands on him. He agreed, so we made the six-hour drive to his home. We had sensed to pray around his home prior to praying for him, and with his permission, we did. Then we went inside, and he was ready to receive Jesus and allowed us to pray for healing.

During this time, my children were out in the backyard playing. My son yelled for me, so I excused myself and went outside to find my sons holding a white balloon with a logo of the American Cancer Society and a purple streamer. I knew it was a sign from the Lord. Signs and wonders follow those who teach, preach, heal the sick, and cast out demons. We were all amazed, especially Uncle Bob. It's been two months since our visit, and he is alive today and very open to learning more about the gospel and Jesus Christ.

Dear Lord, thanks for opening doors no one else could open and allowing us the opportunity to be your disciples and speak Your words. You're such an awesome Father and You show Your love for us in many ways.

Michele Apicella is a member of Christ Community Church in Camp Hill and serves on the ministry team and youth staff.

There is Truth

"In fact, for this reason I was born, and for this I came into the world, to testify to the truth. Everyone on the side of truth listens to me."
John 18:37

Be tolerant. This used to mean to make sure I respectfully disagree with someone. In this sense, tolerance reflects Christian character. Today tolerance appears to be a mandate to accept what I disagree with, otherwise I am intolerant.

I had one professor for numerous classes in college. Because I sought to be tolerant (and to get an A) I was careful to be respectful when I disagreed with her. This fostered a mutually respectful relationship. However this professor would consistently teach that there is no truth that applies to all people, because we each create truth that works best for us based on our circumstances. Therefore, no one can say their version of truth is greater than anyone else's. Truth is whatever works for you.

The last class of my senior year I raised my hand after she repeated her absolute truth about truth being relative. She called on me and with a smile I said, "This is great! When we take our final in a few weeks, I can cheat if I choose to believe that cheating is not wrong. You believe it's wrong for you. That doesn't make it wrong for me. It would actually be wrong for you to impose your view of cheating on me because your truth is not greater than mine." She smirked and got my point.

There is Truth and my standard of truth is set forth in Jesus (John 14:6) and in God's Word (John 17:7). By comparing claims of truth to Jesus and God's Word, what is true becomes evident. We can respectfully disagree without being pressed into compliance with what we disagree.

Jesus, I want to listen to You today. And as I do, help me to uncompromisingly speak Your words of truth in love.

Jeff Comeaux is the associate pastor at The Door Christian Fellowship, Lancaster.

The Big-Boy Bike Ride

"...I prayed for this child, and the Lord has granted me what I asked of him. So now I give him to the Lord...." *1 Samuel 1:27–28*

Learning to ride his two-wheel bike was like any other milestone—full of excitement! So what made this day so different?

"Stay on the right side of the road until we get to the corner. Stop the bike. And together we will walk our bikes across to the other side." Joshua sped away in his excitement!

As his little wobbly self started out ahead of me, it happened!

He pedaled fast! Then faster! And all of a sudden it was no longer my son on his first big-boy bike ride that was so rapidly speeding away from me. It was babyhood and toddler days and little boy fun. My son was growing up.

If I wouldn't have been on my bike, I may have had my arms stretched in front of me reaching ever so desperately to touch him and pull him back to me. Instead, my knuckles were white from gripping so tightly to the handlebars. The waves of nausea rushing through my stomach almost knocked me to the ground. I felt so helpless.

The motor vehicle seemed to come out of nowhere. *Stop! Stop! Stop the bike!* My voice erupted like a volcano. Yes, I was fearful of the approaching car, but was there more to this outburst? Oh, to hold Josh as a baby again and tie his little shoes. Where had the time gone?

As I snapped out of it, I saw Joshua patiently and obediently standing beside his bike, waiting so that he and I could walk our bikes across the street—together.

Thank you for Your help, Lord, because I can't yell stop to Joshua's growing up.

Lisa Dorr is a wife, mother, speaker and Bible study leader.

A Mom's Love

"If I gave everything I have to the poor and even sacrificed my body, I could boast about it; but if I didn't love others, I would have gained nothing. Love is patient and kind. Love is not jealous or boastful or proud or rude. It does not demand its own way. It is not irritable, and it keeps no record of being wronged. It does not rejoice about injustice but rejoices whenever the truth wins out. Love never gives up, never loses faith, is always hopeful, and endures through every circumstance." *1 Corinthians 13:3–7*

My mom was in an accident at work. This close encounter with death reminded me how precious life is. As I was thanking God for His hand of protection and for my mother's life, the Holy Spirit showed me how much like my mother I am.

When I was younger, everyone used to say that I look just like my mom. That wasn't something I enjoyed hearing. I wanted to be my own individual self. Who I am today is a reflection of her influence. My mom taught me to face head-on the storms of life and walk through them with my head held high. She showed me that I could overcome any obstacle and always make it to the other side. She taught me to champion the cause of the underprivileged and to root for the underdog. To be a person of my word and someone others can count on. To stay calm in every situation. To be generous and share what I have. To be strong but tenderhearted. That both laughter and tears are good. To see the fun and adventure in life and not to take myself so seriously. Mostly my mom has taught me to love. I hope my mom sees herself in me and that she thinks I "look" just like her!

Father, we are so very grateful to have "BaBa" today after her accident, and we thank you for blessing her with a long life to influence us all for many years to come.

Sharon Blantz is the proud daughter of "BaBa and Poppy" and serves as regional pastor of single parents and support and care ministries at The Worship Center.

Loneliness of Leadership

"You keep him in perfect peace whose mind is stayed on you, because he trusts in you. Trust in the Lord forever, for the Lord God is an everlasting rock." *Isaiah 26:3–4*

For decades I have been involved in various leadership roles in church, community organizations, and the workplace–usually facilitating, planning, supporting, or advising. Seldom had I been in a "the buck stops here" position, the person who sets the tone for an organization and, by personal example and leadership approach, frees or limits what others do.

In the past year, God has led me into such a place. Amidst the joy of seeing God at work and seeing others' unique contributions have come challenges, pressures, and heartaches associated with relational conflict and problems that do not yield to easy solutions. Faced recently with irreconcilable issues within the leadership team that required a decision, I was forced into the kind of lonely desert place that our Father God loves to invite us to. My conflict resolution skills were inadequate. My heart concern for people was conveying indecisiveness and questions about my capacity to lead. It seemed as if the success of the mission was at risk whatever way we went. In the midst of this crisis, I cried out to God and sensed His still small voice saying, "Look for evidences of my grace already at work. Take that path." Immediately, I had clarity and peace about the way to go and the faith to trust in His providential care for me, for the leadership team, and the course of the ministry. God invites leaders into lonely places where they can experience more of Him and receive His wisdom and love. Go there with Him.

Father, thank you that Your grace is much more than barely adequate. It is sufficient for all situations and satisfies the deepest longings of a heart that has been broken with unsatisfied expectations of others and of myself.

Bruce Boydell and his wife, Joan, envision, equip and empower individuals and emerging leaders of businesses and ministry organizations for the advancement of Christ's kingdom through Lifespan Consulting and Coaching Services.

Not So Fast!

"…Judgment without mercy will be shown to anyone who has not been merciful. Mercy triumphs over judgment!" *James 2:12–13*

I was in the left turn lane approaching the light. I hit the brakes just before an SUV in the right lane shot in front of me to pull into the Turkey Hill on the other side.

A stream of thoughts flowed through my mind: *Those SUVs think they own the road!…He might have been hurt, just to save a couple seconds!…I bet he does this stuff all the time…If he drives that way, what must he be like in other areas of his life?* The cascade of thoughts continued as I pulled into the intersection to make my turn.

I couldn't figure out why I heard a loud truck horn until I shook myself from my brooding. All I saw was the large grill of a semi-tractor trailer truck. Preoccupied with cursing the SUV, I missed that the light was red and I was turning into oncoming traffic!

I continued my trip unharmed, but not unchastised. The still, small voice gently laid out all of what God had seen. I had been "wronged" because the SUV driver had endangered me. But, I had wronged him, too, with self-righteousness and judgment against him, his driving and his vehicle. I brought judgment on myself, simply by reacting to my feelings instead of what the Word of God said.

God tells us what He does for our benefit, not because He is power-hungry. I will be better off (and a safer driver!) when I let "mercy triumph over judgment."

Father, being merciful goes against the nature I was born into. I confess I need a deeper revelation of Your mercy toward me, so that I might offer it to others. Show me today at strategic times how I can put mercy into action, and in Your mercy, transform me in the days ahead by renewing my mind with this Truth. Amen.

Carolyn Schlicher lives with her husband, Darryl, and five merciful children in Elizabethtown.

The Ram is Still in the Thicket!

"Abraham believed God and it was counted to him as righteousness."
Romans 4:3

The past year has been an adventure for me in learning to "let go and let God." A close family member returned to the Lord with a dramatic change in thought, word and deed. He began to repair and become accountable for his previous decisions, demonstrations and destructions. Then a law which had been previously broken was brought into the legal realm.

Suddenly, he was confronted with the reality of his abuse and sin, A recovering addict, with family at home and just starting his new life, he now was in jail.

As a mother, my grief was intense. I knew that this prison was far better than the bondage of drugs. I sensed that I was to release, to "give him up," and let him be God's son alone. My processing caused me to examine many strengths, flaws and identity issues in my parent role. There was recognition, acknowledgment and repentance as I carefully sought the character of God as my template. I gave up all I knew to give to take him as my brother in the Lord.

I have dwelt, in this season, with the story of the ram in the thicket. Abraham believed God first and purposed obedience above all relationships. When we do recognize it and submit the relationship of family or friend to the Lord, we benefit as much as they. The ram is still in the thicket. I know Jesus Christ came and still is with us. I am compelled by His truth to believe nothing is impossible for us, for our families, our brothers and sisters in Christ and our fallen world.

I thank You, Father, for teaching me how to be more like You. Thank you that mercy and grace and justice are Your standards. May Your truth be my example in thought, word and deed. Lord, You are Father, Friend, Faithful and Faultless. There is none like You.

Diana Oliphant is a caregiver and intercessor with a heart for this region and nations.

.

The Perfect Gift

"Which of you, if his son asks for bread, will give him a stone?...If you...know how to give good gifts to your children, how much more will your Father in heaven give good gifts to those who ask him!"
Matthew 7:9, ll–12

After my wife and I decided that we wanted to have children in our life, it was several years before we were finally able to plan for the arrival of our first child. Like all new parents, we approached the day with a lot of excitement and a little trepidation. When our first daughter, Natasha, was born, all doubt was swept away and everything was right with the world.

For 5 minutes.

That's how long it took for the doctor to come back to the hospital bed and say, "I'm sorry, but I believe your daughter has Down Syndrome." This news was a cataclysmic, life-changing event for me. Although I considered myself to be a mature Christian, I think I somehow still believed that I would be immune from certain problems as God would keep them from me. I still believed that God was good, and trusted in Him, but it dramatically changed the way I thought He worked.

Some months later I was sitting in a Bible class listening to the teacher talking about the verses in today's devotional about how an earthly father would not give his son a stone if he asked for bread, and how much more our heavenly Father gives good gifts to us. As the teacher was expounding on this principle, I thought, sarcastically, "Yes God, thanks for Natasha's Down Syndrome, it was such a nice gift!"

In my life, there have only been a few times when I believed God spoke directly to me, and this was one of those times. It was as if His answer to my cynical little prayer burst fully-formed into my mind. He said, "Natasha, just the way she is, is my absolutely perfect gift for you. Your mind and your understanding are just far too small to understand why that is true."

Lord, I may not completely understand why Natasha must face the daily challenges she does, but I have peace that You have Your purposes for all the gifts You have given me. Thank you!

Jay Martin and his wife Gloria and three children attend Lancaster Evangelical Free Church in Lititz.

A Grandmother's Legacy

"Be joyful always; pray continually; give thanks in all circumstances, for this is God's will for you in Christ Jesus." 1 Thessalonians 5:16–18

I loved my grandma's garden with the vividly colored portulacas along the hand-dug beds on each side of the path leading up to her door. I remember well the June roses along the garden fence—red, pink and white. But most of all I liked the old fashioned yellow one, with a fragrance all its own. I can still see the four o'clocks beside the cellar door that fascinated me with their curious habit of only opening their blooms in late afternoon. Geraniums were carefully planted in cement flower pots that adorned her front porch. Grandma loved flowers and everything bright and beautiful.

She also loved to quote old adages. I can hear her say, even now:

"I'd rather have roses and thorns than no roses at all."

"Politeness is to do and say, the kindest things in the kindest way."

"A stitch in time, saves nine."

"Come when you're called, do as you're bid, shut the door behind you, and you'll never be chid."

"Where there's a will, there's a way."

But it was Grandma's prayer life that left a lasting impression on me. I would often see her pause with her needle-work in hand and bow her head in prayer. When my husband was called to the ministry, she was already well into her eighties, but she assured us that she prayed for us every day.

I'm thankful for the legacy of my grandmother. She was a woman of character and determination, yet also patient, kind and understanding. She was appreciative of others, and the joy of the Lord came through in her life.

What legacy will you leave behind? Is the joy of the Lord yours today? If not, look to today's scripture and get God's perspective. His will is for us to be joyful and pray continually and give thanks. Let's do that today!

Lord, I want Your joy to come through in my life today. Help me to pray and give thanks in all things.

Charity Heller is 92 years old. She was a pastor's wife and recently widowed after 67 years of marriage.

The View at the Summit

"No eye has seen, no ear has heard, and no mind has imagined what God has prepared for those who love him." *1 Corinthians 2:9 (New Living Translation)*

The evening is hot. Sweaty hot. The last thing I want to do is run. But I am training for a race and know I have to get my middle-aged body in motion. I am a couple of miles into the run, tired and starting to feel grouchy. I know I am destroying my momentum with my negative thinking, and the last leg of the run is uphill. Will I stop and walk? No! I will not give in. I take a cleansing breath and soldiered on. I will reach the top, while maintaining a steady pace.

I finally crest the top of the hill and gasp—not from heat deprivation or exhaustion—but because of the spectacular sunset painted across the western sky. I stand transfixed as the magnificent orange sphere sinks slowly on the horizon. I am astounded, astonished, amazed and awestruck, dazzled and dumbfounded, all in one heart-bursting emotion.

I've learned that on nearly every run I find a spiritual application for my life. This was no exception. In the spiritual realm, many times we reach a mountain top experience only after times of discouragement. But those spectacular experiences are often the direct result of persevering in the face of daunting circumstances.

Are you putting one foot in front of the other, with no relief or end in sight? Does the hill before you seem overwhelming? Don't give up. God loves you spectacularly and has a grand plan for your life. He will be with you every step of the way. God's awesome like that. Toil to the summit and you will see the view!

Heavenly Father, thank you for loving us and preparing a plan for our lives. Increase our vision and give us Your strength to fulfill all that You have placed in our hearts.

Karen Ruiz is the editor of House to House Publications, Lititz, and likes to run (most of the time).

God Knows Where We Are

"For the Son of Man came to seek and to save the lost." *Luke 19:10*

Have you ever felt lost and alone? I mean really lost and alone? I was driving in heavy traffic in the city of Washington, DC, and I felt lost and alone. Now you may ask, how can you feel alone with all those people and cars around you?

My boss had requested that I attend a seminar to facilitate a presentation on digital publishing. This was the first time I had driven alone in the city, and I followed the directions until I came upon construction. There were many detour signs, and I became confused and disoriented as all I could see were unfamiliar street names. After I realized I had made several loops and was not getting anywhere, I ended up at a red light on the verge of tears and feeling very lost. I began to pray, crying out to God for help.

Suddenly I looked to my right and saw that a white van had just pulled up beside me on the shoulder of the road. I immediately sensed that this guy in the white van had been sent by God. He was looking at me as I rolled down my window and asked him how to get to my destination. He smiled and said, "I'm going in that direction, follow me. I'll take you there." As I followed the van, I praised God for His quick response to my prayer. God spoke into my spirit and told me I wasn't lost because He knew where I was all the time. This is also true spiritually for every unbeliever. God knows where they are and Jesus seeks them to bring them to safety within His covenant of salvation.

Abba Father, thank You for Your love and care over our lives. You know where we are at every moment. Thank You for Your Son Jesus, who pursues and redeems the lost.

Sharon McCamant serves at Susquehanna Valley Pregnancy Services and at the Ephrata Nazarene Church Celebrate Recovery ministry.

Is This Important?

"For the gifts and calling of God are without repentance."
Romans 11:29 (King James Version)

"For God's gifts and his call are irrevocable." *Romans 11:29
(New International Version)*

"For God does not change his mind about whom he chooses and
blesses." *Romans 11:29 (Today's English Version)*

"For the free gifts and the calling of God can never be gone back
upon." *Romans 11:29 (William Barclay)*

Here is a question I have been faced with: Do I, as some have,
change this verse to calling and gifts instead of gifts and calling, as the
Word teaches? My answer is no! Serving as a pastor and teacher (see
Romans 11:29), I know I am gifted and called! I have received the gift
of the Holy Spirit. I am called by our Father to serve Him faithfully.

Over the years as I have counseled pastors, I have noted that some
pastors, for whatever their reason, state they are in the ministry because their father or grandfather served as a pastor, that a prophet has
laid hands on them and the prophet said they will be a pastor, that they
are serving because a relative or friend serves and that they are just
"called" and skip any reference to their gift or gifts of the Holy Spirit.

I have thought about this deeply and think that this is why shep-
herds are missing as flock leaders, some have very relaxed schedules,
serve as controllers and even cause the gifted to not use their gifts in
serving the body of believers.

Less we forget, however, God's gifts are His blessing to us, and
His call is the election to serve in the blessings. This verse in Romans
teaches us that God's pursuing love is everlasting. It is neither harden-
ing nor totally non-permanent. His gifts and call are irrevocable. This
is His agape love of us. So the above actions of pastors are changeable
with total dependence on Him. Our God is absolutely consistent!

*Lord Jesus, I pray for change and that all who serve will know the
gift or gifts given freely to them.*

Bob Burns is pastor of Spiritual Growth Ministries, a guiding ministry to church
leaders in areas of spiritual growth, and serves on the advisory board of the
Potter's House, Leola (an after-prison care ministry).

An End in Sight

"I am the light of the world. He that follows me shall not walk in darkness." *John 8:12*

"Tunnel, tunnel, tunnel..." He pauses, then scurries on, feet flying overhead.

"What thing of beauty and wonder was that?" Hunter asks as his tail flashes by. But now it's behind him, out of sight, out of mind.

"Wait! Wait! What was I doing?" Distracted momentarily, he enthusiastically continues to burrow. "Oh yeah...deep, deep, deeper. Dark, darker...I love it down here in the bowels of the earth."

Seconds later, his head pops out of the tunnel. "Wow! I love it out here in the light."

I'm amazed that no matter where our ferret Hunter is, he always finds his way out, never gets stuck in the middle, no matter his entanglement. He always heads to the other end, where he sees the light. Somehow he knows there is an end in sight.

I've known depression in my life when I could see no end. I felt I was crawling through a deep, dark tunnel, every day slipping farther away from my Rescuer. God wanted to lift me out, but the claws of guilt had twisted the truth of His Word and cast eerie shadows that contorted His image. I buried myself in guilt, closing myself off from everyone—even God. I felt unworthy.

But God created each of us to have an intimate relationship with Him. Sin separates us from God. I asked God to forgive me for listening to any voice above His.

When I finally put my absolute trust and faith in the birth, death, and resurrection of Jesus Christ, when I listened only to the truth of the Bible, I could hear Him calling me out of my darkness. His Words cast a light that led me to the end of myself directly into His arms. I could now receive His healing and love.

Thank you, Father, for Your word that lights the way before me and for Your love that rescues me from the darkness.

Nancy Magargle is a member of Lancaster Christian Writers group.

Giving Of Yourself

"…Always work enthusiastically for the Lord, for you know that nothing you do for the Lord is ever useless."
1 Corinthians 15:58 (New Living Translation)

It seems like yesterday when I moved my belongings to Philadelphia to begin another chapter in my life. It was 1999, and I knew only that I was part of a team sent to reach out to a Latino neighborhood. Exactly what that was going to look like, God had not fully revealed. Immediately upon arriving, the drug dealers were quite visible. In fact, they liked to camp out on our front steps. It was not long until they became friends in an odd sort of way.

However, it was the three children living next door who really tugged at my heart's strings. They loved to come over and hang out. I do not remember how it all took place, but I began to realize the children were struggling in school. Alexis' reading level was two years behind his grade in school which meant every other class was a struggle as well. Katherine's and Juan's grades were also low. I started to help them in the evenings with their homework and encouraged them to read. We decided to start reading the Bible and then discussing what was read. They persisted because they wanted to read the Bible and it helped their reading skills.

Soon, their report cards grades started to rise. Their parents were thrilled with changes they were seeing in the children. All three of the kids committed their lives to the Lord, and today all three are on the honor roll and thinking about college. Alexis wants to be a public defender to help those who do not have enough money to get a lawyer. Juan wants to be a brain surgeon, and Katherine wants to work with kids either as a teacher or a pediatrician. I recently got a note from Alexis that said, "Thank you, Joetta, for being there for me. I do not know what kind of life I would be living today if you were not in it."

Lord, thank you that I can work enthusiastically for You. It's incredible to look back and see what You have done.

Joetta Keefer serves with Hands of Hope, a ministry to the homeless in Philadelphia, meeting physical, emotional, and spiritual needs of hurting people in a practical way.

Fed by Chickens

"And it will be that you shall drink from the brook, and I have commanded the ravens to feed you there." *1 Kings 17:4 (New King James Version)*

We had returned from the mission field in Peru and were beginning our lives again in the States. My wife, Tracie, and I were planting a new church in Reading, Pennsylvania, with our two toddler boys and our newborn baby girl. I was working a full-time job as we planted the church, but my salary was hardly enough to make ends meet, even to keep basic groceries in the house.

During this time of praying and believing God for our family's finances, I was invited to minister in another town. A man there approached me with a very unusual "word" for me. He began to share that God has heard our cry and will answer with many chickens as a sign of His faithful provision in our lives. Of course I thought this was definitely strange—maybe this would happen in Peru or if I lived near a chicken farm, but in the city of Reading? However, having a history of seeing the Lord work in amazing ways, I shared this with Tracie and we trusted God at His word.

Very soon after this, a knock came at our door. Sure enough, a neighbor was standing there with nothing less than a chicken—already broasted, ready to enjoy. She explained that her store made too many and she wanted to share with us. Over the next few weeks, our neighbor continued to come with…you guessed it…more chickens!

If God provided for Elijah with ravens, why could He not feed us with chickens? If the God of the Scripture is alive today, don't you think He is still intimately acquainted with all our ways, all our needs, and will be faithful to be actively involved in our daily lives? The God of Elijah wants to be our God today!

Thank you Jesus, You are the same yesterday, today, and forever!

Craig Nanna lives in Reading with his amazing wife Tracie and three kids, and they together pastor Reading DOVE Christian Ministry Center. Craig also serves as the director for a group of pastors and Christian leaders called the Reading Regional Transformation Network.

God Stories 4

He Makes Us Lie Down

"The Lord is my shepherd, I shall not want. He makes me lie down in green pastures; He leads me beside quiet waters…." *Psalms 23:1–2*

A few years ago I was rushed to the hospital because it appeared that I was having a heart attack. Thankfully, my husband and a close friend were able to go with me. While waiting for the test results, I was in a great deal of pain and fear was beginning to corner me. My heart desperately needed reassurance.

It was then that my friend leaned in close to me and gently spoke these words of life to my troubled soul, "Kathi, there are times when He *makes* us lie down in green pastures."

She explained that in God's sovereignty, He had literally made me "lie down" and I could take comfort in knowing that there were holy purposes in what was happening.

Being in an emergency room was not *my* idea of green pastures, yet suddenly a deep peace came upon me. Much like I would feel sitting by a quiet stream, a sense of stillness entered my soul and I was able to deeply relax.

In spite of the taunting fears my mind had been grappling with— my spirit suddenly grasped the reality that even though I felt like I was walking "through the valley of the shadow of death," I had nothing to fear. God *was* with me. I could sense His nearness and the reality of His presence overshadowed my fears. "The shadow of the Almighty" (Psalms 91:1) easily concealed the concerns I had of death.

Familiar words, memorized through repetition, became life to my soul. I could feel His care and I was once again reminded that the Lord is, indeed, *my* Shepherd.

Thank you, Lord, that Your Word never loses its power to offer life to those in need. Help me to be ever growing in my knowledge of Your nearness and Your care. Amen.

Kathi Wilson and her husband, Mark, co-authors of *Tired of Playing Church* and co-founders of Body Life Ministries, are members of Ephrata Community Church.

Iced-Tea Throw Down

"Peter asked, 'Lord, why can't I follow you now? I will lay down my life for you.' Then Jesus answered, 'Will you really lay down your life for me? I tell you the truth, before the rooster crows, you will deny me three times.'" *John 13:37–38*

Recently, a young man, Nick, whom my family has befriended, came to our house for an evening swim. I had decided to take some time out of my busy schedule to sit on our deck and talk with him. In the middle of our conversation, he asked if I had anything to drink. That afternoon I had just made a gallon pitcher of fresh-brewed ice tea and, truthfully, I wasn't in the mood to share it. The last pitcher I made the day before had disappeared without me getting any of it so I was determined to guard this one for my own selfish reasons.

Without telling an out and out lie, I told Nick that I had water or milk. So he said he would take a glass of water. As I poured the glass of ice water, I justified in my mind that I deserved to keep the ice tea for myself; after all I am the one who made it. I chose to ignore the conviction of my selfishness in my heart and served Nick the ice water.

Many mornings as I am sitting alone with Jesus seeking to know His heart and to do His will, I will often say to Him, "Lord, I will lay down my life for You!" But today He actually responded in an unexpected way to my heart's cry and said, "Will you really lay down your life for me? I tell you the truth, you couldn't even lay down a glass of ice tea for me!" Ouch, that hurt.

You know my heart. You see the good and the bad. You see my godly intentions and the many times I have failed You. Yet, You leave me one simple command, "Love one another. As I have loved you, so you must love one another." Transform this selfish heart into a servant's heart so that all might know that I am a true disciple of You. In Jesus' name, amen.

Anita Keagy, speaker and author, leads Joy Shop Ministries which is dedicated to calling believers to a life-changing commitment of seeking God first every day through the disciplines of prayer and Bible reading.

Photo by Irene Clark

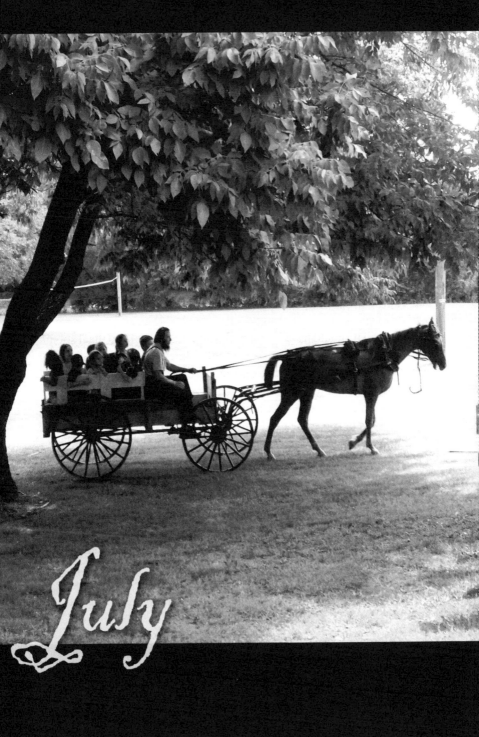

July

Power

"I call to you, God, because I'm sure of an answer." *Psalm 17:6 (The Message)*

One summer, my job involved caring for a young woman with disabilities. I'll call her Amelia. She was unable to speak, so there were many times when she would, understandably, get very frustrated when communicating her needs and desires. Part of my weekly routine was driving her to her place of employment. One day, on the way there, she became angry about something. I couldn't figure out what she needed, even after I asked her several questions that simply required a nod of the head. After all my inquiries and inability to understand, Amelia became so irate that she repeatedly screamed and threw her upper body against the seat of the car. I tried to concentrate on driving safely. I thought, *The sooner I arrive at her workplace, the sooner this episode will be over.*

Though it should have been my first reaction, I realized that I should pray. Amelia was also a Christian, and I knew that it would not be against work protocol to call on the Lord for help. I began to pray aloud, asking God to calm Amelia (and me), and to help me figure out what was wrong. Almost instantaneously, Amelia stopped her outburst, and I could tell she was praying too. I remember holding her hand and feeling the tension release during the prayer. Peace filled the car, and a calm settled over us for the remainder of the trip. I never did figure out what had bothered her; God simply took away Amelia's frustration.

This experience reminds me of the power that comes from calling on the name of Jesus and demonstrates the unbiased authority that the Lord holds—whether we pray eloquently or simply from the depths of our hearts. Perhaps God answered Amelia's prayer that day rather than mine.

Jesus, as I go through each day, may my first reaction be to lift difficult situations up to Your throne of grace. Help me to pray from a pure heart and trust that You hear and answer my pleas.

Maria Buck is the wife of Gary, worship pastor of Petra Christian Fellowship.

Be a Blessing

"I will bless those who bless you, and whoever curses you I will curse; and all peoples on earth will be blessed through you."
Genesis 12:3

It was a hot summer day in the city of Philadelphia. A group of high school students were there, not to goof off, not to do sight-seeing, but in order to bring blessing to the people that they would come in contact with throughout the week. We were in Philadelphia on a week-long mission experience. All throughout the week we were aware of two things: we are extremely blessed, and because of that we are called to bring blessing to those we come in contact with.

This calling to Abraham, found in Genesis 12:1-3, is not only for Abraham, but to all of us who are Christ-followers. This calling is that we are blessed to be a blessing for the sake of the world. The gospel is not just about me and Jesus. It's about those of us who are trying to follow Christ seeking to partner with the king in building the kingdom of God. And one way to do that is to bless other people.

To be a blessing means putting others ahead of yourself. It's about putting their needs before your own needs. So now you may be asking, "So what does this look like?" I am hesitant to give you too many concrete ideas, as I believe you should look around your area and that through prayer and seeking God, He will show you what it means. But, here are some possibilities. It can be as simple as listening to someone who needs a friend. It can look like being a big brother or big sister to a child who needs one. It could mean donating money and time to various organizations. Whatever it means, seek to be a blessing today.

Lord, open my eyes today to see what it means to be blessed, to be a blessing.

Ryan Braught is pastor of Youth Ministries and Nurture and a leader of Veritas, an Emerging Missional community of faith.

What a Gift!

"Therefore we do not lose heart. Though outwardly we are wasting away, yet inwardly we are being renewed day by day. For our light and momentary troubles are achieving for us an eternal glory that far outweighs them all." *2 Corinthians 4:16*

I just celebrated another birthday and I can honestly say it was one of my sweetest. Even though it falls on the day before the Fourth of July and my celebration can be "stretched out" into the next day's independence celebration of our country, that is not what made it one of my most memorable birthdays.

I have been pondering what made it different this year, and I have concluded that it has a great deal to do with experiencing a deeper sense of gratitude to the Lord for the life He has given me. The Lord has not only blessed me with another year of life, but also with family and friends that filled my heart by making me feel extremely loved and appreciated. As wonderful as that is, He also gave me the even better gift of revealing a deeper knowledge of what it means to live with an eternal perspective. One way He has done that is to give me a clearer vision of what priorities really matter.

We know that we are to be kingdom focused on how we live. We are challenged to make every day count for only our Lord knows how many days on earth we will have. All of these statements can sound a bit "elementary," but since they truly are eternal perspective statements, can we really hear them often enough?

Life gets so filled with the temporary, and it is so easy to be consumed with the stresses of this world. Let us instead take great encouragement and comfort from 2 Corinthians 4:18: "So we fix our eyes not on what is seen, but on what is unseen. For what is seen is temporary, but what is unseen is eternal."

Lord, Thy kingdom come, Thy will be done on earth as it is in heaven.

Patti Wilcox is assistant director of Good Works, Inc. in Coatesville.

True Freedom

"So if the Son sets you free, you will be free indeed." *John* 8:36

In the early summer of 1776, wise men met in Philadelphia and crafted a document that stands even today. It laid out the reasons for the War of Independence that was going on in their land. Among these reasons were that certain rights did not come from kings, but rather God. They believed that humanity was "endowed by their Creator with certain unalienable rights, life, liberty and the pursuit of happiness." Many of those who signed that Declaration of Independence ended up paying a great price for that freedom.

However, true freedom is actually found in Christ. Jesus was speaking about freedom to His disciples in John 8:32-36. In verse 32, Jesus speaks about the truth setting you free. Then in verse 36, He mentions how true freedom comes through the Son, who is the Way, the Truth and the Life. Jesus paid the price for that freedom. We can experience freedom living here in the USA, but this freedom leaves us at the grave. Therefore, true freedom is an eternal one which is found by believing in Jesus Christ alone for our salvation.

On this great holiday, I encourage you to pause and thank God for our freedom, especially the spiritual freedom that we have in Jesus Christ.

Heavenly Father, thank you for those men who sacrificed so much that we might have freedom in our land. Thank you even more for sending Jesus so that we can experience true freedom in You.

Kevin Kirkpatrick is the pastor of Berean Bible Fellowship Church in Terre Hill, and a member of the Regional Church council.

Celebrating Interdependence

"From Him the whole body, joined and held together with every supporting ligament, grows and builds itself up in love, as each part does its work." *Ephesians 4:16*

It was a beautiful summer morning on the day we Americans enjoy celebrating Independence Day. My wife, teenage daughter, her cousin and I were on I-95 South headed for Lakeland, Florida.

Our traveling was going great for the first several hundred miles until we realized that the engine was nearly overheating for some unknown reason. Fortunately we were approaching a rest area which provided a safe place to stop. Unfortunately it was a holiday, and all auto service centers were closed in the area. Adding water to the coolant system and taking some counsel from a caring motorist, we were able to reach a parts store at the next exit. It was open! An amazing discovery was made. A small rubber seal in the cap for the coolant system, valued at about 59 cents, had broken. At least seven people reached out to us and blessed us with counsel or assistance in a way that our problem was solved and our trip continued.

I was awestruck as I got the message within this experience. All of the thousands of parts and technologies of the engine were hindered and incapable of fulfilling their purposes because a very small $.59 seal was not doing its part. The plans for reaching our destiny were in jeopardy because of this seemingly insignificant part. We found it totally ironic that on Independence Day we found the wonderful blessing of others going beyond independent thinking. Their gestures of love reinforced our need for each other.

Today, watch for the opportunity you have to answer someone's need. Regardless of how small the role may be, let's celebrate the joy of *interdependence* and bless each other "as each part does its work."

Father, forgive me when I get caught up in independent thinking. I thank you for the way You have designed us with differing gifts and skills to be a blessing to each other. Give me the eyes to see my part to complete it as I fit into Your wonderful plans and purposes. Amen.

Lloyd Hoover serves as a bishop/overseer in Lancaster Mennonite Conference, director of the Potter's House, a leader of reconciliation ministries and a member of the Regional Church of Lancaster County.

The Name of the Lord

"Call upon Me in the day of trouble; I will deliver you, and you shall glorify Me." *Psalm 50:15*

In the spring of 2000, I was praising and thanking God in my car while driving on the Route 30 bypass. It was raining and my car suddenly seemed to hydroplane across the highway. I saw an eighteen-wheeler approaching in my rearview mirror. I screamed, *"Jesus!"* and felt the sense of Him folding over me as a parent would bend down over a child. That is all I remember.

When I woke up in my car, I confess I was disappointed I was not in heaven, but instantly laughed out loud that Satan could not take my life. I knew then God had something planned for me and that I was a threat to the enemy.

According to the accident assessment, I hit a concrete conduit on one side of the highway, spun across to the other side, up the embankment, hit a tree at the top while traveling backwards, rolled back down and spun again in the highway only to end up on the right side of the road safe from the traffic flow. The officer said he could not understand why the car had not flipped. If it had I would have been killed.

The Lord kept me safe, and no other cars were involved in the accident. I do not know what happened to the driver of the eighteen-wheeler. He never stopped, but I am sure he may have a God story some day about a car that spun across the highway.

God was given glory that day as I relayed to ambulance workers, police and doctors what I remembered happening when I called upon the name of Jesus.

Several months later, God called me into full-time pro-life ministry.

Father, Thank you for life and the ability to share it with all those we meet. Be glorified!

Debbie Davenport serves at Cornerstone Pregnancy Care Services and as an intercessor in various settings for the purpose of unity and regional transformation.

God's Leading

"Thus says the Lord, your Redeemer, the Holy One of Israel: I am the Lord your God who teaches you what is best for you, Who leads you by the way that you should go." *Isaiah 48:17*

My mother's favorite song was an old hymn, "He Leadeth Me." I remember her singing that at times and as the years went on, I realized to a greater extent how meaningful that song was to her and that she lived by the words of that song. I am grateful for her example in trusting God's leading in her life.

That hymn has also become meaningful to me. The theme of God's faithfulness comes through and ministers to me again and again. He does know what is best for me, and He does lead me in the way that I should go.

At times my life has taken unexpected turns and certain times have been hard, but regardless of the circumstances I face, I can know that "whatever I do, wherever I be, still 'tis God's hand that leadeth me," and I can rest in that knowledge. In the troubled times, sometimes my mind wants to focus on the hard things and see through my limited perspective rather than focusing on God's faithfulness; but then I can think of the words, "Lord, I would clasp Thy hand in mine, Nor ever murmur nor repine—Content, whatever lot I see, Since 'tis my God that leadeth me." Again, I can choose to trust God's faithfulness and His leading, and that awareness brings comfort and peace within.

As I put my hand in His and trust His leading through my life experiences, I am challenged to respond by walking faithfully in obedience to Him.

Lord God, I thank You for the privilege of experiencing Your faithfulness and Your hand leading me throughout my life's journey. I thank You for the privilege of trusting You.

Betty Metzler serves as a counselor at Petra Christian Fellowship, New Holland.

God's Amazing Ways

"And my God will meet all your needs according to his glorious riches in Christ Jesus." *Philippians 4:19*

After living in Harrisonburg, Virginia, for twenty-four years, our family was planning a major move back to Lancaster County, where my wife and I had grown up. Our house in Virginia had not yet sold, but we needed to move at the end of the month because of a job deadline.

At that time my wife and I were involved in several prayer groups at our church. In one of the early morning prayer groups, we were praying alphabetically through the church directory. Each week, each one of us would call several people to see if they had any prayer requests that they would want to share with the prayer group. We would bring to the group the requests that were shared, and we would join together in bringing them to God. Again and again, we saw God specifically answer those requests. And in this prayer group, God brought an answer that met our moving needs in an amazing way.

A couple that my wife and I contacted (a few weeks before our moving date) shared that they needed a place to live. The house they were building was not yet finished, and they had to move from the place where they were living. As it turned out, they rented our house! We loaded our things into the moving truck during the day on Saturday, and they moved their things into our house Saturday evening. Over the weekend we used their furniture and slept in their bed!

We continued to experience God's perfect timing throughout this whole situation. Their house was finished and ready to move into just as our house sold! That's just like God!

Lord God, thank you for the ways You provide for us and meet our needs far beyond our expectations.

Glenn D. Metzler serves as a chaplain in health care at Landis Homes, a retirement community in Lititz.

God's Protection

"...You will protect me from trouble and surround me with songs of deliverance." *Psalm 32:7*

As I rounded the corner, the Jeep sounded funny, and I felt a sudden thump, thump in the rear of the car on my side. Pulling over and getting out, I noticed the back wheel tilting out a bit at the very top. Closer investigation revealed five empty holes where lug nuts should have secured the wheel to the car.

Surely one or two more revolutions would have resulted in a dangerous accident! Immediately behind the terror of what could have happened came exquisite gratitude for God's plan and provision in this situation. How much does God love me that He protected my life!

Then three thoughts occurred to me. First, most of the time I travel that route, I go much further on the highway. Had I not turned off, I could have lost the wheel in the midst of several lanes of fast-moving traffic. Second, although my GPS gave me incorrect directions, the mistake took me off the highway one exit before my intended stop. And third, because I was driving slowly as I looked for street names, I was able to hear and feel the problem before it became a disaster.

We so often grow frustrated with a change of plans, incorrect directions, or the need to go slowly. However, these may be the very things God builds into our day to keep us from danger or defeat.

How many times in life does God keep us from disasters of which we are completely oblivious? When will we learn to trust God's intervention instead of seeing it as intrusion or inconvenience? Let us praise Him for His protection and deliverance.

Father, please give me patience to trust You to protect and provide for me. Allow me to see Your hand on my life and praise You!

Nancy Sebastian Meyer is an inspirational speaker, Bible teacher and author who ministers from Lancaster to around the nation and brings God's hope to women through *hope4hearts*, www.nancysebastianmeyer.com.

Satisfying Service

"When Peter saw him, he asked, 'Lord, what about him?' Jesus answered, 'If I want him to remain alive until I return, what is that to you? You must follow me.'" *John 21:21–22*

This past summer I participated in a two-week work team. I was part of a group of thirty-nine people from our church that went to the YWAM base in Montego Bay, Jamaica.

One of the things that was very meaningful to me was the appreciation the staff expressed for the work we were doing. Several times I heard them say, "Thank you for coming" or "We appreciate all you are doing for us." Hearing those statements made the trip worth it for me.

One morning at breakfast, Aaron, from the maintenance department, wanted to share the "big picture" with our team. He said, "When we send a team to the nations from this base, and they share the gospel in another land, and those people give their hearts to Jesus, we (our team) are sharing both in that effort and in the rewards of turning someone to Christ." It gave all our work projects deeper meaning to know we were also helping the YWAM base staff in the bigger picture of seeing the nations reached for Jesus.

I find serving the most satisfying when I concern myself less with what God is calling other people to do and respond instead to what He has for me to do.

Lord, thank you for using each of us in building Your kingdom. Thank You for the opportunities each of us have, large and small, to further the gospel. May I fulfill those things You would have me to complete.

Phil Martin and his wife, Doris, attend DOVE Westgate Celebration. Phil works as an engineer for the phone company.

God's Audiovisual

"As water breaks out, God has broken out against my enemies by my hand." *1 Chronicles 14:11*

Just before Christmas I had a huge decision to make that would have been simple except that I was suffering from fear, anxiety and stress. Would I be healthy enough in five months to lead my daughter and a group of high schoolers to International House of Prayer in Kansas City? He reminded me that His grace is sufficient. Facing my fears, surrendering myself to Him, and standing in the authority that I have as a child of God were keys to overcome this potentially crippling, emotional problem.

With sheer faith that God would heal me, I made the decision. In God's lovingkindness, He showed me that I had become lazy in standing against the enemy with the authority He has given me to overcome. I repented. Daily as I applied the armor of God, the fear, anxiety and stress lifted.

We left for the long drive to Kansas City. Each day our group gathered for a time of worship. When it was my turn to lead, I gave the testimony of how God was healing and delivering me from fear, anxiety and stress. I shared about the importance of renewing our mind with God's Word; how it brought me freedom and that taking a stand against the enemy with the Word of God was crucial. As I recited 1 Chronicles 14:7, "As water breaks out," it started pouring down rain outside so hard that my voice was drowned out. God used His own audiovisuals to illustrate His Word and brought confirmation to me that His Word is truth, that I had made the right decision, and His cleansing streams are for me and all who truly seek Him.

Lord, Your Word is truth. I praise you that Your Word endures forever. I thank You that Your Word goes forth today and sets us free. I pray that we would hunger and thirst for Your Word today in every situation. Thank you, Jesus—The Word.

Elaine Hoover is the wife of Lloyd Hoover, bishop of Lancaster Mennonite Conference.

Quieting the Storms

"He stilled the storm to a whisper; the waves of the sea were hushed." *Psalm 107:29*

Recently, I found myself in the state of Florida right in the middle of an oncoming hurricane racing across the gulf and looking to hit the coast with a fury. Its path was predicted to come straight to where I was located within twelve hours. It would be my first experience with a hurricane. Honestly, I was kind of looking forward to it.

That evening the local minister prepared us "out of town-ers" for what was about to happen, speaking from personal experience. But, the visiting minister shared that just as Jesus had calmed the storm (Luke 8:24), we could as well. While the local pastor was being practical and helpful, the visiting speaker was sharing faith to believe for a change on the earth. He shared that the earth is the Lord's (Psalm 24:1) and that He has given it to us to rule over. We prayed peace to the winds and that according to Psalm 107 the storm would be stilled to a whisper.

Watching the weather channel first thing the next morning I heard the weather man say, "Only one other time in recorded weather history have we seen a hurricane do this...this thing just died out and gave up once it hit land...unheard of! It is now simply a tropical storm."

What storms are in your life that you may need to speak peace to today?

Father, we praise You that even the winds obey You and that You have given us this same authority on earth.

Steve Prokopchak helps provide oversight and direction for DOVE Christian Fellowship International's network of churches.

Ask and You Shall Receive

"If you remain in me and my words remain in you, ask whatever you wish, and it will be given you." *John 15:7*

While preparing for a medical mission trip to Uganda, my husband received a request from the pastor for used prescription glasses. The time was quickly approaching as they had only ten days until departure. Scott made several phone calls asking for the glasses. Several places didn't have them, but they were able to give him names of other contacts.

As a result of simply asking, we were able to obtain three hundred and thirty pair of prescription glasses by the end of that afternoon. God's word is so true that all we needed to do was "ask." Many times we don't have just because we fail to ask.

I wish I were going just to see the look on Ephraim's face when he sees all the glasses that were donated. We praise the Lord for His bountiful provision.

"Therefore I tell you, whatever you ask for in prayer, believe that you have received it, and it will be yours" (Mark 11:24).

Thank you, Father, for hearing and answering our prayers and causing faith to arise in our hearts as we experience Your love and faithfulness in our lives.

Karen Jackson serves on the eldership team at Oasis Fellowship in Akron.

Training

"Let us fix our eyes on Jesus, the author and perfecter of our faith...."
Hebrews 12:2

"Leave it. Take it. Drop it. Come." If you have raised a puppy or trained a dog of any age, you are very familiar with these commands. We are currently in the process of training our nine-month-old golden retriever puppy, Chase, to obey the commands of his masters. Because we know that his obedience could ultimately prolong his life, we admittedly become frustrated and impatient when he does not immediately obey.

Training the puppy has given me a renewed appreciation for the process our heavenly Master takes us through—those loving commands he gives because He knows they are good for us:

Leave your simple ways behind; learn to use good judgment (see Proverbs 9:6).

Take up your cross daily and follow me (see Luke 9:23).

Drop the matter before a dispute breaks out (see Proverb 3:20).

Come to me...I will give you rest (see Matthew 11:28).

"Watch me" is the command that makes us the focal point of Chase's attention. He sits straight up and intently looks his master in the face, forgetting entirely about the distractions and temptations that are not good for him. Likewise, Hebrews 12:1-2 reminds us that the tug of distractions and temptations will fade away when *our* focal point is Jesus.

When Chase looks to us and immediately obeys, we reward him with a treat and excitedly encourage his good behavior with affirmations like, "Good boy!" Oh, how sweet it is when we keep our eyes on Jesus and choose to follow Him. It is then that we experience His present blessings with anticipation of the future affirmation, "Well done, good and faithful servant!"

Thank You, Lord, for Your loving patience with us as we go through the training process of life. So that we can persevere in the ways that are good for us, grant us grace to turn away from distractions and temptations and fix our eyes on Jesus.

Chris McNamara works with Life Transforming Ministries in Coatesville and is a Woman of Hope leader at Hopewell Christian Fellowship in Elverson.

Burning Away the Addiction

"Even while these people were worshiping the Lord, they were serving their idols. To this day their children and grandchildren continue to do as their fathers did." *2 Kings 17:41*

I am a believer who also is a recovering addict. The seeds of my addiction probably started when I was five or six years of age, shortly after my mother's death, followed by the oftentimes absences of my father. My addiction is a four-letter word called "work." I am a recovering workaholic.

Work generally isn't considered an addiction. After all, its virtues are extolled scores of times in the Bible. It is rewarded by employers. It is considered a strength in man's role of providing for his family. It is even played out by many women in the work place, or seeking to be perfect moms or even being overly focused on work in the church.

The Lord has shown me that work, as with many addictions, can become an idol. I now am able to recognize it was a contributing factor to divorce after thirty-two years of marriage.

It also can be generational. My father was a workaholic and, probably, his father before him. I now am trying to help mitigate some of these same traits in my sons.

It took a long time to recognize the seriousness of my addiction and then to rely upon the Lord to show me when this tendency starts to re-appear. Today, I have a constant reminder on my car visor that reads: "I don't have to strive; I only have to be obedient."

Lord, help us to recognize when our virtues become our addictions. You love us for who You made us to be. We don't have to strive. Our blessings are found in being obedient to You. Amen.

Casey Jones, who resides in Parkesburg, is an advocate for development of comprehensive marriage and family ministries, including ministries to the hurting, in churches. He is developer of a Transformation Initiative for Building Healthy Communities Through Healthy Families.

Forgiveness

"But if you refuse to forgive others, your Father will not forgive your sins." *Matthew 6:15 (New Living Translation)*

I was unprepared for how my visit to the memorial site of the Dachau concentration camp in Germany would affect me. Reading about concentration camps and touring one of them are two completely different experiences. Walking through the camp, seeing the pictures of the victims, reading their stories, seeing the bullet holes in the wall where executions took place, looking at the ovens in which bodies were disposed of, gives an entirely different perspective.

At more than one point along the tour, I found myself overwhelmed with emotion. I was horrified and heartbroken at the same time. Truthfully, I wondered how anyone experiencing these horrors could ever forgive—until I remembered a compelling testimony from Corrie Ten Boom. Years after her experience in a concentration camp, she tells this story about the time a former guard, at the camp at which she was interned, asked her for forgiveness:

I stood there with the coldness clutching my heart. But forgiveness is not an emotion—I knew that too. Forgiveness is an act of the will, and the will can function regardless of the temperature of the heart. And so woodenly, mechanically, I thrust my hand out. And as I did, an incredible thing took place. The current started in my shoulder, raced down my arm, sprang into our joined hands. And then this healing warmth seemed to flood my whole being, bringing tears to my eyes. "I forgive you, brother!" I cried. "With all my heart!" For a long moment we grasped each other's hands, the former guard and the former prisoner. I had never known God's love so intensely as I did then.

Are you having a hard time forgiving someone today? Forgiving others often starts as a decision of surrender—an act of our will. This surrender invites God to begin working in our lives in a deeper level, allowing Him to heal us. Don't wait any longer.

As You have freely forgiven me, Lord, help me to forgive others.

Karen Ruiz is editor of House to House Publications, Lititz.

His Creation

"Thus the heavens and the earth were completed in all their vast array." *Genesis 2:1*

I often muse as I travel in the mornings and evenings along Routes 10 and 30 in Western Chester County, whether God "planted" me in Parkesburg not that long ago to have the opportunity to more fully appreciate His Creation.

The frequent early morning or evening travel provides a perfect opportunity to marvel at the sunrises and sunsets that never are the same, the colors that never seem to be able to be duplicated by paint on canvas or captured in fullness on film, and to experience the extra opportunities for reflection and prayer time.

Having lost my mother to death at an early age, it also reminds me of Christian artist Danny Oertli's song, "Mommy Paints the Sky", inspired by his young daughter Gracie's question of, "Daddy, did God let mommy paint the sky tonight?" shortly after her mother's untimely death.

In my earlier life, much of my work was in late afternoons and evenings, not allowing for the same opportunities as today. It helps remind me that we have limited opportunities to take advantage of all He provides.

Lord, in times of tiredness, anxiety and distress, help me to see the many blessings that You have provided in Your Creation and take the time to slow down, reflect, and enjoy them. Amen.

Casey Jones, who resides in Parkesburg, is an advocate for development of comprehensive marriage and family ministries, including ministries to the hurting, in churches. He is developer of a Transformation Initiative for Building Healthy Communities Through Healthy Families.

Life to the Full

"The thief comes only to steal and kill and destroy; I have come that they may have life, and have it to the full." *John 10:10*

One morning on my way to my office, I was asking God to guide my decisions for the day. As I was praying I began to realize an inner struggle taking place in the midst of my prayer. My heart was saying I should go to Ephrata Middle School's Bible study. It was the end of the year, and I may not get to see the students for a whole summer. My mind was saying, "You're tired, you're bored with the routine, they won't miss you if you're not there."

I began to wonder if God was trying to get hold of me. Was this urge to go into school the Holy Spirit attempting to guide me? Was my mind coming up with excuses to try things my own way? I began to get excited. What if this was God trying to lead me? My mind was full of questions as my car ended up at my office. I was in my normal parking spot, but I was not feeling normal; my heart and mind where racing. I felt God telling me to go to the Middle School Bible study. Finally, I went, and it was the best thing that could have happened to me.

This day happened to be the last half day of school, and the Middle School was going to spend the morning playing sports and other outdoor activities. The school secretary was frantically searching for people to help lead the activities and I was asked to help lead touch football for the morning. I had a blast playing football with the students. And to think that I was going to spend the morning at the office!

Father, thank you for having the best possible life for us, and forgive us when we try to do things our own way.

Grant Gehman serves as the director of TNT Youth Ministry in Ephrata.

Journey

"Turn me away from wanting any other plan than yours...revive my heart toward you." *Psalm 119:37 (The Living Bible)*

Overwhelmed with grief, tears flowed, freely, down my face as I gripped my husband's hand. Although the doctor didn't want to predict our chances, I pressed for an answer. "The average couple has a 30% chance of conceiving each month. Without the aid of fertility treatments, your chance of conceiving is around 2%."

Nothing prepares you for the news that your lifelong dream of becoming parents may not happen. Although the next several years would be a hard journey of living the difficult reality of infertility, it would be a season of growth and beautiful blessing as we turned to God and aligned our hearts with His.

The months that followed this day were filled with feelings of deep sadness and moments of anger or times of confusion and questioning. I felt myself drift away from the one source that could be my comfort in time of pain, leaving me with my own human inadequacies to cope and attempt to find answers. It wasn't long before I realized that I had to make a choice...to abandon my own way and cling to the One who can be trusted. He spoke, "Trust that my plans and purposes for you are far greater than you can dream on your own."

As I began to embrace the pain and praise Him through my tears, He carried me to a new level of intimacy. His Word became alive as He helped me to relinquish my plans in exchange for His will. Little did I know that four years later, I would be more in love with God than ever before, sharing His amazing love with countless others. My husband joins me on this beautiful journey as he also pursues the lifelong dream that God recently awakened—to serve others through law enforcement.

We may not always understand the trials we face, but one thing is for certain...God's timing is always perfect, His love for us is great, and His plans will always far exceed our expectations.

Thank you Father that our dependence on You reaps abundant joy and that You are given glory through a life submitted to You.

Kristen Long is the director of the Sexual Integrity Ministry with Susquehanna Valley Pregnancy Services.

I'm a Work in Progress

"Cleanse me from my secret faults. Keep back your servant from presumptuous sins; let them not have dominion over me...."
Psalm 19:12–13 (New King James Version)

We've all been hurt by someone; felt that infamous sting of an offense or two or three. But what about the repeated transgressions that go unacknowledged or are minimized and sloughed off by the offender as insignificant? The subtle offenses when left unchecked can dig deep down to the core fertilizing ripened grounds cultivated by unforgiveness...what about them?

Somehow, over the course of my life I learned to stuff and store, falling prey to the delusion that I was a forgiving person. After all, if I couldn't recount the offenses, didn't that somehow mean I forgave?

I marvel at the graciousness of our Lord. Often I will pray the Scriptures depending on where God leads me in my devotional time with Him. For more than a year my heart was consistently drawn to Psalm 19:12-14. Gently, through conviction without condemnation as only the Lord can do, He plainly showed me that I was harboring unforgiveness.

But I was justified, I heard my mind cry. These offenses were painful and unwarranted. Over and over I'd pour my heart out to Jesus and repeatedly I'd hear in my spirit, "He who is without sin, cast the first stone" (John 8:7). I was struck by His patience with me, for this went on for the longest time, until finally I felt the prick—it's not about the offenses or even the offender—it's about my relationship with my Savior, for if I allow unforgiveness in my heart, I am subversively distancing myself from Him.

I'm a work in progress until I can fall into His arms one fine day, but I am thankful that I am no longer deceived by a skewed focus.

Father, I praise Your holy name. I bow before You in awe of Your great mercy and faithfulness. Thank you for Your love that has transformed my life.

Amy Grumbling is a wife, mother of two beautiful girls and a writer.

Nothing is Impossible With God

"However, as it is written: 'No eye has seen, no ear has heard, no mind has conceived what God has prepared for those who love him.'" *1 Corinthians 2:9*

"Jordon will never be able to read," stated the educational psychologist, an expert in testing children with special needs. She had no doubt after testing Jordon for several hours. "Furthermore, he won't be able to drive, be independent...." I lost track of the rest of the "nevers" she was listing about Jordon. I felt crushed—could this really be true? I felt like I couldn't breathe. He was over eight-years-old and showed neither interest nor capacity for reading, among other significant developmental areas. I went home and cried myself to sleep.

When morning came, I got up, shook my head and said "No! I will not accept those words. If it is true, then God, You will have to show me Yourself. Your destiny for Jordon is sealed in Your Name, Your purpose is sure. Please grant us discernment in helping him achieve the purposes You have set for him."

Well, God did show me. Jordon was reading within six months of that bleak prognosis. Not just tediously reading his schoolwork, but reading for pleasure. And with pleasure, I saw God's delight in declaring a hearty "Yes!" over the "never." The darker the night, the brighter the Light!

Lord, thank you for walking with us in our daily challenges. Thank You for showing Your arm is not too short to save and that nothing is impossible with God. Please continue to shine the light of Your love and glory in our dark places. For Your Namesake, Amen.

Cindy Riker is thrilled to be a wife, a mother of four children, a contributing editor, and a Bible study leader for Change of Pace.

Spiritual Refreshing

"Come near to God and he will come near to you...." *James 4:8*

"Stretch out your hands," our worship leader said. "Imagine that you are putting them into the hands of Jesus." I closed my eyes. Jesus seemed to be seated facing me, our knees almost touching. As we clasped hands, my heart melted and the tension from a busy week dissolved. Tears welled up as I basked in his loving gaze. No condemnation, no advice! Just God loving me, and I, in response, loving Him.

The memory of this experience lingers. Simply extending my hands to Jesus became, for me, a profound act of worship. No magnificent cathedral or glorious choir was needed!

Sometimes, it is difficult to feel close to God. But, when we slow down, sit still, and set aside time to be with Him, we discover that He loves to be with us. Just as we need physical hugs daily for emotional health, our spirits crave Divine hugs. Have you received your "God hug" today? Is your spiritual "love barrel" filled? Come to Jesus daily. Like the refreshment of a gentle shower on parched soil, time spent with God will cleanse and renew your spirit.

Lord, giver of all things good, fill my "love barrel" so that it will naturally overflow to others today. Amen.

Leona Myer serves as a pastoral elder at Hosanna Christian Fellowship in Lititz.

It's What's Under the Hood that Counts

"I came so they can have real and eternal life...." *John 10:10 (The Message)*

Sometime back the Associated Press carried this dispatch: "Leslie Puckett, after struggling to start his car, lifted the hood and discovered that someone had stolen the motor."

Leslie had a rude awakening—a car without an engine isn't going anywhere. A life without a clear purpose is like a car without an engine. It's just not going anywhere.

The 17th century physicist/philosopher Blaise Pascal spoke of "a God-shaped vacuum in the heart of every man" which can't be filled by more things—but "only by God." Jesus said, "I came so they can have real and eternal life, more and better life than they ever dreamed of." Jesus Christ is the engine that powers your life and gives it meaning.

If you feel there is something missing in your life, that something is Someone...Jesus Christ. Jesus did for us what we could not do for ourselves. He paid the price of our sins by dying on the cross, and He also defeated sin by rising again on the third day. Our part is accepting this free gift of salvation.

If you would like to ask Jesus Christ into your life, pray this prayer: *Lord Jesus, thank You for loving me. I know that I am a sinner and need Your forgiveness. I know that You died on the cross for my sins and rose from the dead. I want to turn from my sins and give You control of my life. Please come into my life right now, Lord. Help me to follow You always. Amen.*

You are a new creation in Christ! The Bible tells us "The old is gone and the new has come." By making this decision to follow Christ you now have purpose and power. Find a church that teaches from the Bible and make a difference in someone else's life by sharing Christ with them.

Thank you, Lord, for life and purpose. Amen.

Dan Houck is the pastor at The Table Community Church, Lancaster.

Lady

"But if God so clothes the grass of the field, … will He not much more clothe you?" Matthew 6:30 (New American Standard Bible)

In my well-ordered world everything is set to run a certain way. Yet, on one particular Tuesday morning, I found myself taking a sick day (which I never take) to go to the doctor (for persistent allergy problems—which is not even critical), and Tuesdays are the busiest day of my week. As I made the decision, I was a little awed with myself—it was so out of character. I'm one of those people who calls into work while on vacation. Forget sick days!

Within an hour of making the decision, I knew it was a God thing. Instead of going to my own doctor, I ended up taking our senior dog, Lady, to the vet. (My daughter was going to do this on her own.) A gut instinct told me that, since I was home, I should go along. What was to be a routine visit turned into heartbreak.

Within four hours, we had lost a dear family pet to a heart condition so severe that they couldn't even find a heartbeat. As my daughter and I hugged and cried buckets of tears, I was struck with the realization that had I kept my usual schedule, my daughter would have had to deal with this alone. At work, I would have been an hour away and possibly not even heard my cell phone. At the doctor's office, I likely would not have had my cell phone on. So many details of that day had changed uncharacteristically, that we knew it was a God thing. It was as if He restructured our day, even causing me to act out of character, so that my daughter would not be alone for that trauma.

God so cares about the lilies of the fields, the birds of the air, even the grass and trees. How much more does He care for me (Matthew 6:25-31)?

O precious Father, thank you for watching out for each detail of our lives.

Lisa Hildebrand works for Susquehanna Valley Pregnancy Services and ministers as a teacher and speaker in local churches.

It's Cancer!

"And the prayer offered in faith will make the sick person well...."
James 5:15

"It's cancer!" That was the message our family received in early April, 2008. Gavin Wagner, our seven-year-old grandson, was diagnosed with Burkett's lymphoma. Tumors had wrapped themselves around his liver and kidneys. His stomach was protruding rapidly. This rare type of cancer has the potential of doubling in size every eighteen hours.

Gavin had many severe and difficult reactions to the medications such as mouth sores severe headaches, zero white blood cell counts, and loss of hair. However, within a day of chemo the tumors started breaking up and flowing out through a discharge tube.

Praying to God, fasting, anointing with oil, and Hershey Medical was the combination that resulted in effective treatment. We praise God! In just 3-1/2 months and with the last chemo completed, the cancer is gone! He is getting back to riding his four-wheeler, playing and eating normally and even pestering his sister and brothers.

It had been a tough year for his immediate family. Their lives were very much disrupted; but we are filled with praise that prayer was answered and Hershey Medical knew what to do.

Thank you, God, for the healing touch of Jesus that comes to us through prayer, the anointing with oil, and the developments of medical technology. Amen.

Jim Myer is one of the plural, non-salaried ministers at the White Oak Church of the Brethren in Manheim.

Worth Saying

"...So is my word that goes out from my mouth: It will not return to me empty, but will accomplish what I desire and achieve the purpose for which I sent it." *Isaiah 55:11*

I am a PowerPoint ® preacher. That means I use this visual technology to enhance my communication of God's Word. It has required me to become a better prepared communicator and a more disciplined one. This is almost impossible as a Saturday Night Special, and does not happen if you're still writing on Sunday morning. When I first began preaching with this tool, a young lady asked, "What do you do if the Holy Spirit changes the message from Tuesday to Sunday?"

"I just turn off the projector and say what He tells me to say," was my response.

Regardless of how we approach our preaching, most pastors will tell you that *inspiration* is as much a problem as *preparation*. I firmly believe that the Spirit works more effectively through a pastor who prepares than one who puts Him to the test by just standing up and saying whatever pops into his mind. But we still struggle with being sure that what we have to say is something worth saying. Recently we finished Advent and Christmas, seasons that are a particular challenge because people have pretty much heard everything we've had to say on the subject of Christ's birth. Although essentially repeating a previous sermon is not a sin—it does not necessarily capture the full attention of the hearer.

But then I am reminded that the Word entrusted into my care, communicated through my personality and communication, is *the Word of God.* It never returns empty. It always plants seeds for faith. It always brings light in darkness. It always calls people to transformation and obedience. It reminds people of the presence and the heart of God. As long as I keep in my mind the purpose for which God has given that Word and proclaim that message faithfully—it will be worth saying—even if I don't say it very well. Thanks be to God!

Lord, may our words be worth saying today, bringing Your light to all.

Dr. Steve Dunn has been lead pastor of the Church of God of Landisville since September 2001.

How Do We Trust God's Protection and Guidance?

"Trust in the Lord with all of your heart and lean not on your own understanding; in all your ways acknowledge Him and He shall direct your paths." *Proverbs 3:5-6 (New King James Version)*

Sometimes we are able to experience "peace that passes understanding" even when the circumstances appear to be less than stable.

Recently, my wife and I went horseback riding in West Virginia. A normal three hour ride turned into an adventure I will never forget.

We had been on these trails many times before, but this time we went off a trail and ended up on the Tuscarora trail looking at a sign that stated it was 1,200 miles long. Suddenly we realized that the sun was going down quickly. We had no maps, we were low on water and our horses were tired. We decided to pray. One of the horses kept looking to the left into the woods as if she knew the way home.

Finally, we decided to go down a small trail, which took us down the mountain and up another. Along the way we found water for our horses, a break from the sun, and enough beauty to keep our minds off the crisis. It was almost dark when I realized where we were. I asked my wife if she could trot so we could get out of the woods.

We stopped at the first inhabited cabin and met a woman who drove me to our truck, which was two mountains away, and then she cooked us a steak dinner! Only God! She told us about the distressed bears that the state had released this summer where we were riding. God protected us, and my wife's greatest amazement was that I had completed hours of riding with no complaining. Thank God for changing me!

Lord, teach us to trust always, never wandering astray from Your love and protection—always believing in Your deliverance.

Ronald Buch is a senior pastor of Breakout Ministries and is active in marketplace ministry.

Who Is Blessed?

"But his delight is in the law of the Lord…." *Psalm 1:2*

As a member of the Shepherding Team, I am often called on to visit people in hospitals, nursing homes, or in their homes. I find that the Lord teaches me something with each challenge. One woman, I'll call Jane, suffered two serious health problems. I started visiting her months afterward, when she was still bedridden, and unable to speak, though she could nod yes or no. I thought to myself, *I can't just sit here and talk about myself.* Praying for her and reading Scripture are very important, but I felt a need for more—a personal connection.

The Lord brought to mind that I could read other books to her. Besides Scripture and Bible promise books, I began reading from Christian books; a few chapters at each visit. Soon we developed a comfortable routine: we held hands in prayer (the connection of friendship), followed by showing her two or three choices, and ending in prayer. She often chose the Bible first or even as the only source for that day. I would read dramatically in order to be interesting. Jane listened and began expressing her delight with familiar passages. Her face would light up in a big smile. I thought, *do I delight in God's Word? Am I excited to hear or read one more chapter, then another?*

Recently I was reading a story to her where the author expressed a desire to say thank you to a beloved junior high teacher. Jane put her hand on the page to stop me, and she spoke a few words that I did not understand. At first, I wasn't sure what she wanted. Suddenly it struck me! Jane was saying "thank you"—to me! I was touched. I looked her in the eyes and said, "You're welcome," then continued reading.

Who is blessed? You could say both of us. I would say, "Me!"

O Lord, may I live each day obedient to You, no matter what You ask of me.

Sharon Neal is a free-lance proofreader and serves on the Shepherding Team and in women's and children's ministries at Lancaster Evangelical Free Church in Lititz.

Chocolate Rain

"Thanks be to God who always leads us in His triumph in Christ and manifests through us the sweet aroma of the knowledge of Him in every place." *2 Corinthians 2:14*

What happens when an old familiar fragrance blends with the new?

I was out weeding in my garden one morning in my new/old 1854 home in Mount Joy.

I began to sniff a fragrance that I couldn't quite discern. There was a moment when I realized it was "chocolate rain."

The aroma was created when fresh fallen rain kissed the grass and earth in the garden and was melded with the fragrance of the Wilbur factory's morning batch of chocolate. It was a curious little parable from the Lord in that moment. Ways I was used to knowing Him would now be blended with new ways that He would come into my life.

A prayer rose up in me, "Lord, do not let me miss the fragrance of Your presence in my midst. 'Chocolate rain' is such a nice blend of two beautiful smells. Lord, let the new come! Forgive me where I have limited You by using the ways I have previously known You. Forgive me where I have limited my choices of friends to only the old familiar. Help me welcome the new friends You want to attract to my life."

Lord, as the Church triumphant, lead us as a fragrant aroma that will cause the world to pause and wonder. Blend us together in new groupings in the body of Christ that our neighbors, coworkers, and surrounding nations could receive us in new pleasing ways and be attracted to You. Come, Holy Spirit, and blow on our gardens. Waft the fragrance of Christ through the air!

Can you smell the "chocolate rain"?

God, use us in this day to combine our gifts with another so that a new blend of the expression of Christ can come on earth as it is in heaven.

Nancy Clegg is a worshiper and mobilizer in the body of Christ in the region and the nations.

Seek First the Kingdom

"But seek first his kingdom and his righteousness, and all these things will be given to you as well." *Matthew 6:33*

I remember the first time I heard those words stated to me, not knowing they were actually from the Bible. My mother was encouraging me to trust God and give my life to Him so that He could provide and make a way for me. Wow, what a releasing thought it was that God could, or would, make a way for me. I had always felt that I needed to do it all myself and, at that time in my life, it seemed impossible. But all I had to do was to become a kingdom seeker.

Although much time has passed since that first encounter with Matthew 6:33, I still find myself challenged by those words to seek first God's kingdom; it's a present tense challenge and a choice. It's not just that I come to Jesus Christ and live under the Christian banner, but I must walk daily with Him as His kingdom kid.

I came to see that Jesus was not only trying to tell us, but to *model* for us, what His Father's kingdom is all about. He begins in Matthew 4:17 by encouraging us to repent—all repentance is a change of heart and mind toward God. He began to preach the kingdom and, before departing, wrapped it up in Acts 1:3 with final words about His Father's kingdom. Everything "in the middle" is His way of *demonstrating* the kingdom. It's like trying to explain ice-cream to someone who has never tasted it. I have found that it is "better felt than telt."

May God encourage you in His kingdom call for your life this day (Genesis18:14).

Lord, Thy kingdom come and Thy will be done in me today as Your kingdom kid.

Patrick Glennon is the director of the National Christian Conference Center in Valley Forge.

Living a Life of No Regrets on Purpose

"Greater love has no one than this, that he lay down his life for his friends." *John 15:13*

I awoke this morning to feeling like a ton of bricks hit me square between the eyes as the thoughts of our conversation at our small group and Rob's dad's accident collided in my mind.

Time is a precious commodity that we dare not take lightly. I began to weep at the thought of the answer to the question, "Did I do my best?" No, I didn't.

What I wouldn't do to turn back the hand of time to replay all the times I could have invested into Dad Sheehan's life! How I could have been a blessing and chose not to, but instead I was selfish with my words, attitude or time! Time is an investment into eternity. How am I investing my time?

We will be held accountable for every word and action. Do I reflect the love of God and shine forth His light? Is the fruit of the Holy Spirit evident in my life? Am I using my gifts and talents to serve others? These tough and personal questions are needed to shake me into an eternal perspective.

I've had the opportunity to see firsthand the frailty of human life this past week. Life is too short to waste time on things that don't reward eternally. It really does come down to a personal choice in our attitudes and actions in how we respond to others. Are we positive and productive or negative and destructive?

We can't take words or actions back after they have been said or done, and we do not know what a day may bring. I want to live a life worthy of the calling I've received, investing my time and talents into the lives of those around me for His glory and for eternal significance.

Heavenly Father, help us to remember that each moment our words and attitude have eternal significance. Help us use our time wisely.

Diana Sheehan and her husband Rob and children attend DOVE Christian Fellowship Westgate, Ephrata.

Photo by Don Barley

August

Clean!

"Be self controlled and alert. Your enemy the devil prowls like a roaring lion looking for someone to devour. Resist him, standing firm in the faith, because you know that your brothers throughout the world are undergoing the same kind of suffering." *1 Peter 5:8*

Annette and Darryl Oberly attend my church. This is Darryl's story: Darryl grew up as the youngest of a family of four. His family wasn't a Christian family, but he knew they loved him. Unfortunately, their love wasn't enough to protect him from a neighbor's abuse. His family's love wasn't enough to keep him from drugs and alcohol to cover up the inner pain.

After high school graduation, Darryl joined the Marine Corps and participated in several Middle East tours. His drinking increased.

When he returned to the U.S., Darryl lived to get high. Riding a Harley and listening to heavy metal music filled his days. Despite the drug and alcohol abuse, Darryl hung on to his job.

Occasionally he tried to stop his downward slide. He participated in several programs meant to help him become drug and alcohol free, but without success.

Then one night, he rolled his vehicle going around a sharp turn. When he awoke, he fell to his knees and prayed, "God, I don't know who you are. I don't want to live like this anymore."

Darryl went to church and was baptized. A coworker shared the verse above that became an inspiration for Darryl to persevere through temptations.

"I've been clean for 20 years. When you're really ready to surrender to God, He will help you," Darryl said. Although he stayed clean, he backslid in his faith. He stopped going to church.

"I believed in God. I loved Him. But I felt like I couldn't measure up to His standards," Darryl recalled. "I kept praying for God to send someone to me to share His goodness. *(Read how God answered his prayers on the next page.)*

Father, thank you for Your saving love. You never give up on us!

Lou Ann Good, a free-lance writer, is part of DOVE Westgate Celebration, Ephrata.

Longing for God

"In the last days, God says, I will pour out my Spirit on all people."
Acts 2:17

Here is more of Darryl and Annette Oberly's story:

Annette had grown up as an only child. Her family had no church background. She was always trying to please her over protective parents and make them proud.

After graduation, Annette thought getting married would be the answer to happiness. During her first marriage, following God's way was not their life-style. After 10 years with no peace or joy, the marriage dissolved. Annette was alone and felt an emptiness for something. She needed and wanted to know God.

Annette knew Darryl through their childhood because their parents played cards together. Years later, when Darryl walked into her workplace and asked her for a date, Annette was ecstatic. They soon moved in together.

Although they loved each other, something was missing.

"I wanted to fill the void I felt in my life," Annette said. She vaguely attributed the unrest she felt as a longing for God.

"Let's visit the church down the street," Annette said.

They did. There, they found what they had been seeking-Jesus.

"Jesus was what I wanted all my life," Annette said. "We were so blessed with the friendships of the people at the church."

They soon realized that following the directive of Jesus, they should marry instead of merely living together. They soon wed.

Annette and Darryl study the Bible together. Darryl has sensed healing from childhood pain, and a love and acceptance from Christ he had never realized possible.

Annette said, "Pastor Britton's teachings are really opening our eyes, especially the one he taught in Acts 2:17-21. To know that we are filled with the Spirit of the living God—I think about that in my every day tasks." Days of trying to earn her parents' approval are lessening. "I realize it's God's approval I need," Annette said.

Father, thank you for filling our hearts and lives with meaning.

Lou Ann Good, a free-lance writer, is part of DOVE Westgate Celebration, Ephrata.

Thoughts in Flight

"O Lord, you have searched me and you know me. Where can I go from your Spirit? Where can I flee from your presence? If I go up to the heavens, you are there; if I make my bed in the depths, you are there. If I rise on the wings of the dawn, if I settle on the far side of the sea, even there your hand will guide me, your right hand will hold me fast." *Psalm 139:1, 7–9*

Several years ago I took a flight, in a small plane, with a pilot friend around Lancaster County. We took off from the Lancaster Airport and flew over familiar landmarks. It was fun trying to trace our way as we flew. Some places I would lose track of where we were. I was surprised at how difficult it was to figure out where my home was. I was almost lost. It made me feel so small. Weak. Very aware how frail my existence is.

On another flight my trip took me over Florida and the captain announced that the space shuttle was going to be launched to the left of our line of flight. Everyone eagerly went to the windows. The launch was indeed in progress below our plane. I could see a small plume of smoke and the pencil-like shuttle arising into the sky. Humm… no earth shaking rumbles here. It made the the whole process seem insignificant. It made me aware of how tiny the "big deals" in our life seem to God.

More recently my husband and I took a hot air balloon ride to celebrate our anniversary. We took off early on a cool fall morning. We soared up over our Leola home and drifted over Akron. Something that struck both of us was the silence. It was so peaceful only a few hundred feet above the earth. The usual clamor was far away! Maybe it isn't too noisy for God to hear my prayers after all.

If today your world seems overwhelming, remember our God is not confused. He knows us completely. He knows our world completely. He won't lose track of where we are and what is going on in our lives!

Thank you, Father, that you hear every thought and prayer. Thank you for having planned tomorrow already! Thank you for being big enough to care about each detail of our lives.

Sarah Sauder enjoys being a wife and mom as well as graphic designer with DOVE Christian Fellowship International.

God Has a Plan

"May your unfailing love be my comfort." *Psalm 119:76*

It was a beautiful bouquet, filled with cheerful white daisies, royal red carnations and luscious greens, and placed on our kitchen table as an expression of sympathy from our Chapel family on the death of our brother-in-law, Ivan. The shock of Ivan's sudden death at age 56 was so intense that even this floral elegance could not penetrate the disbelief of what had just happened.

Ivan had just begun Day 1 of participating in a bike ride to benefit MCC. He had trained and prepared for the week of riding on the San Juan Islands of Washington State. His life was filled with purpose and joy when suddenly it was cut short by a fatal heart attack.

Staring at this bouquet on the table, I was lost in thought. Life was a blur. What had just happened? "God," I cried out, "what is your purpose in this?"

A response came in a still, small voice from our ever faithful God. "Ivan is just like those flowers. The gardener chooses to cut those flowers in their prime, away from their source of earthly life. He has a plan to create a beautiful bouquet of hope and encouragement. Trust me. I, too, have a plan and purpose for each one in my garden of children, A special plan for Ivan, his family and for you. Trust me to be in the process of arranging your life to further my kingdom."

My spirit was comforted. Ivan's life was complete. We do not need to know the "why." We just have to trust God as He arranges the special plans He has for each of us.

Father, help me to trust You daily in all things.

Brenda Musselman with her husband, Dave, serve the Chapel family at Village Chapel Mennonite Church, New Holland.

My Mount Carmel Experience

"…I urge you to live a life worthy of the calling you have received."
Ephesians 4:1

For the first time, my husband and I needed a four-wheeler to get to a Sunday worship service. In attendance were twenty-four family members and friends. Seated on wooden benches, we faced a nine-foot wooden cross and a stone altar named Mount Carmel. As the sunlight filtered through the trees, a slight breeze carried the birds' soothing songs to our tranquil, outdoor mountain chapel. Overlooking the town of Galeton, in Potter County, we sang *Amazing Grace* with guitar accompaniment. The only major distraction was a snake poking his head up between the stones on the altar as we sang our songs of praise. A symbolic reminder of the presence of evil, even in that remote, secluded area.

Rick shared a devotional about birds. Do our lives most resemble a vulture, feeding on the past decayed stuff in this world, having a predatory nature? Or are we like the hummingbird, feeding on sweet nectar, helping to spread and share what we have received with the world around us? This colorful little bird is efficient, precise, and purposeful in flight. What a contrast between the birds' shapes, sizes, colors, and missions in life. Are we cleaning up the scraps in life or are we using our lives to promote growth, and freely sharing what we have received?

As a believer, I have the gospel, the sweet nectar that gives life. Am I perched high, nested on inaccessible rocks, greedy, self-serving? Or do I daily "hum along" to partake, and purposefully share the gospel, actively participating in life around me to encourage new growth in the lives of others?

Staying at a cabin with a wraparound porch lined with hummingbird feeders, I had the entire weekend to observe and meditate on this object lesson.

Father, we worship You as the Creator of all life. Help us not to act like bird brains, but to walk worthy of our calling, being created in Your Image.

Coleen Gehman is a wife and mother serving with her husband, Bryan, at Lancaster Evangelical Free Church.

Two Choices

"Do you see a man who is wise in his own eyes? There is more hope for a fool than for him." *Proverbs 26:12*

I was having a chat with a new friend, over dinner, after church. Because I wanted to impress this new friend, I tried to keep my foot out of my mouth. The only sure way to do that was to keep mostly quiet, but for me keeping quiet is much easier said than done.

I grew more comfortable and free with my speech. We talked about simple things like the tastiness of the meal and the cuteness of the children wandering the room. I longed for a deeper discussion.

In response to a prolonged lull I remarked, "You're pretty quiet. What's on your mind?"

He responded, "Oh I just like watching people. I'm a pretty good judge of character. I can pretty accurately analyze personalities."

Considering myself one of the most analytical people I know, I jumped at the chance to identify with him in this area. With a proud grin I said, "Oh, I know all about that. I'll bet you get yourself in a lot of trouble with that ability, huh?" I fully expected him to express how hard it is to get people to see themselves as others see them.

My new friend looked at me almost pitifully. After a very short pause he said, "Actually no. I seldom get into trouble with it."

I almost said, "Well, you must not be very good at analyzing people!" But the Holy Spirit stopped me, and I simply sat there waiting in silence. With a tender kindness he explained, "When you analyze people and you see flaws in them, you have two choices. One is judgment and the other is intercession. I choose intercession."

He was so profoundly right. I had more than put my foot into my mouth. I had exposed myself, exposed my sin to him. But rather than feel embarrassed, a calm washed over me. I was thankful for his wisdom and I trusted that in the moment he had looked at me with kindness in his eyes, he had paused to intercede on my behalf. The Lord had intervened and spoken life and correction into me.

Today, Lord, I ask You to teach me Your ways and mold me according to Your purpose. Thank You for a teachable spirit in order that I may receive Your instruction. In Jesus' name I pray, amen.

Falaq Lucas is from Coatsville.

God Stories 4

His Path

"Trust in the Lord with all of your heart and lean not on your own understanding. In all of your ways acknowledge Him and He will direct your path." *Proverbs 3:5*

My husband, Steve, had worked at the same place for almost thirty years. Gradual promotions came to him, until one day the company decided only college graduates would be promoted to staff positions. Suddenly, Steve was given the option of night-shift on a machine or to be laid off.

Not having much time to decide what to do, the Lord gave Steve a great idea. He said to me, "I don't really have a choice. I know they will need someone to do my job when I'm gone. I don't know if they know, but I do design work for the other companies they serve. I'm going to tell them and see if they would be willing to subcontract the work out to me."

As ridiculous as it sounds, that's what he did. The man responsible to replace Steve was happy and relieved that he didn't have to find someone to do this part of the job, because it would have been difficult to find someone able to do it. The replacement asked the manager if it would be okay if they subcontracted the work to Steve. The manager said he had no problem with it!

Now, they are paying Steve more for doing the same job, plus he picks his own hours. That was eight years ago. Amazing God!

Father, You have a destiny planned for all of us before we are born. You said the steps of a righteous man are ordered of the Lord. We ask You to position us to be at the right place, at the right time, doing the right things, for the right reasons. In Jesus' name, amen.

Dorinda Kaylor is a regional intercessor.

More Than Just Words

"Let each generation tell its children of your mighty acts; let them proclaim your power." *Psalm 145:4*

Storytelling is an art form that allows much creativity. It teaches, educates, entertains and is also a way to instill truths. Oral storytelling is improvisational. As a non-scripted account, it exudes expression and life. Although the body of the story is the same, the flare and details are expressed differently each time it is shared.

As youngsters are tucked into bed, most express interest in listening to a story. This is a wonderful opportunity to share a "God Story" with passion from your heart. Psalm 78:4 tells us to "...tell the next generation about the glorious deeds of the Lord, about His power and his mighty wonders."

Children observe adults in myriads of situations. They learn from watching. They also learn from listening to your personal stories. Are you willing to capture a moment from your life and convey a truth to the next generation? Will you proclaim the goodness of Father God through a past situation that challenged you?

The Lord gave the message to Joel "...Pass the story down from generation to generation." You will build the faith of your children by retelling how God supplied your needs. Those following you will be strengthened to persevere through their wilderness, as they remember the testimony of God bringing rain and refreshment in your times of drought.

My children are young adults; however, we still recall stories as we take road trips together. My son-in-law and daughter-in-law are my new audience to hear how God blessed us as a family. Collectively, we are making memories—"God Stories" to pass to future generations.

God, I want my words and stories to declare Your faithfulness to me so that others are encouraged to seek You and lean on You in their time of need.

Nancy Leatherman resides in Manheim Township. Since both of her children are married, she is delighted to be a mother of four.

Beseech My Son!

"Now, my God, let, I beseech thee, thine eyes be open, and let thine
ears be attentive unto the prayer that is made in this place."
2 Chronicles 6:40 (King James Version)

Early one morning while I was sleeping I heard this word come
into my spirit as I awoke saying, "Beseech my Son!" I was meditating
on what I had just received. I knew these words were for me personally, as well as possibly others the Lord may be speaking to who have
a desire to increase their passion in their prayer life toward God. I was
feeling that my prayers were not effective or connecting with the heart
of God. As I researched the meaning of *beseech* and its context in Scripture, I discovered it is an action word that calls us to "ask, call upon,
plead, beg, appeal, urge, implore." The Bible says God rewards those
who earnestly seek Him.

In Psalms, David prays, "O God, you are my God, earnestly I seek
you; my soul thirsts for you, my body longs for you, in a dry and weary
land where there is no water." This word helped me to realize that I
personally needed to increase passion in prayer and also that *beseech* is
an action word—prayer is action; I needed to go after God, and expect
great things from God and believe in faith that He will answer.

*Dear Lord, my prayer is that You would stir in us that desire, and
passion in our prayer life—in my prayers personally as well as
others who feel their prayers are powerless and ineffective. We
desire to connect with Your heart Lord, and pray for those thing that
are aligned with Your perfect will. We see that You are already
increasing our desire to connect with You in our day; our cry is for
more, Lord, so come! Come to our region and revive our hearts for
You in our prayers.*

Hershey Sensenig serves as executive chairman of Village Chapel Mennonite
Church. He and his wife Lisa are involved in reconciliation ministries and other
prayer initiatives.

Rainy Morning

"I will declare that your love stands firm forever, that you established your faithfulness in heaven itself." *Psalms 89:2*

It was a rainy morning and an end to a difficult week. I was still trying to untangle my husband's estate.

Problems mounted with every heavy sigh I took. How would I manage all the legal, emotional and financial issues I was facing? How would I be "mom enough" for my thirteen year old daughter or my two grown sons? How would I cope with taking care of my elderly mom? And what would heal this open wound where my heart once was?

It was time for the daily trip to the mailbox, something I dreaded. I might as well take the dog out for a walk. Poor fella, he looked lost too.

As we picked our way along the road, I kicked at the stones and mumbled almost to myself, "All things work for the good....Well, Lord, I know that is what the Word says, but what good could come from this mess?" I had an immediate sense of God's presence. A sweet tenderness enveloped me as I was impressed to turn around. I heard the Lord say, "Look up!"

As I looked, I saw the most beautiful rainbow encircling my house. The colors were vibrant, yet misty, like a water color painting. It was as though God was hugging me with the most amazing array of heavenly colors of His love!.

As I gazed at the bow in the sky, I was reminded of God's covenant and of God's promises....I will never leave you or forsake you...and I was immersed in His peace. The heavens were declaring God's faithfulness to me!

Lord, I thank You for Your hand of deliverance in my life. I thank You that You are a covenant keeping God. Thank you for demonstrating your great love for us, in that when we need to be turned around and redirected you paint rainbows in the sky for all to see! You are, indeed, faithful, Almighty God!

Cindy Nolt is an elder at Breakout Ministries.

Contact Faith

"My message and my preaching were not with wise and persuasive words, but with a demonstration of the Spirit's power, so that your faith might not rest on men's wisdom, but on God's Power."
1 Corinthians 2:4

It's a warm summer day, and our baseball team is having batting practice before we leave town for our afternoon game. I noticed the boys all gathering in the outfield, and it appeared that one boy was crying. I went out with a few other moms to see what happened. The kids said that Tyler had lost his contact. He just got them yesterday, and it's a trial pair to see if he is able to wear them. He doesn't have any extra lenses nor did he bring his glasses. So I boldly said, "Okay boys and moms, let's pray and ask the Lord to allow us to find this contact.

Immediately the adults chuckled, thinking that it was impossible to find a small clear contact lens in the grass. As we gathered and I knelt down to begin praying, I extended my hand outward and looked down. Immediately I had a contact lens at my fingertip! Praise the Lord!

The adults and kids were amazed! My son and I knew the Lord put that contact right there. He gave me a big grin, and I smiled back. We then got Tyler some contact lens solution, and I was able to share with him some tips to keep him from losing the lens again.

I was grateful that the Lord revealed Himself in such a powerful way that day because the story of finding the contact lasted for hours at the baseball field. And that young boy knew that God cares about everything, even a contact lens.

Dear Lord, I thank You for the gift of faith that You have given us to step out and declare who You are in the midst of all situations. You are my Rock.

Michele Apicella is a member of Christ Community Church in Camp Hill and serves on the ministry team and youth staff.

God's Wisdom Through Others

"Trust in the Lord with all your heart and lean not on your own understanding…." *Proverbs 3:5*

Some years ago, while taking my family on a summer vacation to the Western United States, we visited an area north of Helena, Montana. Instantly, we all fell in love with the beauty of the "Rockies", the fresh, clean, air, and the people who lived there. Upon returning home, I contacted numerous real estate companies in the Helena area, determined to move my family West!

Sometime during my search through properties on the market my friend and father-in-law gave me some advice in a very gentle way. He said, "Joe, before you move your family west take the time to visit the area in the winter." I listened, and the very next winter we went on a ski/snowmobile trip to Montana. Understand, in those days, we loved snow and winter, but never knew winter to be 25 degrees below zero at mid-day!

When we returned home, all the Montana real estate material got trashed. A wise man is always ready to listen to wise council.

Father, let us be eager today to listen to wise council in order to understand Your desires for us.

Joe Nolt is an assistant to the director of DOVE Mission International, Lititz.

AUGUST 13

All the Barriers

"And Jabez called on the God of Israel...." *1 Chronicles 4:10*

I don't know about you, but I can put up barriers that hinder God from blessing me with all He has for me.

Oh, that I would have the boldness of Jabez—he did not allow any barrier to stop him from all God had for him (1 Chronicles 4:9-10). So what did Jabez do?

1. Jabez called on the God of Israel. He went right to the source—his Creator, his Provider, his Father.

2. Jabez asked God to bless him: He didn't go with a list (which I tend to do)—he wanted the God who knew him best to bless him with *all* God had for him.

3. Jabez asked God to enlarge his territory. He was willing to go beyond his self-imposed border. Jabez had to look past his abilities and look at God's. God would equip him for the work He had for him.

4. Jabez asked God to keep him from evil, so he may not cause pain. That was his mother's label. Jabez wanted God to help him be who *God* created him to be—not what others (parents, friends, himself) "labeled" him to be. He wanted the label of others to be replaced with who God said he was.

And, you know what? God granted his request. I, too, have experienced, many times, God working in my life to help me move beyond my self-imposed borders and my false labels. To remove any barriers that keep me from all God has for me. God desires to do that for *all* of His children. Will you join me and pray with the boldness of Jabez? When we do, we can expect God to grant our request too!

Father, You are our source. May we open our hearts to Your work as You remove the barriers that hinder us from embracing all You have for us.

Kathy Nolt works alongside her husband in business. She is also administrative assistant for the Regional Church of Lancaster County.

Legacies

"...I will pour My Spirit on your descendants, and My blessing on your offspring." *Isaiah 44:3*

"Tami, you'll never guess what this wooden table was used for," my dad said. "I can still see Great Grammy laying out the intestines, squeezing out the contents, and checking for holes by blowing through the opening. Then she stuffed it with freshly ground sausage meat. This crock was used for making homemade sauerkraut and that crock held *schmeirkasa*. This six-quart strawberry holder was made from dynamite boxes from the days when your grandfather used to be a coal miner. He also fashioned this smaller box with a row of metal teeth to more quickly pick huckleberries that grew abundantly on the coal region hills."

After traveling with my air force husband for twenty-three years, we had finally settled near home. I was enthralled with discovering the "treasures" in my Dad's barn—objects reminiscent of my family's legacies of hard work and creativity. I enjoy filling my home with these pieces of the past so that I can tell my own children and guests about my cherished inheritance.

In our dining room is a wedding gift from my mom's father, an antique painted glass plaque, symbolizing another type of rich legacy. Having hung above his farmhouse kitchen table for as long as my mom could remember, the plaque's words defined my grandfather's simple and reverent way of life:

Rules for Today: "Do nothing that you would not like to be doing when Jesus comes. Go to no place where you would not like to be found when Jesus comes. Say nothing that you would not like to be saying when Jesus comes."

Heartfelt memories often accompany our fondest heirlooms. But the richer treasure is one that continues through generations, not fading with time.

Dear Father, thank you for all the delightful inheritances You have left me. I ask You to continually remake me from the inside out, so they have a spiritual baton to carry to the next generation.

Tamalyn Jo Heim, with her husband, Bob, wants to carry on this legacy through their talks on marriage, parenting and their Bible studies on teen purity.

Hurricane

"Great is your love towards me...." *Psalm 86:13*

After receiving life-threatening injuries in an accident four years ago, I expected a tough physical recovery, but the intensity of the accompanying emotional journey surprised me and shook my world.

Though I'd been following God for twenty years, my desires and beliefs were caught up in a hurricane and it felt like I had no control over the direction of its path. I'm generally optimistic, believing that tomorrow will be better than today, but my days swirled with questions, doubt and anger. I went from looking forward to the future to wanting to die.

In the midst of the pain, God's Spirit helped me search for truth. I read, journaled, prayed and received counseling. Hours spent soaking up the sun or studying the full moon helped me connect to God in a new way. Actively looking for the good (daisies, hugs, encouraging words, chocolate) every day helped me accept and adjust to my new normal. I recognized the healing that comes from expressing my raw, honest emotions to Him, and I felt His love as I grieved the life-style changes the injuries forced on me. With time, I was able to live in the balance of being honest about my disappointments, while celebrating the miracles of my recovery. Light-bulb moments were rare; instead, it was a daily choice to believe my Creator is good and He loves me. Absorbing that truth helped me step out of the hurricane, even without answers to all my "whys."

I'd like to skip this chapter of my life and the ongoing effects of it, but I don't have that choice. The choice I have is life today. I can't change the past and I can't predict the future, so I will embrace each day as if I might die tomorrow, while making plans to live to be 120!

Thank you for Your love and help me be aware of it all around me.

Janet Oberholtzer celebrates life with thankfulness, good coffee and dark chocolate. She is director of Women of Hope at Hopewell Christian Fellowship.

In the Race

"I press on toward the goal to win the prize for which God has called me heavenward in Christ Jesus." *Philippians 3:14*

Most of America tuned in to watch Michael Phelps try to reach his much-heralded eighth gold medal at the Summer Olympic Games in China. The emotional story of a single mother dedicated to providing an active outlet for her ADHD son was the main human-interest focus of the media coverage at the 2008 games. Encouraged by a perceptive swimming coach, Michael pursued a dream that led him all the way to the top of the awards podium eight times. We all applauded his accomplishment along with his mother, proud to claim him as our own new Olympic hero.

That last race was a 4x100 meter relay. It is easy to forget the names of the other three swimmers, but if the first two had not parted the waters, so to speak, for Michael, his record time would still have lost the medal. The last swimmer, Jason Lezak, plunged in for the race of his life. His amazing 40.06 split has been called one of the greatest swims of all times. Phelps's name is known throughout the world. Sports enthusiasts will remember Lezak, too. Few will carry Weber-Gale and Jones in their minds for very long. All four won the gold.

What is my part in the race for which God has called me? Have I trained and prepared? Do I dive in to do my very best? Is my eye on the prize for my own gain, or do I give my all to contribute to the success of others as well? I want to go for the gold to please my Lord, and hear His "Well done!" when the race is over. With His help, I will stand with many teammates to receive the prize and share in His glory.

Lord, help me to give my all to race for you and towards you. May I encourage many others along the way.

Joan Boydell works with her husband Bruce in Lifespan Consulting, and serves the pregnancy center movement through Care Net.

Taste and See

"Taste and see that the Lord is good; ..." *Psalm 34:8*

This verse became a prayer and a reality for my daughter last summer when she was diagnosed with celiac disease. A routine visit to our pediatrician raised concerns as to why Keri, at age 13 had not been growing. She has always been a picky eater so this was my explanation; however, her doctor ordered blood tests. The results came back quickly and we were told that Keri had celiac disease. I had never heard of this disease, but we soon became well informed. The only course of treatment was to follow a strict lifelong gluten-free diet.

Well, this was going to require some major changes as Keri's favorite foods such as pancakes, waffles, donuts, and chicken tenders all contain gluten. I was discouraged when I focused on all the foods that she could not eat, so I asked the Lord to help direct my attention towards all the foods she could eat. Since she was a picky eater and strong willed, I knew I would need His help. So my prayer, and the prayer that I asked others to pray for Keri was that she would "taste and see" that gluten-free foods are good.

"The Lord is good..." Yes, indeed! He revealed His love and goodness to us in many ways during this time. He provided many people who shared their experiences with this condition. Keri tasted and found that she liked many of the new gluten-free foods. The Lord used her strong will to help her stick to the diet even at school and her friends' homes. As her body began to heal, she felt better, developed a hearty appetite, and had a lot more energy. In fact, a new silly, fun personality emerged. In one year from the diagnosis she has gained over thirty pounds and has grown five inches. It is such a blessing that the Lord revealed this problem to us while Keri is young, providing the opportunity for her body to grow during her adolescent years.

Thank you Father for inviting us to come to You with our needs and for revealing Your great love and goodness to us in so many ways.

Cheri Miller is a wife, mother, teacher at Lancaster Mennonite Schools, intercessor for SVPS and member of Middle Creek Church of the Brethren.

Choosing a Legacy

"You will show me the path of life; in Your presence there is fullness of joy; at Your right hand are pleasures forevermore." Psalm 16:11

I heard a teacher make a statement which really touched my heart. She said, "You cannot do anything about your inheritance, but you can determine your legacy." That sent me to the dictionary for definitions. They were quite similar, except for one entry under legacy which stuck with me. It read "something handed down by a predecessor, *a legacy of mistrust."* I began to understand that my legacy could well be turning my history into His story.

Mother and I traveled to the Midwest, our homeland, the heartland of America last summer. Our first evening there we attended an outdoor orchestral program. We placed lawn chairs in the front row and sat down. The orchestra was seated below us in a large gazebo. A long sloping hill separated us. Quickly, all sides were filled in and the program began. Some were seated on blankets with small children. Older children were playing at the far end of the property with jump ropes, soccer balls and tag teams.

As the first selection began, I was delighted to see small children come to the edge of the hill, lie down and begin rolling down the hill. When they got to the bottom, they came back up and did it again and again. I was fascinated at the peace, safety and lack of interruption that was exhibited. Even in the older children, there was no shouting, distraction or disharmony displayed. I felt inside, "This was your background. It was a safe, harmonious place in which to play, grow and learn." The children knew the conduct standards in all settings. I need to pass this love and admonition of the Lord forward...exampling is contagious!

Thank you, Father God, for the legacy of Your love. Thank you for the order, teaching and affirmation which is Your legacy for each and every one of us.

Diana Oliphant is a caregiver and intercessor with a heart for this region and the nations.

.

A Morning in Eden

"God saw all that he had made, and it was very good." *Genesis 1:31*

A couple of years ago, John, a friend of mine, and, like me, a priest serving in the Diocese of Allentown, noted that the Appalachian Trail passes through our diocese on its way from Georgia to Maine. We had both done bits of that section that runs through Schuylkill, Carbon, Lehigh and Northampton Counties. We decided to close the gaps.

We started a three day, two night hike, at Swatara Gap, in Lebanon County, on a hot and humid June day. We crossed the Swatara Creek and ascended the steep gap, walking the trail as it enters Schuylkill County on the ridge of the Blue Mountain. After sharing the heavier pack throughout the day, we made it to the William Penn Shelter where we spent the night. The power of a nighttime summer thunderstorm inspires awe. Having a roof over your head during one moves you to thanksgiving.

The next day we got back on the Appalachian Trail. The day was much fresher after the previous night's storm. We were happy to meet another friend, Patrick, where Route 645 crosses the trail. We were even happier to see the hoagies he had in his hand.

After lunch we continued on and made it to the beautiful Hertlein campsite just as the sun was starting to set. We pitched our tents at the confluence of two mountain streams, prayed evening prayer, had a bite to eat and retired for the night.

We awoke to a day even more beautiful than the previous one and decided to celebrate a simple Eucharist on a rickety table. A cathedral could not have provided a more beautiful setting. As we listened to the Scripture readings, the sun came over the ridge and created hundreds of beams of light through the trees. We all felt that the Lord was truly present! I know there are places more beautiful and scenes more dramatic, but that morning I found myself in Eden, "…and it was very good."

Dear God, You have given us the beauty of creation as a foretaste of heaven. May everything I do today, in thought, word and deed, prepare me for eternal life with You.

Tom Orsulak is pastor of St. Peter the Apostle Roman Catholic Church in Reading.

Supply and Demand

"My God shall supply all your needs according to His riches in glory." *Philippians 4:19*

No one would argue that black gold—oil—is in short supply in the midst of a world that has a great demand for it. But there is also a much more serious situation, and that is the search for eternal living water, which can permeate a dehydrated soul and refresh a desert-like life.

In Psalm 92, David compares his spiritual need to that of a physically emaciated deer, whose tongue is parched and whose body is weary from the intense heat of the day: "As the deer pants for streams of water, so my soul pants for you, my God. My soul thirsts for God, for the living God."

As a young teenager, I lived in a home where there were not a lot of extras. Earthly possessions were quite simple and limited; money was almost nonexistent. Supply and demand took on many faces in my life. School was hard because learning did not come easy. Dad was out of work a lot because of a drinking addiction. But one of the greatest times of my young life was when, by the "skin of my chinny chin chin," I was accepted into college. Who would have ever thought that a skinny, undernourished, backwoods, slow-talking kid would go to college!

God became not only my supply, but even more, my source. Too often one can create an "on-call God." He becomes a resource instead of *The Source* of our life. The tendency is for one to want their needs and desires met on their time schedule. But when the Lord becomes your source, it's like the trickle of water from a small mountain stream that ultimately turns into the river of God's goodness that flows into an ocean of loving service to others. When His life flows through us, we become wiser, more winsome, and a living witness to others, of His grace.

Lord, may I never underestimate the depth of the riches of Your "Oil." Thank you for lighting my life in order that I might help others see the way. You are not just a resource, but my Source.

Dr. Sandy Outlar serves as the Headmaster at Lancaster Christian School.

He Will Change You

"You are the God who preforms miracles; you display your power among the peoples." *Psalm 77:14*

There are times in our lives when only God can change a situation.

I am a Vietnam veteran who was seriously injured in Vietnam in June, 1969. An entire amo pit exploded with me in the center of it. Due to this explosion, I suffered a head injury that left me with tunnel vision. I could only see things in front of me, so I had to turn my head to see peripherally. It felt like my head was on a swivel. I lived with this problem for many years.

I attend a church that prays for the sick every Sunday. I would always go for prayer believing that God was going to touch me, but nothing happened.

On Mother's Day, about 10 years ago, God touched me.

We were in the praise and worship part of the service. About 30 minutes into the service something happened. The whole building seemed to light up. I didn't know what was going on. I thought that some of the lights were blown out and came back on again. I was looking around to see if anyone else was affected. I went on to worship the Lord and then finally I realized what had happened. I had received a touch from the Lord. As I stood there, I noticed that I was able to see my wife standing beside me. I didn't have to turn my head to see her. Tears started to roll down my cheeks. Praise God, I was healed!

When you have an encounter with God, He may or may not change other people, but He will change you. God can change your impossible situation, too, when you seek Him with all of your heart and just believe.

Father, thank you for healing me. Your Word says in Hebrews 13:8 that You are the same yesterday and today and forever. You are the Great Physician, and You continue to heal Your children today.

Andy Parsons works part time as a pastor at Wernersville State Hospital.

Outworking Jesus

"Are you tired? Worn out? Burned out on religion? Come to me. Get away with me and you'll recover your life. I'll show you how to take a real rest. Walk with me and work with me—watch how I do it. Learn the unforced rhythms of grace. I won't lay anything heavy or ill-fitting on you. Keep company with me and you'll learn to live freely and lightly." *Matthew 11:28–30 (The Message)*

I wear many hats, but do I rest in Him? Is running around trying to be all things to all people walking in God's grace? The Lord stopped me with the piercing sword of His Word. "In returning and rest you shall be saved; In quietness and confidence shall be your strength...But you would not."

How presumptuous it is to try to outwork Jesus. Even He rested! He was not stressed or worried, harried or burned out on religion. He only did what He heard the Father tell Him to do! What peace and grace!

When I hear myself saying, I "should," I "need to," I "have to," I get resentful. I am not a fruitful vine but an ugly weed. I haven't learned the unforced rhythms of grace. When I'm overly busy, running to meetings, wearing myself out, I develop an attitude that stinks...all because I am not recovering my life in Jesus!

I have discovered why Jesus said we would always have the poor among us. We will always have demands on our time and resources. Jesus didn't say not to work, He said work *with* Me! Rest *in* Him!

Lord Jesus, I thank You for teaching us to exchange our heavy burdens for Your unforced rhythms of grace and imparting Your life which is true life! I lay down my agendas and take up Yours today! Forgive me for trying to live in my strength when it is Yours I need. Amen.

Cindy Nolt is wife, mother, grandmother of seven and elder at Breakout Ministries. She is active in intercessory prayer, oversees the hospitality ministry and teaches Bible studies and leads small groups.

God Does Answer Prayer

"And Jabez called on the God of Israel saying, 'Oh, that You would bless me indeed, and enlarge my territory, that Your hand would be with me, and that You would keep me from evil....'"
1 Chronicles 4:10 (New King James Version)

The Prayer of Jabez, was the hot book of the year. Since my friends at church were discussing the book, I decided to give it a cursory, once-over. After all, as much as I had studied Scripture, I had no idea who this Jabez was and figured he was not as strategic as the local scuttle-butt supposed.

I skimmed the book, superficially, praying Jabez's prayer, then put it aside to be referred to in the future, if needed.

A few months later, I was admitted to intermediate care at Hershey Medical Center, with one of the worst setbacks my Multiple Sclerosis had ever given me. My body would not respond to my commands. My legs would not support me; my arms would not move; even breathing was an effort. I was terrified. I needed my husband with me through the gloomy night.

In God's providence, the nurses would not allow him to stay, but they did have a CNA (Certified Nursing Assistant) by my bed all night. Sleep was futile so she filled the endless black with her cheerful chatter. By the next morning I felt a budding relationship with her. Giving her my phone number seemed natural.

Sometime later I received a phone call. She was intoxicated and needed my help. Our discussion that night expanded my self-imposed boundaries. When she needed a place to live, I opened our home.

Through her addictive life-style, the Lord enlarged my territory to witness the effects of drugs and alcohol. There were times when all that connected to reason was God's divine presence. What began as a withered flower has blossomed into a beautiful woman living for Him.

Lord, help me see people through Your eyes. Thank you for enlarging the boundaries of our lives.

Joan Patterson is the Lower Windsor Township tax collector.

What is Your Name?

"But the Lord said to her, 'My dear Martha, you are worried and upset over all these details! There is only one thing worth being concerned about. Mary has discovered it....'" *Luke 10:41–42*

Martha expected ministry to take place in her home, so, in the morning, she began preparing fresh vegetables, fruits and baked goods. The table was adorned with a tablecloth, the serving dishes, and silverware that would be needed. Mugs and glasses were arranged near where the hot and cold drinks would be served.

The house was already clean. Martha was organized and planned enough time to accomplish the tasks so her home would be peaceful and ready for the first guests. She was comfortable in her hospitality role. She'd had years of experience and, quite frankly, she received compliments for her expertise in hosting various affairs.

The ministers Martha was hosting prepared their hearts to deliver the message and prophetic words. About an hour before guests were to arrive, the ministers realized something was missing so Martha ran an errand with enough time to return prior to starting time. Upon her return, she was instructed to leave "Martha" in the garage. She would become "Mary" for the remainder of the evening. It would be time to put the work aside and sit at the feet of the teacher to learn, to listen, to be refreshed and refilled spiritually.

If you love to welcome guests and the gift of hospitality comes naturally, you receive joy being "Martha." However, if you are able to lay aside the busyness of caring for others and make time for Jesus as Mary did, you will find true refreshment. Discover the pleasure of sitting in His presence. That is what Mary chose.

As I care for others, by preparing natural food, remind me, Father, that my heart needs spiritual refreshment for fellowshipping with Jesus.

Nancy Leatherman frequently opens her Manheim Township home to guests.

Patience is a Virtue

"Be still before the Lord and wait patiently for him." *Psalm 37:7*

We've all heard the phrase, "Patience is a Virtue." Well, lately it seems like my husband and I have been learning that the hard way. Shawn has been looking for a new job for a little while, and was finally interviewed for a worship leader position at a local church. He has been desiring to be a worship leader ever since I have known him. The pastor told him that there are other candidates for the position, and they're not in any hurry to hire someone. They don't want to rush into it, because they want to be sure they have the right person, which is understandable. It might take a couple months. Shawn is still in the running, but he has to wait.

I've been wanting to finally buy a house of our own. And we almost did. We had put an offer on a house on a Thursday, but it went up for sheriff's sale that Monday. The bank owns it now. We were told we'll have to wait until it goes back on the market again. So either God doesn't want us to have that house, or it's just not the right time. So I'll have to wait.

Being patient does not come easy or naturally at times. We are stubborn sometimes, and we want our own way. We don't always see the big picture, but God does. Isn't that comforting to know?

Father, help us all to learn the value of being patient. Help us to understand that Your timing is perfect, and Your ways are best. You only have plans to prosper us and not harm us. And You only want what is best for us, even though we don't see that at times. Thank you for that. Amen.

Jennifer Paules-Kanode is a DJ for WJTL Radio.

When God Says "No"

"In his heart a man plans his course, but the Lord determines his steps." *Proverbs 16:9*

As I wrote in yesterday's devotional, my husband and I were waiting to see if we got a house and if my husband got a worship leader position. Well, needless to say, neither one of them opened up.

It turns out, someone came along and bought the house with cash. And the church decided to keep looking for another person to fill the worship leader position. Of course, both my husband and I were disappointed.

As humans, it's hard for us to understand why God says "no" sometimes. According to our finite minds, everything seems perfect and in God's will. So why does God say "no" and allow disappointments in our lives? Well, we may never know the answer to that question, but the Lord does. And I know one thing: God has our best interest at heart. In Jeremiah 29:11, it says, "'For I know the plans I have for you,' declares the Lord, 'plans to prosper you and not to harm you, plans to give you hope and a future.'" Isn't that a great promise to claim? Hold on to that today and continue to wait on the Lord.

Dear heavenly Father, while it's disappointing when You tell Your child "no," we take comfort in the knowledge that You care for us and only want what's best for us. We rest in that assurance. Amen.

Jennifer Paules-Kanode is a DJ for WJTL Radio.

Again Lord?

"Oh, that you would bless me indeed, and enlarge my territory."
1 Chronicles 4:10

Again Lord? But, when I bought the book I thought you wanted me to buy it for someone else! Don't you remember that we've already worked through this book seven years ago? In fact, this is the book that started my life journey that led me to working in full-time ministry as the director of CCWS Medical. Don't you remember, Lord?

The *Prayer of Jabez* book tells of a man's journey into blessings and service. It's Jabez's heart cry to serve more, to do more, to reach more and to care more.

As I read this amazing little book seven years ago, my heart began to cry out to the Lord that I might desire to serve Him more, do more, reach more and care more. I had no idea at that time what my heart's cry would lead to. Many times I am asked how I got into full-time ministry. I always chuckle. I then share the story of Jabez and how God chose me to do His full-time ministry. I was not looking for this position; in fact, I was quite content in my daily life...until I began reading this book.

The honest prayer became, "Here am I, send me Lord!" Since that time I've been on an amazing journey with Him. During this seven year journey, I've experienced some very difficult situations, I've learned more about who I am in Christ and I've had the time of my life! How did I get to have this opportunity? It's not that I chose to do this, instead He chose me. It's all very humbling!

Thank you, Lord, for calling me into full-time service. I match my prayer to Jabez's: "Oh, that you would bless me indeed, and enlarge my territory, that Your hand would be with me, and that You would keep me from evil, that I may not cause pain." Amen.

Karen Pennell serves as CEO of CCWS Medical, a life affirming pregnancy care medical center ministry with two locations in Chester County (West Chester and Coatesville). CCWS Medical has the awesome opportunity to introduce parents to the humanity of their preborn babies through ultrasound technology.

Constant Change

"The Lord Almighty, the God of Israel, says: Reform your ways and your actions, and I will let you live in this place. ... If you really change your ways and your actions and deal with each other justly, ... then I will let you live in this place, in the land I gave your forefathers for ever and ever." *Jeremiah 7:3, 5, 7*

Transformation has almost become a meaningless word in our language. But I like the way Jeremiah gets right to the point in the verses above. We measure change by looking at "ways" and "actions." As Christ's disciples, we want them to become more like His (2 Corinthians 3:18). Since He loves us and we love Him, this process is easy, right?

Change is difficult, because the work of receiving His love and giving it away requires not merely mentally assenting to a need for change but also emotionally responding with a will to pursue the change. A heart of brokenness is the fertile soil for the seeds of redemption and healing: "... 'This is the one I esteem: he who is humble and *contrite* in spirit, and trembles at my word'" (Isaiah 66:2, italics mine). A heart of change is produced when it accepts God's Word, the ultimate authority. Without brokenness, no hope for change exists.

The human heart has many ways of hiding the need for change. Most people would rather put up with brokenness than expend effort to change its source. One difficulty is the need to accept responsibility for new ways and actions. Agreeing that a problem exists implies a need for resolution. At the risk of being labeled stubborn, rebellious or indifferent, it's easier to deny the problem. The other extreme is to do too much. Becoming performance oriented leads to self-righteousness. Although good works might impress other people, from God's perspective a person's good deeds are like "filthy rags" (Isaiah 64:6).

Like most people, I usually tend toward one or the other extreme. I have to allow God to break my heart and remind me that constant change is here to stay.

Lord, produce true change in my life. Realizing I cannot change others, I am responsible to cooperate with You to see change in myself. Show me the blockages and give me the grace to give up control.

Dr. Edward Hersh provides counseling and healing prayer ministry to individuals and families, trains lay counselors.

Demand a Blessing

"I tell you, although he will not get up and supply him anything because he is his friend, yet because of his shameless persistence and insistence he will get up and give him as much as he needs."
Luke 11:8 (Amplified Bible)

Margaret, an anointed woman of God, was on the phone. She had called Dial-A-Prophet, the recent prayer phone line that I had started. It was evident that Margaret was very discouraged. Her financial struggles had been an unrelenting storm beating against her faith. Some people had told her to keep waiting for the Lord. Others had even questioned her faith.

As I talked with her, I remembered my dream the night before. In the dream, I was standing next to Jesus. There was a small child there who boldly reached out to hold his hand. Jesus grabbed the child's hand. I, too, wanted to touch Jesus so I also grabbed his hand.

I shared this dream with Margaret and explained that God wanted us to exercise our faith as a little child. I explained that a child makes unrelenting demands of the parent by crying louder and louder until the need is met. I declared that we needed to make a demand on heaven for her need. So we prayed, respectfully demanding of God, that Margaret's financial need would be met right now.

Immediately after we prayed, I had an idea to call someone and ask that person to contribute to Margaret's need. I called the person and he said that he was excited about being given the opportunity to help her.

Before the day ended, Margaret not only had the money that she needed, but God also threw in an extra hundred dollars to bless her. We had made a demand on heaven and it was God's good pleasure to bless His children.

Dear heavenly Father, thank you for hearing the demanding cries of Your children and providing all our needs.

Rev. John Paul Peters is the president and founder of Eagle Focus International Ministries, a ministry designed to teach listening prayer.

I Need a Second Touch

"Jesus asked the man, "Do you see anything?" The man replied "I see people; they look like trees walking around." Once more Jesus put his hands on the man's eyes. Then his eyes were opened, his sight was restored, and he saw everything clearly." *Mark 8: 23–25*

It is natural to go through our day seeing people as trees as did this blind man. This is the only recorded miracle that occurred in two steps. Jesus first spat into his eyes. This blind man declared he could see people, but they looked "as trees walking around." Jesus was not satisfied with partial vision, so He touched him again a second time and "he saw everything clearly."

How easy it is to go through life and see people as trees. To do so costs us little, and requires little time. We stay clean, and it keeps ministry impersonal, safe at a distance. Most importantly we stay on task. This is certainly not the Jesus model! Jesus' ministry most often came in busyness and in the form of an interruption. His ministry was personal, intimate and quite unorthodox at times. Jesus got dirty. He stopped, he listened, he looked, he touched, he wept and he was grossly misunderstood at times. In all this, He gave all.

Our temptation today as believers is to put on our "spiritual sunglasses" and selectively interact in a world of broken and hurting people. We see them partially but not completely as Jesus does. In addition, the world cannot see our eyes as we intentionally shield ourselves from them.

Just like the blind man in this miracle, I, too, need a second touch today. To see not as trees walking around but to see people as Jesus does—clearly.

God, grant me the vision today to see people as You created them.
May I see them clearly and be the hands, feet and voice of Jesus.

Brian E. Martin serves as lead pastor at Weaverland Mennonite Church in East Earl. He and his wife Shirley are the parents of four children.

A Heart like David's

"The Lord is my strength and my shield; my heart trusted in him, and I am helped: therefore my heart greatly rejoiceth; and with my song will I praise Him." *Psalm 28:7*

Have you ever cried until you couldn't cry anymore? I know I have. Chances are, many of you have, too.

Certainly, David had his share of grief. Once, returning to Ziklag, he and his men discovered their wives and children missing and the city burned to the ground. 1 Samuel 30:4 says, they "wept until they had no more power to weep." *Until they had no more power to weep.* To be in such a place of brokenness and grief is to be without hope. At that moment, David saw only the ashes of his life.

But notice what he did next. It says he "encouraged himself in the Lord his God." Most versions say, he "found strength in the Lord." As a shepherd, David poured out his soul before God. He worshiped when fear gripped his heart; he worshiped when joy flooded his soul; he worshiped under the conviction of sin. This was the pattern of David's life.

We may never face anything as devastating as what happened at Ziklag. However, should circumstances (or seasons) in life move us to despair, we can be like David. We can turn to Jesus with weeping and worship. We can bless His holy name. We can seek His face and direction. I love God's answer to David in 1 Samuel 30:8. He said to "pursue" the enemy and "recover all." Only God can give beauty for ashes.

Lord, I want a heart like David's. One that worships You on the mountain, in the valley, and everywhere in between. One that abides in Your presence and offers up praise even in the midst of sorrow. For You are blessed and glorified—and I am encouraged and strengthened through the praises that You inhabit (in me).

Ann Place attends DOVE Christian Fellowship in Elizabethtown where she has been involved with worship for many years. She and her husband, Richard, have three grown children.

Photo by Ann Rodriquez

September

Thunk, Thunk

"...The kingdom of heaven will be like ten virgins who took their lamps and went out to meet the bridegroom. Five...were foolish and five were wise. The foolish ones took their lamps, but did not take any oil. The wise...took oil in jars along with their lamps." When "the bridegroom arrived, the virgins who were ready went in with him to the wedding banquet." *Matthew 25:1–4, 10*
(New International Version Study Bible)

Thunk! Thunk! Thunk!

I was driving back to college, after a short break, and had been on the road for hours. Although I had heard this "thunk" for miles, I dismissed it as road noise. Besides, I'd driven this route countless times before and never had any problems. An issue with the car was the furthermost thing from my mind—until the noise got louder, and the "thunks" came faster, and it became obvious that the noise was coming from under the hood and not the road.

I pulled off the interstate, found the nearest Texaco, located the pay phone, and called my dad. "Uh, Dad, I'm hearing this weird noise coming from under the hood. What should I do?"

"Have you checked the oil lately?"

"Well, no." To my surprise I couldn't find any oil on the dip stick. I went inside the station and purchased some oil. After adding almost two quarts, I started the car and then checked the dip stick again. *Whew, I found a reading! A* quick call to my father, and I was back on the road. As I drove along the interstate, I realized that my car had been dangerously low on oil. But, I had become too comfortable thinking my car was reliable, and hadn't recently checked the oil.

Have you checked your spiritual gauge lately? Have you become too comfortable with life? Is your guard down? Spending time in the Word and daily communicating with God keeps us spiritually ready at all times!

Lord, thank you for Your inspiring words that keeps me spiritually filled.

Jill Printzenhoff is an earth science teacher at Lititz Christian School.

But Dust

"Our mouths were filled with laughter, our tongues with songs of joy." *Psalm 126:2*

One Sunday morning the no-nonsense, poker faced preacher was elaborating on how we are nothing but dust and ashes from the Scripture found in Genesis 18:27, "...though I am nothing but dust and ashes." A confused little boy pulled on his mother's sleeve and asked, "Mommy, what's butt dust?" It takes a child thinking literally sometimes to help us see the humor in serious situations.

Laughter has physiological affects too. The University of Maryland Medical Center had a team of researchers led by Dr. Michael Miller who discovered that laughter is linked to the healthy function of blood vessels. This healthy function actually helps to prevent heart attacks. Further, laughter has been found to help us feel better, it stretches muscles, it causes us to breathe more deeply providing more oxygen, it's like a mild workout and researchers have also discovered that 10-15 minutes of laughter will burn 50 calories!

So, perhaps laughter is like a good medicine after all. Find a friend to laugh with today. Don't forget to laugh with your spouse and your children...they'll love you for it.

Father, may we have fun building Your kingdom today and may we bring laughter to another.

Steve Prokopchak helps provide oversight and direction for DOVE Christian Fellowship International's network of churches.

Turning to Jesus

"Come to me, all you who are weary and burdened, and I will give you rest." *Matthew 11:28*

The night my husband said he was leaving our seventeen-year marriage for another woman was the night my dreams were shattered. I had spent a lifetime thinking I was in control, and in one moment it all came to a screeching halt. God had brought me to a crossroad, but the decision was still mine. Would I finally admit that I desperately needed Jesus in my life, or would I continue to live my life on my own strength?

Praise God, I chose to fall on my knees and cry out to God for His divine intervention in my life. That night was just the beginning of a very long journey, but one that I would not trade. The lessons I learned were the foundation on which I have now built my life.

During this time, Jesus taught me to lean on Him. He held me closely through all my trials and wiped away every tear. I knew that His shoulders could withstand my burdens, but his tenderness and provision gave me comfort. His daily outpouring of love gave me the courage and strength that I needed to get up each day and start again.

It has now been ten years since my husband walked out. I am a single mother who has successfully raised three wonderful boys. Two have graduated from college and the third will be a new freshman this year. God has used these years to teach me that I never have to walk any path alone. Even though my husband rejected me, I was accepted by my Savior. Praise be to God for His grace and mercy!

Thank You Lord Jesus, for loving me just as I am. Help me to continue to lean on You and to always remember to lay all my burdens at the foot of the cross.

Karen Helm serves as the records coordinator at Messiah College.

It Always Pays to Pray

"…Pray continually." *1 Thessalonians 5:17*

On a flight from Chicago O'Hare airport to Hong Kong, a man seated in the rear of the plane suddenly went wild. He was visibly drunk and started pushing flight attendants, pulling the phone off the wall and cursing everyone in sight. Passengers seated in the rear of the plane surged forward in fear. I immediately began to pray for wisdom and safety for all of us. One of the pilots came to the back of the plane to find out what was happening, and I met him in the aisle. "Could we help you, sir?" I asked.

"Yes, you can," the pilot said. The pilot handed me a pair of hand-cuffs. "I need some strong men to subdue him before he hurts some-one."

"Sure," I said, as if I did this all the time! I asked a few of the friends I was traveling with to help. We grabbed him, handcuffed him, pushed him back into his seat and secured him in his seat belt. He strained and struggled to break free, so we took turns holding him down (and praying) for the next few hours so he wouldn't rip the seat off the floor. Finally, we made an emergency landing in Anchorage, Alaska, and the FBI came on board and escorted the troubled man off the plane.

After the plane was again in the air, the purser and flight attendants thanked us profusely and asked if there was anything they could do for us. "I would like upgrades for the rest of my life," I quipped. They smiled and told me that was not possible. But they did give each of our team members an upgrade on our flight home from Hong Kong to America. We all felt like big shots. My daughter, Katrina, now tells my friends the story, concluding it with, "My dad will do anything for an upgrade!" The real lesson from this story is this: It always pays to pray! I believe God heard our prayers and kept the incident from escalating into something far worse.

Lord, teach us to pray in every situation.

Larry Kreider serves on the executive team of the Regional Church of Lancaster County and as the International Director of DOVE Christian Fellowship International, Lititz.

New!

"He which hath begun a good work in you will perform it until the day of Jesus Christ." *Philippians 1:6*

I wasn't saved until age 51. I came from a non-Christian, dysfunctional family background. When the Lord began an incredible reformation project in my heart, my relationship with my family and any friends were nearly non-existent. Since that time, through miraculous changes, He gave me a new life, healing me, my marriage and relationship with my son. He gave me an entire new set of brothers in Christ to encourage me.

Recently, I was given a Christian book to evaluate for our counseling ministry. The book was called *Beyond the Darkness*. The content of the book was focused on the impact of childhood abuse, especially sexual abuse, on our Christian growth. It took me eight weeks to read the 15 chapters in the book. Each chapter opened up an area of my life that needed healing. Each verse from Scripture addressed a lie that was hidden so deep inside of me that I couldn't even see them.

Though The Lord had brought me a long way in the 13 years, there were issues that had not yet been addressed. Thank God He chose that book and that time to show me those issues that were holding me back. He showed me the lies that I believed because of my childhood experiences. The Holy Spirit gave me the power to choose the truth about my identity in Christ. He showed me that the guilt that I was still carrying was totally forgiven by the shed blood of Christ. Then the Holy Spirit impressed on me "Now you must forgive yourself and look to God alone for your identity." What a weight came off my shoulders! I felt bondages falling off and freedom that I had never experienced.

Dear Lord, thank you for Your faithfulness to change me from glory to glory. Even though You gave me a new heart and new mind, even though You gave me a new identity, You still take me step-by-step to show me that new life that You gave me. Amen.

Robert S. Rew, M.S., Sc.D., is a missionary, president of Encuentro Ministries Board, Christian counselor, scientist, teacher, and president of Rew Investment & Rewsearch Consulting.

SOS

"My grace is sufficient for you, for my power is made perfect in weakness." *2 Corinthians 12:9*

For the past week I have felt very grumpy and unhappy, especially toward my little brother. When I thought I knew why I was mad at him, I went up to my room to write it out. Sometimes God talks to me through what I write.

As I wrote, thoughts began to pop into my head. *If you act the way you're acting that doesn't make you any better than him.* I finished writing, and by the end God had started working on changing my heart. I started praying. I was tired of being tired and grumpy. I started to want God to break me down so He could rebuild me the way He wanted. And you know what He did? He did just that. I had to allow Him to work. I asked him to make me into a humble, cheerful servant—to help me keep my eyes focused on Him, and to have His joy again.

In allowing myself to get mad, I had given the devil a foothold that I didn't want him to have. The only way to find the strength to fight was through Jesus.

Once I said I was sorry to God and asked for Him to help, He did. I realized that while I was getting mad at circumstances, God was there holding out His joy and strength to me, but I had chosen to turn away from it. He was so willing to give me help and true joy. God's power is made perfect in our weakness if we allow Him to show that.

God, You are awesome. Please make Your power perfect in our weakness today. Help us to keep our eyes on You. Amen.

Elisabeth Schlicher is a home schooling student along with her four other siblings. She attends DOVE Elizabethtown.

Just a Short Flight

"To man belong the plans of the heart, but from the Lord comes the reply of the tongue." *Proverbs 16:1*

I sat down wearily on the commuter jet beside a young man whose "hoodie" sweatshirt completely covered his face. He obviously wanted to be left alone, and with all my preparations for our prayer journey to Belgium, I didn't mind the opportunity to read quietly.

But prior to our trip I had committed to Jesus all travel interactions, willing to share with anyone He sent my way and asking for wisdom and opportunity from the Holy Spirit. Sitting beside my young traveling companion, I reminded God, "I'm willing to speak to him, but I won't force anything. If you want me to share, You'll have to open the door." I pulled out a book and began to read.

Suddenly the young man sat up and tossed a small book into my lap, suggesting that *"this* was a good book to read." I picked it up and saw that it was a religious prayer book on "proper" daily living. I paged through its contents, sighing inwardly at its lifeless "letter of the law" contents. I prayed for words to speak that would bring *true* life.

For the next 45 minutes of our short flight, we shared together as God gave scripture after scripture for this *seeker* who was looking for a relationship with God, but was mired in religion. I absolutely marveled as the Holy Spirit ordered every word and every verse.

As the flight attendant called for us to prepare for landing, we prayed together about his future as an inductee into the armed forces, and for God's fathering and guidance for his life. He was no longer hiding under a hood, but smiling and bright-eyed as he thanked me and we parted ways to catch our connecting flights.

Thanks Father, that You love people through us and You prepare the way. I love being Your child, and following Your lead! Amen.

Janet Richards and her husband Rusty lead *Pray Big!*, an international ministry of cleansing, healing, reconciliation and restoration.

We Walked Through the Fire

"'For My thoughts are not your thoughts, nor are your ways My ways,' declares the Lord, 'For as the heavens are higher than the earth, so are My ways higher than your ways and My thoughts than your thoughts.'" *Isaiah 55:8–9 (New American Standard Bible)*

Almost seventeen years ago my husband was diagnosed with a brain tumor. He was only thirty-three years old. He was given about six months to live, but we were blessed with six more years together.

At the point of his passing, we had three children, ages six, three, and eighteen months. A month or so before he died, we knew that it would take a miracle from God to save his life. Modern medicine (which truly is amazing) had exhausted all that they could do for him.

We sat on the couch one evening watching the children play, and tears welled up in my eyes. How could it possibly be God's best for these children to grow up without the influence of their daddy? The things he could teach them! The example he would set—was all an intricate part of who they would become. I spoke the reason for my tears to my husband. His response made me cry all the harder, but it also filled me with great peace. He said to me, "We will continue to pray for healing, but if it's God's will for them to be raised without me, then it is God's best. Who am I to ask for less than the best for my kids?" He spoke with tears and conviction and my heart flooded with peace. God is so faithful to His Word, and as we passed through the waters they did not overflow us. When we walked through the fire, we were not burned (Isaiah 43:1-3).

Thank you, dear Father, for bringing us through the high waters and the flames in our lives. You are amazing.

Lisa Hildebrand works for Susquehanna Valley Pregnancy Services and ministers as a teacher and speaker in local churches.

No Limitations

"But those who wait upon God get fresh strength. They spread their wings and soar like eagles, they run and don't get tired, they walk and don't lag behind." *Isaiah 40:31*

Have you ever been in a holy place, a place that quieted your heart, that made you listen for the footsteps of angels, and know that our Father Himself leaned down to touch, a place that made your heart kneel?

Recently I was privileged to be in that place. Our Life Skills class room held nine teenage children who live with limitations. Every morning we started with "Praise and Prayer" and this particular morning Matthew had a heavy heart. He said that his grandmother was in the hospital, and he was scared.

Our normal routine is to have each child voice a praise and prayer and then they take turns praying aloud. This day Matthew was the first to pray. He bowed his head and prayed, "Thank you, God, for this day. My grandma is in the hospital and she needs healing. I'm really worried. Would you help me, Lord?"

How simple, how profound! As his heart poured out through his words the room had a holy quiet descend. He had opened the door of heaven with his heart.

Each child in turn prayed quietly as we went around the room. It seemed everyone sensed the Father's attentive ear, knowing that there are no limitations for them in this area, feeling free and following their hearts. We continued in that holy place for a short time after the last amen before leaving the eternal and walking back through the door of the temporal.

Father, these precious ones are limited but their hearts and spirits are not. Teach me, Lord, the trust and humbleness that they have, that the simplicity and honesty of their hearts is what You hear. Would you help me today, Lord to be like them?

Christina Ricker is a past instructional aide at Living Word Academy's High School Life Skill classroom who learned from the children.

Clothed in Splendor

"I gave you expensive clothing of fine linen…I gave you lovely jewelry. You looked like a queen, and so you were! I dressed you in My splendor," says the Sovereign Lord."
Ezekiel 16:10–14 (New Living Translation)

I was about to experience a woman's worst nightmare…arriving at a conference luggage-less. As the airline attendant assured me they'd do everything they could to locate it, I ran down a mental checklist of what I was missing—clothing, jewelry, makeup, hair products…ugh.

Day by day, no luggage. And day by day, my Father poured out His blessing providing both physical and spiritual clothing for me.

The physical clothing came through a friend who was my size and happily shared her outfits with me. My morning visits to her room yielded more than just clothing for the day. As we stood at the bathroom mirror together, experimenting with her makeup and jewelry, we began a deeper, more honest relationship with each other.

While I was blessed by clothing that fit, it was still awkward wearing someone else's. I didn't feel like *me*.

But that was another part of the blessing of this challenge—a deeper understanding of my identity as God's daughter.

God spoke to me about my image, my identity and what made me truly me. Of course it wasn't the outer clothing I wore, but the spiritual clothing, the clothing that identified me as His. He talked to me about wearing white linen garments of righteousness and gold refined by fire, and about being clothed in splendor and wearing His fragrance.

My luggage was found after the conference, but I had learned to be content through those days. After all, I was dressed like a queen, wearing resplendent white garments, sparkling gold and a divine fragrance.

Abba Father, keep speaking to me about my true identity as Your beloved daughter and queen. May I wear the spiritual clothing You provide for me and reflect Your beauty.

Lisa Hosler serves at Susquehanna Valley Pregnancy Services and with teams uniting for regional transformation.

September 11, 2001

"For God has not given us a spirit of fear, but of power and of love and of a sound mind." *2 Timothy 1:7 (New King James Version)*

In the wake of the September 11, 2001, terrorist bombing and destruction of the World Trade Center towers, many of us were faced with fear and intimidation. The magnitude of physical destruction and the sense of violation shook people to the core of their being. I, and many others, had anything but a sound mind over this time.

As different people were responding to this tragedy differently, I heard of one Christian ministry that felt led of the Lord to confront the fear that was associated with it. They scheduled a meeting on the one year anniversary, right in downtown Manhattan, to confront any intimidation or fear people were feeling in regards to this terrorist attack. This really got my attention as the right thing to do, so my son and I traveled to New York for the one year anniversary of 9/11. It was a great night of worship, faith and victory over fear, and as you know there were no follow up terrorist attacks. It also proved to be a great lesson for my son in confronting opposition and fear.

In the book *Good to Great* by Jim Collins, he talks about how to confront the brutal facts of our reality without losing faith. We must be honest with where we are at before we can move from that place. Facing fear starts with an honest assessment of what it is that is intimidating and confronting us. I have found it helpful to then take some specific action in the opposite spirit of whatever the fear I am facing.

God does not want us to live lives full of fear and timidity. He wants us to live life full of faith and confidence in His goodness. We must look fear in the eye and confront it. Perhaps it will be helpful to have someone pray for you or take someone with you as I did with my son.

Lord Jesus we know it is not Your will for us to be full of fear and intimidation. It only causes us to shrink back from the things we are destined to do. We ask now, in Jesus' name, that You would show us the root of any fears we have. Give us freedom from that fear and show us any actions we can take to solidify this freedom.

Brian Sauder helps provide oversight and direction for DOVE Christian Fellowship International's network of churches.

My Clock

"Ask, and it shall be given you." *Matthew 7:7*

It had been a long day, and I was too tired to attend the evening ministry without some needed rest. Fifteen minutes was what could be spared, so as I settled in bed I looked at the clock: 5:02. Lord, wake me up in fifteen minutes. No sooner had my head touched the pillow, or so it seemed, when the cat jumped upon me and disturbed my peace.

Angrily, I grabbed her and put her out. Grumble, grumble. All I asked for was fifteen minutes and she interfered.

As I crawled back to bed to try again, I looked at the clock to see how much time was left, when I read 5:17.

Father, You gave me exactly what I asked for. Forgive me for my attitude in receiving.

Thelma Nye is worship coordinator for Agape Fellowship in Christ Church in Harrisburg and is a S.E.E.R. intern at Gateway House of Prayer.

Climbing Off the Ladder

"And the king will answer them, 'Truly I tell you, just as you did it to one of the least of these who are members of my family, you did it to me.'" *Matthew 25:40 (New Revised Standard Version)*

I'm always amazed at the many ways in which God reveals Himself to us. For me, those moments of revelation are most evident when I put myself in the position to serve others, a posture that's not always been comfortable for me.

I spent my young adulthood "climbing the ladder" and serving myself. But as I have grown in Him, claimed my discipleship with confidence, and discovered my heart for those less fortunate, I realize that the posture Christ calls us to is one that places us on our knees to serve others. We must get down off the ladders that lead to nowhere and start crawling down the path that makes an eternal difference.

We live with a resurrected Lord that calls each of us to be His hands and feet to meet the needs of this world. We are called out of our churches and into our communities to take His love and healing power to those who need it most. And we are called to stand in the gaps.

The amazement comes when He reveals himself to us—when we see Him in the faces of those we are serving. We aren't just taking Him out, we are meeting Him there! What a privilege it is to put ourselves in a position that enables us to meet Him again and again!

Heavenly Father, we thank You for revealing Yourself to us as we serve You. We ask for You to provide opportunities for us that we may encounter You again and again, as we strive to make a meaningful difference in our homes, in our communities and to one another every day. Amen.

Shauna Ridge serves as the director of Lay Ministries at Hopewell United Methodist Church in Downingtown.

Believe God for a Miracle

"...You are sterile and childless, but you are going to conceive and have a son." *Judges 13:3*

"There's no chance of you conceiving without having major surgery." Those were the words I hoped so much that I wouldn't have to hear. Those words were even harder to hear, because ten months earlier, July 2, 1981, we lost our first child, a son, at five and a half month's gestation.

Unfortunately, I had carried him about 6 weeks after he had died, undetected. That apparently caused an infection, which led to adhesions, and ultimately, blockage of my fallopian tubes. This blockage was confirmed by three tests.

An appointment for a consult was scheduled at Johns Hopkins Hospital for early August—three months away. For three long months there was nothing to do except hope and pray. So our consistent prayer was that if God didn't want me to have surgery I would conceive before my appointment. Meanwhile, the pain of facing possible infertility was increased every time I saw a pregnant woman or a mother holding an infant in her arms.

My appointment was scheduled for a Monday. About two weeks before my appointment, I missed my period, or… was it just late? I couldn't go for a pregnancy test until 10 days after I missed my period—that would be the Saturday before my appointment. The results wouldn't be available until Monday morning. (My appointment was 1:00 that afternoon.) That Monday, our first miracle was confirmed. I was pregnant!

Our daughter was born April 4, 1984. A son was born May 10, 1986, and our third miracle, a son, arrived June 12, 1988.

Laproscopic surgery would later reveal that there were no longer any adhesions, and my pelvic organs were totally normal!

Dear Father, thank you for our three miracle children. What an amazing gift You have entrusted to us. Give us wisdom to raise them to become followers of You.

Marian Riehl serves as a Stephen Minister at Manor Church near Mountville.

A Full Harvest

"But a few seeds did fall on good ground where the plants grew and produced thirty or sixty or even a hundred times as much as was scattered." *Mark 4:8*

When my daughters were young, I chose Christian education for them. However, the nearby Christian school was led by a principal who did not agree with my denomination's tenets of faith. He was so against these tenets, in fact, that he actually defamed me to my seven-year-old daughter.

During this same time, a friend was moving a very large piece of glass, when he was so severely injured that he was transported via life flight to a distant hospital.

An evangelist was ministering at our church that same week and offered to pray for hospitalized friends and family members. Although my husband refused to go, I felt compelled to do so. We traveled quite a few miles to visit and pray for the friend, who was eventually healed.

I was struggling with how people could be so uncaring—and expressed this to the evangelist on our return trip. He reminded me of the above passage from Mark, and stated that perhaps it meant that some Christians only choose to embrace thirty percent of the Lord's teachings, some sixty percent, and others one hundred percent. He asked me how much I wanted to embrace, and I immediately said one hundred percent. He exhorted me that it is therefore my responsibility to love those who choose to walk in less than one hundred percent of the Lord's light.

I grew through this biblical revelation, one that empowers me to ask the Lord for His unconditional (agape) love even for those who choose less than one hundred percent of His revelation. After all, that is the way the Lord loves each of us.

Thank you, Lord, for loving others through us. Thank you, too, for teaching us valuable, lifelong lessons through every trial. Only You can give us a 100 percent yield. Have Your way!

Denise Colvin is blessed with four daughters and ten grandchildren. She and her husband, Rich, a volunteer pastor, minister to older seniors in a residential setting at The Villa St. Elizabeth in West Reading.

Set Aside

"If you keep your feet from breaking the Sabbath and from doing as you please on my holy day, if you call the Sabbath a delight and the Lord's holy day honorable, and if you honor it by not going your own way and not doing as you please or speaking idle words, then you will find your joy in the Lord...." Isaiah 58:13–14

A Sunday School teacher was talking with a preschool class about the story of Creation, and she asked them what God did on the seventh day. A dark-eyed three-year-old raised her hand and said, "I think He mowed the yard."

Setting aside Sabbath time is a way of gaining a proper perspective on the rest of the time we are given in a week. In another century, Matthew Henry wrote this about Sabbath: "On Sabbath days we must not walk in our own ways (that is, not follow our callings), not find our own pleasure (that is, not follow our sports and recreations. In all we say and do we must put a difference between this day and other days."

Matthew Henry might be shocked by what has happened to Sundays since he wrote those words. There is virtually nothing one cannot do on a Sunday that one cannot do any other time during the week.

Sabbath days are intended to give us time to reflect—to stop long enough in a world which rushes by so quickly that we can fail to look for the holy or fail to see it as it passes. Without carving out the time to think about what is good, what is just, what is perfect, and what is true (Philippians 4:8), we just might forget to think about those things.

Sabbath doesn't have to be Sundays, but it has to be intentional time where we focus on God's thoughts and not our thoughts. When we don't, we may discover that it is *we*, not God, who have taken center stage in our drama of life, and that is a pretty good definition of sin.

Lord, it is difficult for us to take time away from our time to give You the time that You gave us in the first place. Help us to find the time we need to give You back the time You gave to us, and teach us to listen for that still, small voice crying within us—Your voice. Amen.

The Rev. Dr. Randolph T. Riggs is pastor of First Presbyterian Church in Lancaster and president of the Lancaster County Council of Churches.

One Question

"Then the Lord God called to Adam and said to him, 'Where are you?'" *Genesis 3:9*

The first recorded question God asks is a great one.

On our first trip to India, Fran and I stood before a class of students soon after our arrival. We were not sure of our location in the subcontinent of India and surely did not know what time it was after flying through many time zones! Even though disoriented, we functioned mainly because we had a relationship with a person living there.

When God questioned Adam, it wasn't that He could not find him. He knew exactly where the tree-huggers were. Adam and Eve had lost their way, and God knew it! So God began His search for the lost that continues even to our day. Christianity teaches that God looks for us even when we are not looking for Him.

Where am I location-wise, vocationally, socially, educationally, emotionally, relationally, physically and spiritually?

Do I have the patience and courage to name my reality in each of the above? God's question of "Where are you?" reveals the grip I have on my own reality. This can easily be confused with where I'd like to be, but that is not the question. The question is always present tense and certainly not past tense!

Solomon tells me that I have the ability within myself to search for the answers to God's inquiry (see Proverbs 20:27). Only when I face and embrace my current reality can I move forward. This is not to suggest that I acquiesce to the pressures of the present but instead allow the lamp of the Lord the freedom to search my innermost being. Having a friend showing us around India brought assurance that we were not lost. With the guidance of the Holy Spirit, I'm finding my way through the remaining seven areas of "Where am I?"

Dear Jesus, reveal to me my location so that my service to You will be worthy.

Richard Armstrong serves as assistant director of The Worship Center Global Ministries in Lancaster.

Finishing, Not Fainting

"He gives power to the weak, and to those who have no might He increases strength." *Isaiah 40:31*

The days of fasting, hiking and heat left me weak. I had needed some time alone with God to learn to rule my flesh by the power of His Spirit within me. Now relaxing in a new trail shelter, I thought, "This certainly does not compare with the Apostle Paul's 'light afflictions' I was reading about in 2 Corinthians 11!" Did God have a surprise planned for my descent down the mountain? Turning toward home, this out-of-shape pastor was soon in serious trouble. After two hours of hiking over rocks under a fifty pound pack, I missed my connector trail, was sweating profusely, panting and becoming dizzy.

Quoting Isaiah 40:28-31, I pressed on, determined to rule my flesh, not bail out, but find God's strength to prevail. I crossed over the mountain peak, hoping to intersect my trail. The going was arduous, over rocks, vines and fallen trees. I was soon resting again, nauseous, cramping and nearly blacking out. I imagined helicopters and dogs searching the mountainside for me. I thought of abandoning my pack, calling for help, but the issue was—is my God sufficient?

Finally, after two more hours I stumbled onto the trail, found a large rock, and fell to the ground, hugging that cold, wonderful rock like an old friend! I slept, but awoke quite nauseous, dizzy and cramped from my toes to my neck!

I decided to make a cell call to seek God's leading. I wouldn't reveal my condition, and if my friend was not alarmed, I would know God was preserving my life. Well, my friend was exceptionally jovial about my trail odyssey, so I determined to get to my feet and finish. By God's grace I made it home that night, with the knowledge that I can live every moment in the strength of His Spirit within me.

Father, remind us always to live in Your strength, and not faint when the trail gets rough.

Lee Ritz pastors Destiny Christian Ministries in Reading.

Trucks

"Be still and know that I am God; I will be exalted among the heathen and I will be exalted in the earth." *Psalm 46:10*

While driving to work one morning, I was passing a tractor truck on a four lane highway. As I got beside the truck, it started coming over into my passing lane and forced me off the road. I lost control of my car and started spinning around several times landing right in the middle of the northbound lane, facing south. I thought I was in the clear, and then I looked up and saw two tractor trailer trucks bearing down on me, side by side. Just then, my CD player played the song, "Still, Be Still."

So I did just that! I sat and watched the trucks coming for me realizing that when they hit me, I would surely die. The closer they got, my car started to rock, gravel was hitting my car, and I could smell burning rubber from the trucks' tires. But all of a sudden, the trucks separated and went around me. There was absolutely no damage to me or my car!

In the days that followed, the Lord impressed two profound things upon my heart. Number one, was that if I had tried to take things into my hands, and move to right or the left, I would have surely died. But by being obedient to "Be Still and Know I am God," the Lord was able to do the impossible for me. And, the second thing was when we take the hands off the steering wheel of our lives, the Lord is faithful to maneuver, change, or stop whatever is going on because nothing is too hard or difficult for Him. Amen!

Thank you, Lord, for being our refuge and strength, and very present help in time of trouble.

Sharon Roseboro is the leader of the dance ministry of Lancaster Evangelical Free Church in Lititz.

Time to Pray

"I will call on you O God, for you will answer me: give ear to me and hear my prayer." *Psalm 17:6*

How did it happen?

Either the train was five minutes early or I was five minutes late. I was caught on the wrong side of the tracks.

I usually tried to cross those tracks before the train came through town, so I could get to school that was ten miles away. I chose to get there early to prepare both mentally and spiritually for the school day.

I sat there stewing over my delay, which could easily be up to fifteen minutes.

God spoke to me saying, "You want to spend time with me, why not now? I am here."

I shoved the car into park, and began my journey of prayer on the road. I first thanked God for the prompting invitation. Then I prayed for the engineer as he waved and smiled crossing in front of me. I returned a smile. Knowing my wait could be as long as 50-60 slow moving boxcars, I relaxed, took a deep breath and continued my talk with God. We talked about my family at home finishing breakfast before heading to their schools, my pastor-husband headed for the church office, my fifth grade class and other children, teacher friends, the principal, and even the janitor were added to the list. On and on we went with needs around the world, and soon the road was clear and I continued my drive, God with me all the way.

It was a beginning for me.

God is everywhere, ready to get in touch whenever we reach out, anywhere, any time.

When caught in delays at checkout counters, I pray for the person ahead of me and behind me. In long lines, the Spirit prompts where prayer is needed. I keep reminding myself to redeem the time; it is God's time.

Dear God, it is hard to imagine what my life would be like without prayer. Thank you for being available anywhere, anytime, and for hearing and answering my prayers.

Ruth Rudy is an elementary teacher, pastor's spouse, volunteer with MCC, mother and grandmother.

The Holy Spirit and a Four-Year-Old

"At that time Jesus, full of joy through the Holy Spirit, said, 'I praise you, Father, Lord of heaven and earth, because You have hidden these things from the wise and learned, and revealed them to little children. Yes, Father, for this was Your good pleasure.'" Luke 10:21

I was not sure what to do with my four-year-old daughter; she would not stop crying. Every morning, it was the same: she and I would sit down together, I would read the Bible to her, and before I had closed the binding, she was weeping uncontrollably. I tried to have her explain what the matter was, but she only shook her head and cried even harder. Her older brother had never acted this way.

My husband and I were at a loss. We decided to keep reading the Bible to her every morning, and keep hoping that she would feel better after time went by. However, her crying only became worse as the weeks wore on. As I prayed for my daughter, God made me realize that His Holy Spirit was convicting her. My little four-year-old was already beginning to become sensitive to the Lord.

I sat her down next to me, the tears flooding into her eyes, and asked, "Sweetheart, do you want to ask Jesus to forgive your sins? Do you want to ask Him to become your heavenly Father?"

With an expression full of relief, my daughter nodded her head and prayed to receive the gift of salvation from God. Tears were filling my own eyes as I dried her wet cheeks. I looked down and saw a smile of inexpressible joy spread across her face. From that day on, she never cried during our morning Bible lessons again.

Jesus, You have cleansed us from all our sin. Thank You for Your gift of everlasting salvation and freedom from guilt. Amen.

Mandy Satta is a full time student at Lancaster Bible College and Graduate School.

Even the Storms Have to Listen

"I tell you the truth, anyone who has faith in me will do what I have been doing. He will do even greater things than these, because I am going to the Father." *John 14:12*

My mom started a wonderful tradition a couple years ago with my sister, sister-in-law and me. Twice a year we go to a bed-and-breakfast for the night where we do a craft or watch a movie and just have a great time together. We usually end up going to garage sales or thrift shops the next day, then out for lunch before heading home.

In May we decided to do something a little different. We went to Sea Isle City for a long weekend. We were having a wonderful time at garage sales on Saturday when we noticed the sky getting really dark. When we got "home," we turned on the TV and saw that they were calling for tornados in the area. The sky got blacker and blacker, and then the storm started. The lightning was coming in a straight line from heaven to earth. It was nasty. We were in a trailer in a campground, and we were getting pretty worried. Where do you go in a trailer if a tornado comes through? I began thinking that this worrying is not right. Instead, I can do something about this. So I walked over to the window and said, "storm in Jesus' name you are going to go out around us. You are not going to harm us."

Within a very short time, the lightning stopped, the winds died down and the rain was just a gentle shower. It soon stopped completely, and the sun came out. Jesus spoke to the weather and it obeyed Him. He says in John 14 that because He is with the Father, we will do even greater things than He was doing while here on earth.

Thank you, Jesus, that You have given us the authority to do even greater things than You did while You were here on this earth. Help us to always remember that it is You working through us. We can do nothing on our own.

Brenda Boll serves as an elder, along with her husband Steve, at Newport DOVE. She is on staff at House to House Publications.

A Promise in the Darkness

"...Never will I leave you; never will I forsake you." *Hebrews 13:5*

The sky was bright and sunny that morning, there was not a cloud in the sky, but I felt a storm within me. As I drove to school, I felt so distant from God, as if He were a million miles away.

Depressed, I prayed, "Lord, I need to know you are still with me. I need to know you are close...Please, give me a sign today...If you are really there, will you turn off all the lights at school?"

It seemed like an impossible request. There was not a storm cloud in the entire sky, and I heard of no projection of rain for the whole day on the Weather Channel. I decided I would just have to swallow down my misgivings and accept the void in my chest as a mere passing fancy that would dissolve as soon as I got over my emotions.

The school day passed slowly, hours of sitting in classes and catching up with friends were all that I did. Behind it all, though, I still kept wondering if God had heard my prayer.

As I was sitting in class, a clear voice came over the loudspeaker, "Attention! This is an announcement that the electricity in the building is being tested. The lights will be turned off for just a few minutes now. Please remain seated and in your classrooms."

The room filled with chatter and laughter as the lights flickered and went out. I, however, sat there silently and with my mouth wide-open in amazement. Tears filled my eyes, and in the darkness, I picked up my Bible, and hugged it lovingly to my heart.

"Thank you, Lord," I whispered, "Thank you for not condemning my doubt, and for being so sweet to me."

Lord, I praise You for You are always with us, and no matter what, You will never forsake us, even when we doubt Your wonderful promises. Amen.

Mandy Satta is a full-time student at Lancaster Bible College and Graduate School.

Our Forever Family

"Yet to all who received him, to those who believed in his name, he gave the right to become children of God—children born not of natural descent, nor of human decision or a husband's will, but born of God." *John 1:12–13*

In March of 2008, my wife and I made a trip to China for the purpose of adoption and returned with our son Bennett. Our adoption story began in the fall of 2005 when we started getting serious about adopting. We took time to pray about what country to adopt from and what agency to help us in the process. We filled out forms and more forms. We sat through classes and read books to help prepare us to be parents. All the work was done by July 2006, and then began the wait. We continued to pray that God would bring our "forever family" together.

"Forever family" is a term used in adoption to contrast the adoption family with other family, foster care and orphanage situations that were temporary for the child. When a child is adopted, he or she has found their forever family. Just as God adopts us, making us His children, and giving us an eternal place in His family (1 John 3:1, Romans 8:15-17), so an adoption places a child and parents together to be forever family.

In November of 2007, we saw our son, Bennett, on a list of waiting children that were ready for adoption. We expressed interest in Bennett and were matched with him. After more paperwork, we traveled to China. It was an amazing experience to meet our son for the first time on March 4. We are so blessed by our son, who brings us so much joy, and thankful to God for bringing our forever family together.

Lord, I was separated from You by my sin, but You made a great sacrifice that I might be reconciled to You, and You adopted me into Your forever family. Thank you for the gift of eternity with You in heaven. Allow me to be a tool of Your work in bringing others into Your family.

Brad Sauder works as a computer programmer and attends DOVE Westgate where he serves as a small group leader.

Am I Really Supposed to Live Like This?

"May those who delight in my vindication shout for joy and gladness; may they always say, 'The Lord be exalted, who delights in the well-being of his servant.'" *Psalm 35:27*

The first car that I ever owned had a problem with its transmission, and it would leave a puddle of fluid under my car when it sat in the same location for a length of time. I got into the habit of always looking under my car to check for a leak before I drove it away. Sometimes the leak would be bad enough that it would leave a trail of fluid as I would drive away. Consequently, I developed the habit of always looking in my rear view mirror as I drove away to see if I was leaving a trail of fluid on the road. For many years after this I still maintained these habits expecting something to be wrong with my car, even though I had better vehicles that were mechanically sound and didn't leak fluid at all.

Was I really supposed to live like this? As I pondered it, I concluded that this was an expression of a poverty mentality that had attached itself to me early in life. I asked the Lord to help me break free of it. It took some time, but I can say that I am free from it today. I now enjoy driving the vehicles God has given us without the nagging fear that something is wrong mechanically or will go wrong with them. He does delight in my well-being.

I believe we must be totally convinced that God is an abundant provider—not just sometimes when He is in a good mood but as a part of His nature He provides abundantly for us.

Father, we give You thanks today that You are a God who enjoys providing abundance for us and our families to do Your will on the earth. Help us to break free today from any poverty thinking that might be manifesting itself in any way in our lives. We say, "The Lord be exalted, who delights in the well-being of his servant." Amen.

Brian Sauder is the author of the book *Prosperity With a Purpose*.

Is my Heart Unveiled?

"But we all with unveiled face, beholding as in a mirror the glory of the Lord, are being transformed into the same image from glory to glory, just as from the Lord the Spirit." *2 Corinthians 3:18*

From the day of our salvation to the end of our lives we are to walk with Lord in sickness and in health for richer and in poor, for better or for worse until our death. We walk with an unveiled face but do we walk with an unveiled heart?

Looking back over our lives from the day of our salvation until now, have we changed, have we grown? Transformation of our heart is daily. As we walk with the Lord we will go through different seasons, a time in God's wilderness, a time of being under siege from every direction, a time of feeling unwanted or being used. These are the doors that we walk through so that God can transform us into His image.

God wants to walk with Him just as Adam did in the cool of the day and to have His glory resting on us. Sometimes we ask, "Am I making any progress in my walk with God, have I backslid or am I standing still?" When we see someone every day or almost every day we see little change, but when we see someone we haven't seen for a long time, we'll often say, "Have they changed!"

Let's not become complacent because we do not see change or it seems to take forever. We need to evaluate ourselves from time to time to see if we are allowing God to transform our hearts or if we are getting colder or, even worst, standing still!

Lord, unveil my heart that I may see any place where the enemy may have a foothold. This is my prayer—that I may walk blameless before You, that I may walk in the light as Your Word is the light of my path. Amen.

Jeff Burkholder is chairman of Elizabeth Township Board of Supervisors and youth leader at DOVE Christian Fellowship Westgate.

God Never Fails

"Not one of the good promises which the Lord had made to the house of Israel failed; all came to pass." *Joshua 21:45 (New American Standard Bible)*

Life has its challenges. God never promised that life would be exactly the way we want it. A number of years ago I was diagnosed with a disorder for which there is no cure at this point, even though there has been research all over the world. No one knows the cause nor how to cure it. It has changed my life in innumerable ways. The typical response would be to ask, "Why me?" And I must admit that there have been days that I have asked God that question.

Recently in studying the book of Joshua I was especially encouraged and challenged by Joshua 21:45. As I memorized and meditated on the verse, I considered what some of the good promises are that God has made. One promise that is very meaningful to me is also from Joshua. It is from chapter 1, verse 9, where God says that He is with us wherever we go. I think this means more than just place to place, but also from life situation to life situation. In the New Testament He also promises to never leave us nor forsake us (Hebrews. 13:5).

The daily challenge is to trust God even though I don't physically see Him. Even though I can't see everything God is doing, I do trust Him for the future, for I know that none of His promises will fail.

Lord, help us today to remember Your promises and to trust You fully to bring them to pass.

Beth Holden is a wife, mother and grandmother. She is a former nursing instructor. She and her husband, Bill, serve in various ways at Lancaster Alliance Church.

Seeing God in the Details

"Delight yourself in the Lord; and He will give you the desires of your heart." *Psalm 37:4*

At the age of forty-six, I had never been on a real vacation. I may have gone to the beach for a day or fishing for the weekend, but no vacation. In the summer of 2007, a group of women were going to the beach for a few days. I was invited to go. I really wanted to go, but being a single mom, I could not afford it. Before I had a chance to give my answer, a woman who works in the church office came up to me and handed me a wad of money from an anonymous person. I knew God was providing for me to go.

When we got to the beach house we were renting, I asked what I owed for my share of the rent. I was told someone had taken care of it. I had such a great time! God knew just what I needed. Also, one of the women with us was someone I did not know very well. That trip was the start of a good friendship. Isn't God so great?

Father God, thank you that You know exactly what we need. You work things out better than we can imagine.

Julie Gehman attends Ephrata Community Church.

Smile!

"Love is kind." *1 Corinthians 13:4*

How do you make a trip to the grocery store or the post office more fun? Take a two-year-old boy along! You may not think taking a toddler to such places would add much value to the trip. Let me explain!

This past year my husband and I traveled to China and brought home our son, Bennett. This toddler knows how to brighten up any room. He smiles at others. An occasional cheery wave adds to the fun. So, how does this make an errand more fun?

Well, people smile back. Sometimes they add a chuckle with it. Sometimes they wave back. And then I find myself with a big grin, too.

How simple is that? Joy gets spread through the room!

Father, thank you that Your ways are simple enough a child can understand them. Help us keep our grown-up priorities in line with Your plans for how we live.

Sarah Sauder enjoys being a mom as well as graphic designer with DOVE Christian Fellowship International.

Two Paws and a Nose

"Wake up, wake up, Deborah! Wake up, wake up, sing a song!"
Judges 5:12

"I am not taking you out now!" I was having a hard time waking up this morning and the last things I wanted were two paws and a cold wet nose on the edge of the bed.

By the urgency and frequency of the pounce I knew "Star" really needed to be walked. Between 4:30 and 5:00 am. I like to get up, have quiet time, coffee and get ready for the day before walking Star. She is usually just fine with that. I could tell by her "dog dance" that wasn't happening today. I angrily got up thinking to myself that my mother-in-law would have responded sweetly to her dog which made me dislike myself even more. I continued in my self-absorbed little snit as I wrapped winter gear around me.

Meanwhile Star continued her dance on the porch. Why couldn't I have mercy on our beautiful little Star. Pre-storm cold smacked me as I opened the door.

Standing by the road, my view always goes across the valley and as the frigid air quickly blew the sleep away I saw the start of a new day. Pink sliced through the bottom of night as it pierced my attitude. I used to stand and pray over the valley during Star's walk turning the ordinary into purpose. When did I stop? God opened the day with color and brisk newness and purpose. Words to a Carmen song started blowing through my mind, "Revive us, O Lord, Revive us, O Lord. Cleanse us from our impurities and make us holy. Hear our cry and revive us O Lord."

Thank you, Lord for waking me quickly this morning even if you used two paws and a nose. Please Lord, forgive me, cleanse me, revive me that I can meet every instance today with thankfulness, praise, and purpose. I want to wake up and sing to You. And Lord, please may revival spread across this county and nation like the break of dawn. Slicing through the darkness and bringing Your Light.

Christina Ricker is an intercessor at Petra Christian Fellowship, and a wife, mom and Nana.

October

Simplicity of Faith

"...unless you change and become like little children, you will never enter the kingdom of heaven." *Matthew 18:2–3*

"You are going to Uganda for missions and not working this summer?" My father repeated my last sentence. "How will you have money for your senior year?"

"God will do it," I said. "He's done it for three years, even though I didn't earn a lot." I was so sure.

My father paused. "Well, I'm sure I can't change your mind," and that was that.

I returned from my trip, which had quite an eventful ending because we were detained by authorities for a week! The next morning, my father said, "So, how do you pay for the semester only one week before classes?"

"God will do it somehow. I did this for Him with His promise that He will take care of me," I said. My father looked down and chuckled.

"I suppose I should tell you that..." and the story of God's provision unfolded. An administrator approached Dad that morning. Somebody backed out of a grant program. They needed an upperclassman replacement or money would be forfeited. Then the papers must be signed today. If not detained, I would have flown differently and been 500 miles away right now. If not obedient to God, I would have missed this miracle.

Twenty years later, I am humbled at my complete abandonment to knowing God would provide. It wasn't false bravado or cockiness that let me say those things. It was quiet knowing, confidence in what was to be. When we replace simplicity of faith with complexity of life, we lack.

God, Your Word says I am Your child, but I think that discusses my family relationship with You. I forget that it points to a natural faith in You to provide, protect, and love. Open my eyes to the children around me who exercise this so well.

Carolyn Schlicher, her husband Darryl and five children live in Elizabethtown.

Photo by Josie Wilson

God, Our Provider

"The mind of man plans his way, but the Lord directs his steps."
Proverbs 16:9

It was October during my daughter's senior year of high school. She was applying to three colleges. We didn't agree on her first choice; I questioned her reasons for going there. I didn't want her to miss out on where God wanted her to go. I asked God to work it out for her if this was the college He wanted for her. If not, I asked Him to close the door tightly.

Meanwhile a fourth college contacted her. She was interested, so she went on their website. After looking at the information, she felt this was the college God was directing her to. In January she applied, knowing it was a little late to do so and that this college was also more expensive. To make a long story short, she was accepted to three of the four colleges she applied to. The only one that did not accept her was the one I had prayed about. God closed that door tight. God has provided for my daughter's first year of college, and we are confident that He will continue to provide for the rest of her schooling.

Thank you, Lord, that You are our Provider. You can see all and know how to direct our paths.

Julie Gehman attends Ephrata Community Church.

The Stain-Lifter

"…Though your sins are like scarlet, they shall be as white as snow; though they are red like crimson, they shall be as wool." *Isaiah 1:18*

I was on my lunch break and thought I would go to a nearby grocery store, grab a few groceries and do some sampling of the foods they serve as you shop. I reached for a folded tortilla chip to dip into their homemade salsa. Next thing I knew, all of the salsa ran down in the front of my "very white top." I looked down to see the damage and saw six blotches of salsa and a chunk of tomato looking back at me.

I quickly headed toward the back of the store for some water and a paper towel, dodging the men in suits by picking up a melon and pretending to be interested in it, trying to cover up my stains. The water and paper towel only made it worse. So I dashed to the detergent aisle to grab one of those stain sticks I saw advertised. I ripped it open and dabbed my salsa stains. Then I proceeded to go to the checkout line and looking down, I discovered that all of the stains were gone. When I told the cashier my story, I felt like I was in a commercial. As I paid for the stick, I noticed it said, "Instant Stain Remover—Not a Pretreater."

Basically isn't that what God tells us He is to us? An instant stain remover.

Thank You God for forgiving our sins and not pondering over them or hesitating to forgive us. You know all things. Even when we try to cover them up, You still forgive and love us.

Lisa M. Garvey serves with the Hosanna Christian Fellowship Prayer Team Ministry.

Making a Difference

"...we must help the weak, remembering the words the Lord Jesus himself said: 'It is more blessed to give than to receive.'" *Acts 20:35*

I was a young 18-year-old teacher aide, fresh out of high school, hired to teach in a newly funded Federal Program for people with both deafness and mental retardation, incarcerated in a state institution for the mentally retarded.

Clyde, a man both deaf and blind, was housed in the infamous ward with a reputation for having the most violent men in the institution. I had never met a deaf-blind person before. I tapped him on the shoulder—immediately, he reached out his hands to grasp mine. I awkwardly finger-spelled "h...i" into his palm. He immediately spelled "hi" back, then handed me a Braille book. "Teach me!" he signed.

During the next few weeks, I learned Braille and began to teach Clyde during my lunch break. Language and communication began to come back to Clyde. He seemed to be so bright and gentle...so what was he doing in an institution for the mentally retarded and locked in a violent ward? He had been locked up for over ten years.

I began to voice my concerns to the administration, but they said Clyde had an IQ of 57 and he belonged in the institution. As a teacher-aide, I had no "clout" to make any changes in a system that treated people as if they were animals. I turned in my resignation and enrolled at a local college to major in Special Education. I thought if I became a teacher, I would have the ability to make changes.

But, I could not get Clyde out of my mind I reported his situation to another government agency. Clyde was re-tested, and amazingly the results indicated that Clyde's IQ was at least 140! Several months later, Clyde was living in his own apartment with a full-time assembly job at a Ford motor plant and making more money than I made! Let's not give up on seemingly hopeless situations in our lives and those around us.

Lord, help me to give with no expectancy of return. I know I can make a difference in someone's life today. Help me to be an advocate for others.

Jim Schneck is a free-lance interpreter for the Deaf, an advocate for the multi-disabled and a doctoral student.

The Solid Rock

"You will keep in perfect peace all who trust in you, all whose thoughts are fixed on you! Trust in the Lord always, for the Lord God is the eternal Rock." *Isaiah 26:3–4*

It was a beautiful summer day, and I was enjoying a weekend of camping at Raystown Lake with my husband and his family. I walked the bank of the large body of water, enjoying the peacefulness.

After some time of meandering, I sat on the bank and began taking pictures of the incoming waves splashing against a weathered brown rock. Looking through my viewfinder at the water, I suddenly felt tipsy, as though I were moving! Dropping my camera to my lap, it didn't take long for the feeling of movement to pass and I verified that I was, indeed, still stationary! I then brought my camera to my eye again, this time focusing on the rock. No problems there—I quickly realized that the unstable feeling came only from focusing on the water, and that when my gaze was fixed upon the *rock*, it was clear that it was not *me* that was moving, but the water instead.

As I sat pondering this phenomenon, I thought of how easy it is, in this ever-changing world, to lose sight of the Rock that is Jesus and to allow our eyes to be drawn in by the fluctuating waves of our culture. When our eyes are on the waves, our emotions have full reign to bring fear, feelings of instability, insecurity, anger and other non-fruits of the spirit into our lives. But if we keep our eyes fixed on the Rock, He will keep us in *perfect peace* as we trust in Him, as promised in Isaiah 26:3. As we continue to live in a world that is, in general, ruled by emotion and impulse, let's remember to keep our eyes fixed on the One who is the eternal Rock.

God, in this time of uncertainty and chaos in the world, I pray that You will enable me to keep my eyes fixed solely on You. Fill me with more and more of Your insight and Your perspective, and may Your peace be in me and shine through me, spilling out to others. Thank You that You are the solid Rock, in which I can put my hope.

Ann Rodriquez is the administrative secretary at DOVE Christian Fellowship, Westgate Celebration in Ephrata and leads worship at her home church, DOVE Elizabethtown.

Never Give Up!

"You need to persevere so that when you have done the will of God, you will receive what he has promised." *Hebrews 10:36*

Laura was a young, 17-year-old girl with a slight hearing loss, mental retardation and severe behavior problems. She was unable to speak with her voice, but began to learn sign language in order to communicate. I had the "joy" of working with her. Most of the other teachers couldn't stand her! She was dirty, smelled bad and pinched. Laura's favorite disgusting habit was to eat cigarette butts—and to spit on you when she was angry.

One day during a summer class, I was determined that Laura was going to go through the entire lesson completely without spitting on me. Every time she spat, I would start at the very beginning of the lesson and repeat it. After one hour, my shirt was soaked, but we got through the lesson!

Laura was so needy. Although I dreaded working with her, I was determined to not show her I didn't like her. I acted like I was so happy to see her, when in reality I wished she was sick at home. In time, Laura began to respond and behave. I found that I also had changed and actually was glad to see her.

I thought she would never learn her name. Every day for one and one-half years, I worked with her daily to get her to respond to her name and learn how to spell it. For awhile, I thought it was hopeless—she would never master it. Then one day, she spelled her name perfectly and even went on to spell her last name, which was very long.

By the time I was done working with her, Laura had learned over 800 signs and could communicate some things very well. She actually became one of my favorite students. Don't ever, ever give up! Because, God has not given up on us!

Lord, help us to persevere to help others today. When we persevere we are doing Your will.

Jim Schneck is a free-lance interpreter for the Deaf, an advocate for the multi-disabled and a doctoral student.

Awesome Comfort

"Even though I walk through the valley of the shadow of death, I will fear no evil, for you are with me; your rod and your staff, they comfort me." *Psalms 23:4*

The anticipation of the phone to ring seemed more then we could bear. The Transplant Clinic called the day before, alerting me of a kidney and pancreas that were a match! Confirmation in being the closet match from the fifty or more people waiting for those same organs would come in eight to fifteen hours. This was the fourth such phone call I had received in these regards. The devastating words of "sorry, they went to someone else," was something I wasn't looking forward to hearing again.

At 5:00 a.m., my husband, Jay, and I were "be-bopping" down the turnpike listening to praise and worship music and calling people regardless of the unreasonable hour to alert them that my wait was over and to start their prayer chains. It was surreal, a peace and excitement I cannot explain…it was a definite "God thing"!

The whirlwind continued upon arrival at the Transplant Clinic. I was bombarded by the flurry of four to eight nurses and staff intent in their task as they scurried in and out of my room.

Lying on the gurney, I was wheeled off to surgery, now alone in what looked like a dark, dingy basement. In the extreme stillness and quiet, it was the first time my mind began to wander. I felt an uneasiness settling over me. At that moment, Scriptures started "clicking" in my mind…verses I was unaware I knew by heart! With arms outstretched, Jesus appeared to me, I saw myself draped over them. What an awesome comfort to me that God showed Himself in that way.

Heavenly Father, thanks for always being with me, seen or unseen, You provide me with comfort. Plant Your word in my mind so I will always be able to draw upon it, trusting and knowing You intimately.

Nan Schock serves as a Stephen Minister at Manor Church, south of Mountville.

OCTOBER 8

How Long Will You Mourn?

"And the Lord said unto Samuel, 'How long will you mourn for Saul?...fill your horn with oil, and go....'" *1 Samuel 16:1*

A spirit of heaviness settled over me. The joy I had always known as a Christian gave way to prevailing sadness, as an entire season of life seemed to end without the realization of certain prayers being answered.

After months of mourning, the Lord got my attention one day by asking whether (or not) I really believed that Jesus' suffering was enough to cover the particular pain that I was feeling. Pondering that question, the Holy Spirit immediately began to minister truth to my spirit through the words of Isaiah. "Surely he hath borne our griefs and carried our sorrows...the chastisement of our peace was upon him..." (Isaiah 53: 4-5).

Sooner or later we all experience grief. Just as Samuel lamented over his broken relationship with Saul, sometimes we find ourselves unable to get past the losses in our lives. Whether associated with a broken relationship, the loss of a loved one, a job, a home, or some other cherished possession or dream, there comes a time when God may ask of us, "How long will *you* mourn?"

God desires to fill us with joy, renew our strength, and help us go on living. He said to Samuel, "...fill your horn with oil, and go!" He was calling Samuel to anoint a new king. He had plans for Samuel's life and a destiny for him to fulfill. And, God has a plan for our lives beyond what we can often see or understand.

Lord, when I experience loss and disappointments that seem like almost more than I can bear, help me to face them in the light of Your presence, standing on the truth of Your Word. Thank you for working all things together for good in my life and for filling me with the oil of joy and renewed hope.

Ann Place attends DOVE Christian Fellowship in Elizabethtown where she has been involved with worship for many years. She and her husband, Richard, have three grown children.

My Heavenly Prescription

"This is the day the Lord has made: we will rejoice and be glad in it." *Psalm 118:24 (New King James Version)*

While moving forward into my season of life as a widow, I tend to look, or I should say glance back, by using the rear view mirror of my mind instead of the windshield of my "now."

Before I realize it I'm about to wreck my vessel. Suddenly, my Father God gives me a loving jolt and my attention is full throttle on my day as I'm headed with clear vision, looking through the windshield of my "now."

It does take my will to choose to be glad to be in this season of my "now" pathway of life. I can truly rejoice, ever becoming glad in each day that the Lord has made for me.

My solution is God's "Son-glasses" that I wear at all times for daily protected vision. How wonderful to experience my Lord's daily provision no matter what greets my day.

Father, as I travel on my pathway of life, I thank You for the comfort in knowing that Your Word is the lamp unto my feet and the light that has radiated truth upon my daily path.

Elta Seaman is a mother and grandmother and serves at Ono United Methodist Church as a Women of Faith leader.

Hidden Treasures

"My purpose is that they may be encouraged in heart and united in love, so that they may have the full riches of complete understanding, in order that they may know the mystery of God, namely, Christ, in whom are hidden all the treasures of wisdom and knowledge."
Colossians 2:2–4

My wife and I traveled to Montana for a ministry related trip. We came up against many obstacles prior to our leaving and it looked very dim if we were to even go on the trip. However we both felt a sense of call and decided to move ahead in spite of the pressures that were mounting. Upon accepting the call to go, the peace of God came upon us and our family, realizing then that we made the right decision.

When we served in Montana, God used us in ways I never imagined, and we discovered so many of God's hidden treasures. If we would have given into the pressures of life that we faced, then we would have missed out on a treasure He desired for our lives.

Someone asked me, "What was your rationale for going on this trip?"

To which I replied, "The decision to go was not based on rationale but purely on faith in Christ."

When we listen to God's voice, the steps He shows us may not always be the easy road, or the most comfortable situation, or always seem to make the most sense. It may be that He is calling us into embracing something new. It will take faith in God and not our own understanding. If the road we chose to walk on is by faith, and not our fears, many hidden treasures will be discovered in our lives.

Lord, thank you for revealing hidden treasure to Your children who seek Your face. I pray that You will embolden us to follow Your plans for us, as we walk by faith.

Hershey Sensenig serves as executive chairman of Village Chapel Mennonite Church. He and his wife Lisa are involved in reconciliation ministries and various other prayer initiatives.

On My Own Two Feet

"What is impossible with human beings is possible with God."
Luke 18:27

I am running...on my own two feet! I can run!

As I put one foot in front of the other, my thoughts mingled with words from doctors four years earlier, *"You might never walk again."*

Now, I was not only walking, but running on my own two feet. I could only run a few minutes at a time, but I could run!

My husband and I, along with our three boys, were on a cross-country trip in California in May 2004. Suddenly, they were watching a helicopter fly away with me in it, not knowing if they would see me alive again. Sadly, they surveyed the accident scene—five semi-trucks and our motor home, with severe damage to the corner where I had been sitting. Thankfully, no one else was hurt.

The trauma surgeon, a believer in God, assessed my critical state and asked for wisdom as he evaluated my extensive injuries—collapsed lung, wounds the size of Texas, splintered femur, Humpty Dumpty pelvis and multiple other wounds and fractures. At first, amputation seemed like the only answer to the massive wounds on my left leg, but praise God, a ten-hour surgery saved it.

A pre-accident workout for me was running two to ten miles, so three months later, after dozens of surgeries and hours of therapy, I was thrilled to be walking on my own two feet, even if it was only ten steps across the room with assistance.

Though living with constant pain and limitations, God's Spirit gave me strength to endure the seemingly endless therapy and to pursue additional surgeries that brought more healing. Gradually, I could walk for exercise and as my legs strengthen, the impossible began to seem within reach. One day, on a walk, I cautiously picked up the pace and broke into a jog. What seemed impossible is possible with God!

Thank you, Maker of all, for creating us with the amazing capacity to heal.

Janet Oberholtzer is a runner and also director of Women of Hope at Hopewell Christian Fellowship.

Live Well!

"Thus says the Lord of hosts, the God of Israel, to all the captives whom I have caused to be carried into exile from Jerusalem to Babylon: 'Build yourselves houses and dwell in them; plant gardens and eat the fruit of them…multiply there, and do not be diminished.'" *Jeremiah 29:4–6 (Amplified Bible)*

It was my birthday and I knew exactly what I wanted—healing. For the past year I lived in a land of suffering, exiled to a place where my body fell apart piece by puzzling piece. Like Humpty-Dumpty, no one could put me back together again. All year long I relentlessly asked God for healing. I didn't want to live like this—in this land of suffering and brokenness! Surely He would give me what I wanted for my birthday. After all, I was His daughter and He loved me. So on my day of days I sat down with Him, ready to receive my present—His Word of healing to me.

Have you ever longed for a gift, been sure of its arrival, opened it with hope and confidence…and found something totally other? Me, too.

God didn't grant me healing. Instead, His Word to me from Jeremiah 29 was, "Daughter, this is where you live now. Continue to live and live *well*, whether in this land of suffering or in a land of prosperity and peace."

God didn't say no to my request for healing, but He didn't say yes either. Instead, He instructed me to live well right then and there, *in the midst* of that painful place. He had plans for me, but their time had not yet come. I was to trust Him and get on with the business of living well.

God, thank you that You see, know and love me even when I'm living in a land of suffering. Give me sufficient grace to live well in this place until You come to take me home.

Jenny Gehman is a mentor, speaker and author, who lives (well) with her husband and son in Millersville.

Prayer for My Children

"All your children shall be taught of the Lord, and great shall be the peace of your children." *Isaiah 54:13*

It was a day when reality hit for me as a mother. Pressure had been mounting in my heart to the point of despair. Do I even want to see my children grow up in this crazy world? Do we have a chance of them even becoming decent citizens, or at most, godly people? It was the 70's, and we observed many children taking the path of drugs, being rebellious, creating a heartache for their parents who were "good" people. I had seen little around me holding out hope beyond the usual!

I finally ran to our bedroom, and collapsed on the floor beside the bed, kneeling before my only source of life and hope for the future;

"God," I cried out, "Please just have our children grow up to be good people, help them not to embarrass us in any way, if they can just be law abiding and honorable, Oh Lord, help!"

Suddenly I was interrupted with an inner voice I recognized as my Lord not wanting me to go further with this prayer. It was one of those defining moments that I knew I was being confronted with Truth.

"Oh no, you don't want what you are asking for, your request is grossly lacking the thoughts I have for your children. What if I desired to use each of them uniquely in service to Me that you know nothing of? What are you doing here asking for so little? Will you accept My challenge to you to be careful to teach and train them in My ways and let Me direct their paths?"

I was crying profusely now. "I am so sorry, please forgive me, but I need Your help to even know how to pray for them as I should."

God took me at my word, and gave me a new prayer to pray, "Lord, grant each of my children a relationship with You that is genuine, fulfilling, totally satisfying." This was, for me, a whole change of demeanor and posture in prayer and was the beginning to hope that purified my heart for these many years. He is faithful!

Lord, thank you for continuing to bring us to health and wholeness through hearing Your voice and listening when You speak. In Jesus' name, Amen.

Naomi Sensenig serves as a deaconess at Lancaster Evangelical Free Church in Lititz.

Angels

"Be not forgetful to entertain strangers: for hereby some have entertained angels unawares." Hebrews 13:2

Most of us, when we were children, were told by our parents never to talk to strangers. These words of wisdom to children however do not always apply to adults. Recently as I was driving in my hometown, I saw a stranger carrying two bags of groceries along the highway. He quickly jumped into my car after I asked if he needed a ride. The man happened to be an unemployed Army veteran. He honored me by saying the words, "God bless you," to me as he exited my car.

So many strangers bless me as I do my prayer walks by offering me food, water and shelter. Should I not do the same to strangers in my own area?

In the last five years, I have visited many churches of different denominations in West Virginia and Ohio. In all of them, I entered as a stranger. In some of the churches, I left as a stranger, but in many of the churches I became a family member united by the blood of Jesus. In those churches, I heard the words, "How may I help you?"

Today, if an angel would unknowingly enter your church today, would he be treated with love or would he be mostly ignored? If the church in America would treat all strangers as if they were angels, perhaps a true revival would occur throughout this nation and throughout this world.

Father, open our eyes to the strangers, whom we meet. Help us to see them through your eyes. Help us to hear them through your ears. May we show them the love that You have shown us through Your son, Jesus. Amen.

Jim Shaner is a board member of Chester County Women's Services Medical and founder of One Nation Under God – Walk Across America.

Continue in Love

"But wisdom that comes from heaven is first of all pure, then peaceable, gentle, willing to yield..." *James 3:17*

Several years ago, our church conference passed a vote in favor of a denominational merger. Conflict due to differing opinions on issues that surfaced resulted in tension, potential for division, uncertainties and many questions.

How would our opinions influence areas within our own congregation where we served in leadership? How would we continue to be faithful while facing disappointment and frustration due to a perceived lack of ability to handle conflict in healthy ways? In prayer, I asked for His wisdom and opened His Word to Ephesians 5:1-2. "Be imitators of God as dear children. And walk in love..." His words washed me with peace and beckoned me to continue in love through the conflict, transition and uncertainties. His wisdom also granted me a willingness to yield to His voice through prayer and intercession.

A little over a year later I shared some of what I was discovering through prayer in a seminar at our annual conference assembly. Soon afterward, questions and arrows of doubt entered my mind. Was I obedient to share what He asked me to? Was this an appropriate setting to share? Should I even continue sharing these discoveries with others? While conversing with an acquaintance after the closing worship, a young friend of his whom we had never met before, approached my husband and I saying, "I'm hearing a phrase for you and your husband that I think is from the Lord. I'm hearing, "continue in love." In amazement, the same words of wisdom He had given me over a year earlier, now spoken through a complete stranger, chased away doubt, washed me anew with His peace and encouraged me to continue in love yielding to His pure voice and gentle guidance.

Grant me, Father, heavenly wisdom for every situation I may face today. Grant me faith to trust in Your wisdom through uncertainties, conflict, or transition the future may hold.

Lisa Sensenig has served in prayer, speaking, writing and Anabaptist reconciliation.

I Will Make a Road

"Watch for the new thing I am going to do. It is happening already-you can see it now! I will make a road through the wilderness and give you streams of water there." *Isaiah 43:19*

We moved into a farmhouse which the Lord miraculously provided. The one drawback was that it had a lane half-a-mile long which suffered serious washouts almost every time it rained. One man received a hole in his gas tank from one of the ruts while visiting us!

I would have to go out and shovel and rake the dirt and stones back into place. It was during one of those repairing episodes that I found myself complaining to the Lord about all the time required to make our driveway a good road for people to drive on. We would have as many as sixty people at our Wednesday night Bible study, so I couldn't neglect to fix the driveway.

At this time, I heard the Lord say to me, "You're a lot like this driveway. You continually need manicuring, nurturing and instruction because I want you to be a roadway for people to come to me."

I didn't know the scripture about God making a roadway, but that night I opened my Bible, and in the good news translation, I read Isaiah 43:19, "Watch for the new thing I am going to do. It is happening already—you can see it now! I will make a road through the wilderness and give you streams of water there." This began a season in my life of unusual, but wonderful, times of teaching by the Holy Spirit.

Thank you, Lord, that You make a road through the wildernesses of our lives and lead us to streams of refreshing water.

Pastor John W. Shantz of Spring City Fellowship Church, Spring City.

Pay Attention!

"When I consider Your heavens, the work of Your fingers, the moon and the stars, which You have ordained." *Psalm 8:3*

"So, what was your most challenging course?" I had congratulated Andy, my son's best friend, on completing his bachelor's degree. Andy was beginning medical school in the fall.

I wasn't expecting his answer. "Cell Physiology, which is the study of the internal mechanisms of the cell."

"Really!"

"Yes, the cell is extremely complex."

Isn't it interesting that what we think of as one cell—something that is small and, therefore, should be basic and simple, is not only the foundation for all living organisms but also pushes the boundaries of human intelligence into all its processes?

God's creation is chock-full of intricately complex, yet awe-inspiring beauty. Tonal frequencies and chord intervals result in harmonic music pleasing to the ear. The death of a seed, in the ground, sprouts into a stalk that holds rows of yellow kernels that tastes sweet, thereby adding enjoyment to the process of nourishing our bodies. The nerve fibers and combination of chemicals in our nose are tantalized by the alluring aroma of a magnolia blossom ready to burst fully into bloom, symbolic of the desire of young love. The delicate softness of an infant's skin or the lush moss covering a forest floor is exquisite to the touch because of small nerve endings in our fingers or our toes. The spectrum of light wave frequencies enables us to see various colors: lemons, strawberries, blueberries and oranges. If we take the time to carefully observe a plant, we might discern a camouflaged praying mantis or a leafhopper. When we marvel at stars located billions of light-years away, we reflect Frederick Buechner's statement, "We learn to praise God not by paying compliments, but by paying attention."

Elohim Creator, help us to open our eyes and our other senses to enjoy Your creation surrounding us, thereby praising You in endless ways of which we would have never dreamed.

Tamalyn Jo Heim enjoys the majesty of God's creation with her husband, Bob, and children: Bobbi Jo married to Steve, Joshua married to Kari, Kendralyn and Rebekah.

Follow Me!

"Philip found Nathanael and told him, 'We have found...Jesus of Nazareth, the son of Jospeh...Come and see.'" *John 1:45–46*

It was an odd sight. A large tour bus in my neighborhood on a Sunday morning trying to turn around on a narrow street. Out of curiosity I watched. Out of pity I went out to see if he was lost. The door split open. The bus driver had a weary lost look written all over his face.

"Do you need directions?" I asked. "Yes," he said hopefully, "I am trying to get to Route 30."

"I can tell you how to get there." He was relieved. Using lots of hand motions, I gave detailed directions to make sure he would not get lost. "Go left to the first intersection. There's no stop sign, go right, not straight. Then at the stop sign go right. Soon after bear right at the bend in the road. Don't go straight. At the light go left..." The bus driver's relief had evaporated. He was lost again.

My strategy changed. "I'll get my van and you can follow me. I'll take you to Route 30." He took a deep breath, sat up and was ready to go. He followed me and as I pulled over at the on ramp he passed me honking and waving. He was no longer lost.

God has placed people all around me today who do not need another person telling them where they should be in life or what to do; they need someone willing to walk with them to show them how to get there. Just as Philip invited Nathanael to go with him to Jesus, I have seen the same joy as I saw on the bus driver's face when I walk with someone to meet Jesus.

Jesus, help me to do more than give directions today to those who are lost. Soften my heart so I can invite others to follow me so that together, we can find You.

Jeff Comeaux is the associate pastor at The Door Christian Fellowship, Lancaster.

Yes, I am!

"Afterward the Lord asked Cain, 'Where is your brother? Where is Abel?' 'I don't know,' Cain responded. 'Am I my brother's keeper?'"
Genesis 4:9

I credit Rev. Dr. James L. Smith of the Second Baptist Church in Coatesville for the answer to Cain's question used as a heading for this devotional. In an inspired sermon on this passage Dr. Smith recounted his background growing up amidst the temptations of the lonely street life, and how his encounter with Jesus set him on the path to understanding how significant godly men are in each other's lives.

I do not have any natural brothers but I have learned about brotherhood through fellowship with other Christian men, my relationship with my brother-in-laws and in the fascinating observation of my own sons. Even at a very young age, my oldest son in many ways demonstrates what it means to be his younger brother's keeper and my younger son demonstrates the powerful bond of trust that results.

As many young boys do, these two spend at least one portion of their day "wrestling" each other, "practicing Karate," or just plain old hitting each other. As a watching father I took note of how aggressive my younger son was with his older brother. One day my sister pointed out how he played much more sensitively with children other than his older brother. I realized he is more aggressive with his older brother because he trusts his older brother not to hurt him back. Likewise, my oldest son holds back, usually inflicting just enough retaliation to let his younger sibling know he can mean business when he wants to. Witnessing the emotional maturity my oldest son demonstrates in his relationship with his brother, and the trust my younger son places in him teaches me much about what the Lord requires of brothers in this sin-stained world.

My prayer is that throughout the body of Christ represented in this devotional, and through the global church, we would know this relational intimacy of brotherhood as children of God in a trusting relationship with Him and each other.

Father, through each person You have created, demonstrate today what it means to be their brother's keeper. Amen.

Bill Shaw is executive director of Life Transforming Ministries in Coatesville.

A Spiritual Legacy

"Good people leave an inheritance for their children's children...."
Proverbs 13:22

When we were young, each birthday was a celebration. Along the way somewhere that thrill died off. Lately, however, I'm starting to look at birthdays differently, not with regret but with gratitude. Birthdays really are a cause to celebrate, because life is a gift.

I've begun to think more about what I'll be leaving behind when my heavenly summons comes. The Bibles tells us that "good people leave an inheritance for their children's children...." When I die I'm not sure that I'll have all that much to leave my children or grandchildren in terms of this world's goods. However the Paris Hilton's and Lisa Marie Presley's of this world bear witness that inheritances which can be measured in dollars are often more a curse than a blessing.

But there is a kind of legacy we *can* leave to those who follow us, one which always blesses. That is a *spiritual* legacy, a legacy of a life lived according to godly values, a demonstration of passionate and joyful commitment to the things of God. Won't that serve those who come after us much better than dollars and possessions which might distract their attention from God or lead them to depend less upon Him?

On the day I leave this world, I want to feel contentment in knowing that I have fulfilled God's calling on my life, and in that niche have made a difference. If it is clear to those who someday gather to bid me farewell, why I have tried to live as I have—if I have accurately reflected the precious Friend Jesus has been and is to me in that journey, and if I have instilled in them at least the seeds of a hunger to live for God's glory in His calling for them—then I think I will have succeeded in leaving behind a wonderful inheritance.

What legacy are you creating? Think about it.

Help me, Lord, to live in such a way that my life draws other people to You.

Pastor Joe Sherer is senior pastor of Mount Joy Mennonite Church. He and his wife Mary Lou have three daughters.

Confession

"The tongue is a fire...so is the tongue among our members, that it defileth the whole body...But the tongue can no man tame...."
James 3:6, 8

In June 2006, my husband had his left knee replaced. After the surgery he was unable to exercise because of a breathing problem. He would get out of bed and sit on his recliner all day long until it was time to go to bed at night. This went on for months. Every time he would walk a short distance he would have to sit and gasp for breath for a couple minutes before he could continue to wherever he was going.

It was very upsetting for me to see him suffer, but in the spring of 2007, I was getting very frustrated by his not being able to do anything. A couple times each day I would tell him that I was so sick and tired of him just sitting in his chair and not doing anything.

Then, *I* started feeling so tired that I could hardly move around. Around this time, I received a magazine from a ministry that had an article about the importance of our words and what we say and how it can affect not only our spiritual health but our physical health as well. I realized I needed to change my words. As soon as I stopped speaking about being tired and being sick of things, I started feeling normal again.

Thank you Father for sending an article for me to read that would open my eyes to the truth. Help me to keep my tongue under control.

Doris Showalter is a wife, mother, grandmother and great-grandmother and attends Mission of Love Church, Ephrata.

Jesus Really Cares

"...Ye have not, because ye ask not" *James 4:2 (King James Version)*

For several months I had a nagging pain in my left thumb. As time went on I started having severe pain.

I went to the doctor who suggested I go to a specialist and get cortisone shots in my thumb. Shots and I really do not get along, so I tried not using the left thumb. That didn't work so well.

My husband and my son tried to convince me to go to the specialist and get the shots telling me that it would only hurt for a short time and I would no longer have the constant pain. I stubbornly refused to listen.

One day I was in the kitchen, picked up something and the pain flew into my thumb, causing me to cry aloud with pain. This time my husband was very firm and told me that Monday I was to call and make an appointment with the specialist to get the shots. That Sunday morning when I went to church I told the pastor that I needed to be anointed with oil and prayed for my thumb. At the end of the service he anointed me with oil. Later that day, I had an annoying ache but not the severe pain like I had before the pastor prayed for me. The next week I could bend the thumb and had no pain. It has been many months now and I am pain free. I thank Jesus for touching me that morning and healing my thumb.

Jesus cares about every little thing that bothers us and all we need to do is ask Him. He will help us.

Father, I thank You for loving me and for touching my body whenever I am hurting. You are the Great Physician.

Doris Showalter is a wife, mother, grandmother and great-grandmother and attends Mission of Love Church in Ephrata.

We Can Pray

"When you pass through the waters, I will be with you…For I am the Lord, your God, the Holy One of Israel, your Savior." *Isaiah 43:2–3*

Children are profound teachers of spiritual truths. I was reminded of this while on a family vacation to the shores of Delaware.

We had planned for an evening of fishing on the bay. We gathered our fishing gear, boarded the boat and headed out to toss some lines and to watch the sun set. Moderately familiar with the bay and its numerous sandbars, we were confident that we could safely navigate across the open water towards the inlet where the fishing is best. With the boat going nearly full throttle and the refreshing wind and the sound of splashing waters, we had hopes of a relaxing fishing trip.

Our perfect evening came to a lurching halt when we hit a sandbar hidden under a mere seven inches of water. We scrambled overboard and tried to rock the boat free with no success. The hours passed slowly. The sun was setting. Passing boats ignored our dilemma. Land was a far swim and a night spent on the boat was even less appealing.

In those increasingly anxious hours as we discussed options, my four-year-old son offered his opinion, "Dad, I know what we can do! We can pray!" He then led us in prayer while kneeling in the boat.

While attempting to pass through the waters, we had overlooked the One who cares for us. Yet God is always near. I often make life too complicated and then neglect to ask for the Lord's help. In time, the water rose with the tide as we drifted free, arriving safely home as darkness settled over the bay.

Lord Jesus, thank you for caring for me as I "motor on" through the waters of life often unaware of dangers just below the surface. Remind me to simply pray and to pray simply, with child like trust. Amen.

Wesley D. Siegrist pastors Erb Mennonite Church, Lititz.

An Unworthy Vessel Comes Back to the Father

"But now, O Lord, thou art our Father; we are the clay, and thou our potter; and we all are the work of thy hand." *Isaiah 64:8*

God's word, through the ministry of Christian music, lives to testify that it has the power to change hearts and mold broken lives.

Nine years ago, I was introduced to WDAC, The Voice of Christian Radio, 94.5, after relocating here from Philadelphia. As a youngster of four years of age, God used Christian music to speak to my young heart, convicting me of my need of a Savior. Similarly, in years since, I renewed my Christian covenant through hearing a Christian broadcast that WDAC airs, and responding as God powerfully spoke to me. Many times throughout my life, when I was broken, shattered, and afraid, God spoke, assuring me that I was never alone. Over my shoulder stood the Potter, molding this unworthy daughter into a vessel for use in His service.

How thankful I am that God's spirit still strives, is strong, yet moving and sweet, powerful and mighty. It helps me to realize my dependence upon God's grace in my daily walk with Him. I have learned I can come into the presence of Jesus and worship God in spirit and truth, knowing the music of the gospel has long been the key to my heart. Over and over, He has melted and molded me, "Empty and Broken, I came back to Him, a vessel unworthy, so scarred from sin." "He did not despair, He started over again, and I bless the day, He didn't throw the clay away." The songwriter further utters my true testimony, "A vessel of Honor, I am today, all because Jesus didn't throw the clay away."

Father God, as I come into Your presence, gratitude is the song of my soul. As I stand in awe, I lift my hands in praise. Thanks for allowing a U-turn in my life to change my direction.

Lucinda Gabert serves as part-time receptionist at WDAC. She is a member of the Lancaster Christian Writers Association and worked in Medical Transcription while homeschooling her sons.

The Face of God

"Wisdom lights up a person's face, softening its hardness."
Ecclesiastes 8:1 (New Living Translation)

The reflection in my mirror revealed a face that was aging. Dark shadows appeared under my eyes, wrinkles had replaced smooth skin, the crisp contours of youth had rounded. "Emily, you're getting older," I observed. Then I wondered, if years of work and stress show on my face, what must God's face look like after millennia of shouldering the burdens of His children?

The apostle John tells us that no one except the Son has ever seen the Father, but Scripture gives us hints about that divine face. If wisdom lights up a person's face, softening its hardness and if God is the source of all wisdom, then we can be sure that He must have the softest face of all!

One day, in the future, we will no longer see as in a mirror. We will see our heavenly Father face-to-face. What joy will be ours when we can reach up and touch the soft cheek of the One who is the Alpha and Omega of all wisdom.

Father, as You conform me to the image of Your Son, may my face reflect Your beauty and may my words communicate Your Wisdom.

Emily Parke Chase works with the Capital Area Pregnancy Centers of Camp Hill and is author of *Why Say No When My Hormones Say Go?*

For Crying Out Loud!

"...Blessed are those who have not seen and yet believe."
John 20:29

All of my children were fairly independent as babies, but only when one of their parents was nearby. If my oldest could not see me, she would get a little nervous and call out for me in that baby language of hers.

One day, she was in the other room playing while I was making dinner. She must have panicked in missing my presence and started to cry. Since my hands were covered in raw meatloaf, I could not go to her right away. So I called out to reassure her. But Hannah was crying so loud, she could not hear me and kept right on crying. I knew she was safe, and I had a good reason for not coming. She did not know that. She couldn't hear my comfort above her own misery.

Have you ever been "crying so loud" you couldn't hear God's voice reassuring you? Did you miss Him telling you He was right there beside you and it was all going to work out soon? Although it is probably one of the hardest things for us to do, there is good reason why God needs us to be still before Him at times. We tend to do a lot more talking than listening. And that may keep us from hearing exactly what we need.

Dear Lord, I will take the next minute to be quiet before You. I am opening the ears in my heart. Help me be receptive to Your timing and to hear correctly all that You have to say. Amen.

Tracy Slonaker is a wife, mother of three, and director of Christian Education at Harvest Fellowship in Colebrookdale.

Lord of the "Ups" and "Downs"

"Peace I leave with you; my peace I give to you; not as the world gives do I give to you. Do not let your heart be troubled, nor let it be fearful." *John 14:27 (New American Standard Bible)*

My wife, Gayle, and I had a stress-filled year beginning with July of 2007. First, Gayle was diagnosed with uterine cancer, had major surgery, and 30 radiation treatments (as of this writing, she is cancer-free).

On Labor Day weekend, I had a heart attack and 2 or 3 mini-strokes (for which, unbelievably, I only missed six days of work, and unfortunately had to give up some very good food).

At the end of September, our oldest son, Brandon, his wife, Rachel, and our then 6-month-old granddaughter, Lillyann Grace (who, by the way, is adorable) moved in with us.

In May of 2008, Gayle's mom went to be with the Lord after fighting cancer for eight years.

A month later, Brandon revealed to us that he felt God calling him to the pastorate, was hoping to start seminary by the fall, and would be moving that little girl (did I mention she's adorable?) about 160 miles away from us.

Some of these situations caused feelings of helplessness, but we've had many years of walking hand in hand, not only with each other, but also with the Lord, while trusting in His amazing provision. So we never lost hope. Space limits me from telling you all the stories, but suffice it to say that the Lord has chosen to allow us to go through our share of challenges through the years. More importantly, however, is the fact that He has carried us in His strong arms through each and every one of those challenges. And He has shown us, each and every day, that the journey is a blessing.

Father, thank you for being Lord of the "ups" and the "downs" as You walk with us each step of the way.

Mike Stike is operations manager and Morning Show Host from 4:00 to 9:00 AM at 94.5 FM, The Voice Of Christian Radio, WDAC, in Lancaster.

Rock of Help

"Then Samuel took a stone and set it up between Mizpah and Shen.
He named it Ebenezer, saying, 'Thus far has the Lord helped us.'"
1 Samuel 7:12

Recently my family shared in an annual weekend at a mountain cabin. We have been doing this for about twenty years. I happened to be reading in 1 Samuel over this time and the above verse was in my mind and heart. On Sunday we gathered for a time of family worship. All of us came with an awareness of the challenging situation that one member of our family was facing. I thought back over the past twenty years and realized that each time we gather someone is facing a loss of job, a major transition, a significant health challenge, a troubled relationship, or some other significant circumstance. The challenge always seems daunting at the time, and yet we come together a year later finding ourselves on the "other side." Each time God has come through as our *Ebenezer.*

One of the first years we vacationed at this cabin my father buried a treasure along a trail between the cabin and the stream. Each year we follow the map which leads to that treasure and each year we dig up the jar and marvel that the treasure remains. This year that treasure became to me sort of like that stone that Samuel set up between Mizpah and Shen. Each year it will remind me that thus far the Lord has helped us.

Take time today to reflect on the life of your family or community. Can you affirm the Lord as your Rock of Help? Perhaps you could set up your own *Ebenezer* stone as a reminder and encouragement of your confidence in God.

Father, thank you that You are an ever present help in our time of need. Today we rest with confidence in You as our Ebenezer—Rock of Help.

Barry Stoner ministers in the marketplace.

My Only Source

"What is more, I consider everything a loss compared to the surpassing greatness of knowing Christ Jesus my Lord, for whose sake I have lost all things. I consider them rubbish, that I may gain Christ."
Philippians 3:8

I was jogging when I was memorizing this verse, and it hit me that God was speaking directly to me about a great loss I was to bear...what could it be?

I had already lost a husband to a plane crash eighteen years prior. Would God take another husband from me? No, I thought, the most precious thing to me is our youngest daughter. My heart was in anguish as I realized God wanted an answer from my heart. I told Him that whatever He wanted was alright with me. I had no clue what awful events were about to happen. Within a few weeks, our precious fourteen year old Lacey, was diagnosed with a horrible brain tumor. Being told there was no hope, I was faced with the greatest loss in my life. I wondered how strange it was that God had forewarned me about this.

In those brief days at the Children's Hospital of Philadelphia I prayed for God to heal her completely or take her home quickly. I couldn't bear to see her suffer, and I knew heaven was so dear to her heart. How she longed to know all the answers to her many questions about eternity. God did both, He healed her completely by taking her home to be with Him.

I will carry this pain in my heart until I can hold my dear child again, and this time it will be forever. No matter how great the loss, it has caused me to love the Lord more and hunger after Him with all my heart.

Father God, You are God of all comfort who is my only source of strength and comfort. I consider all things loss for the surpassing greatness of knowing Christ Jesus my Lord.

Jeannette Y. Taylor and her husband Dick are full-time staff with the NAVIGATORS. Jeannette also volunteers with REST Ministries in Coatesville.

Grace All-Sufficient

"But he said to me, "My grace is sufficient for you, for my power is made perfect in weakness." Therefore I will boast all the more gladly about my weaknesses, so that Christ's power may rest on me. That is why, for Christ's sake, I delight in weaknesses, in insults, in hardships, in persecutions, in difficulties. For when I am weak, then I am strong." *2 Corinthians 12:9*

For the glory of God alone, may I share a word of testimony from a woman named *Ruth*?

Ruth contracted polio while serving with her husband in Beirut, Lebanon, as missionaries, on Christmas Day of 1954. She spent the last 30 years of her life on earth completely paralyzed below the neck.

In 1982 she was interviewed, and at its close, was asked if she had a final word to share. Her response was as follows:

"Yes, I would like to say that I think the biggest miracle—even more of a miracle than if the Lord healed me—is that every single day He gives me joy and peace and grace. You know, I just can't get over that because it would seem that after twenty-seven years that would run out, yet every day it is a joy just to be alive and to experience more of Him. I hear of others being bored with life and I just can't get over the joy the Lord gives to me. God's mercies are renewed every morning."

Ruth is my aunt and is now in heaven. Twenty-six years later, her life's testimony of daily reliance on God's all-sufficient grace stays in my mind as a reminder of the true definition of God's power.

Our Father, we come now to thank You, specifically for Your wondrous grace—that both saves and sustains us. In Jesus' name, Amen.

Peter W. Teague, Ed.D. is president of Lancaster Bible College and Graduate School and co-founder with his wife, Paulette, of Jessica and Friends Community.

God Had a Better Plan

"For I know the plans I have for you," declares the Lord, "plans to prosper you and not to harm you, plans to give you hope and a future." *Jeremiah 29:11*

Growing up in the city of Chicago, I had to overcome a lot of diversities in life. My mother had nine children that she practically raised by herself. I can remember days when we didn't have food to eat or shoes to wear. My mothers struggles where more than she could bear. At the age of fifty eight, she had a stoke, and went home to be with her heavenly Father.

Both of my parents were illiterate, neither one could read or write, and that became one of my struggles as well. I found myself looking for love and acceptance in the wrong places. At the age of fifteen I had a beautiful daughter, and nine years later I had another beautiful daughter. Two years passed and I decided to marry my childhood sweetheart, the father of my children. He was a drug dealer, and I thought this would give me a chance to live a better life. We moved to Florida, where his mother and siblings lived. My life became a nightmare, as my husband became very violent and abusive.

Five years later, we move back to Chicago and I left him, but by this time I had a crack cocaine habit. I was back and forth in this relationship for years in order to supply my needs. My oldest daughter, at twenty-eight was a crack addict, and killed by a serial killer. This was so devastating that I could not see my way out.

But God had a plan, and today I know that all things work together for good according to His plan, not mine. God has blessed my life tremendously with a very rewarding job as a counselor for women. He has made it possible for me to be an encouragement to other hurting people.

Jesus, please give me Your priorities and character. Mold my heart to reflect Yours. Fill it with Your compassion and love. Your graciousness and gentleness, Your mercy and joy, Your passion for people and for goodness and holiness. Give me Your integrity and intimacy.

Mardester Thomas is a counselor in the Women's Shelter at Water Street Rescue Mission, Lancaster.

November

Lord, Thank You for the Reminder

"And we know that in all things God works for the good of those who love him who have been called according to his purpose."
Romans 8:28

I had been called into my boss' office and terminated. I was humiliated that I was being fired based on a lie. Asked to work out two week's notice and transition all of my accounts to the remaining employees, I carefully noted the status of each account over the next ten very long days. *Why me, Lord? I'm an honest and hard worker! Why me?*

With my children in school, I was now free to help my mom even more in the care of my terminally ill aunt. She was in the final stages of bone cancer, and the brunt of the work fell on my mother whose livelihood also depended on a business she ran from her home. While my siblings and I had been helping with night shifts, what my mother really needed was uninterrupted time to work.

So I sat for hours the first day, talked with my aunt when she was awake, and cared for her needs. While she slept, I prayed. *Lord, why have you allowed this? Why now? Is it simply to care for my aunt?*

The next day, my aunt asked me to shut the do or. *"What is it that is different about you?"* she asked. *"There's something about you that is different from the rest of the family."*

Quietly and simply I explained the message of salvation. When I asked her if she was ready to give her life to the Lord, she was. We prayed together as she invited Christ into her heart.

Now exhausted, my aunt fell asleep. It would be her last lucid conversation. The next morning she went to meet her Lord and Savior.

Father, I thank You for reminding me it's not about me and that You can use me when I am broken.

Jeanine Tobolski serves as the director of Early Childhood Ministries at Calvary Church in Lancaster.

Abandoned?

"I will never leave you nor forsake you." *Hebrews 13:5*

I have suffered with abandonment issues for a long period of time. During a prayer time, I was asked how I felt when this happens in my life. The first word that came to mind was *lonely*. As we prayed, my prayer partner asked the Lord to show me a time in my life when I first felt that way. She took me back to a time in my life when I was a teen. I remembered sitting in my room when my dad came in. He sat at the end of my bed and told me he would go to church and pray for me about the struggles I was having. At this time I didn't have a relationship with God; I didn't even know I could. I came from a very devout Catholic family, and my problems were not part of how I was being "raised."

As my dad left my room I felt so alone, yet this time I could see Jesus sitting with me on my bed! I began to weep, and my partner asked what it was that I saw, which I shared with her. She asked if He was saying anything to me, and as I focused I could hear Him say, "I was with you even then and have not left you since." How amazing!

Even as a rebellious teen, one not even interested in God, He was still there. He has never left me, even from birth. That brought me such great comfort, and now when I'm left alone, I know truly that I am not. His Word has told me so, and now He has confirmed that with me.

Thank You, Father, for never leaving us. Even in our times of rebellion and sin You are there. You are true to Your Word. Help us to always remember that.

Eileen Christiansen is a leader/youth leader of Celebrate Recovery, a twelve-step Christ-centered program in Sadsburyville.

The Lord Will Direct My Steps

"In his heart a man plans his course, but the Lord determines his steps." *Proverbs 16:9*

"A man's steps are directed by the Lord. How then can anyone understand his own way?" *Proverbs 20:24*

Some years ago I traveled from Pennsylvania to visit some "Florida snowbirds," a retired couple from our congregation who wintered every year in the Sunshine State. The trip was coupled with an invitation to preach in the church they were attending and the desire to visit another church in Pensacola. Those were my plans!

Besides the planned events, there was time to relax, enjoy some lunch outings, and see the sights. On one of those relaxing days, as we were driving back to the couple's travel trailer, Jean and I made the "spur of the moment decision" to visit Pinkie. Pinkie, a good friend of Mike and Jean, was recently widowed. We arrived at her home and it wasn't too long until we knew the Lord had sent us. It was a tough day of grieving for Pinkie. We visited for a little while and before leaving, prayed with her.

In the years that followed, Pinkie would often comment how much that visit meant to her. And, Jean and I have often recalled that day. Our conversation, that desire to visit Pinkie, that "spur of the moment decision" was the Lord directing our steps. I had planned a trip to Florida, but the Lord determined and directed my steps.

Father, You lead my steps even when I don't know You are doing it. Thank you. Lead me today, Lord. Make me sensitive to Your Holy Spirit. Help me hear Your voice. Perfect Your will in my life today. In Jesus' name, amen.

Daniel Wagner serves as senior pastor of Towerville Christian Church in Coatesville and as president of the Ministers Alliance of Coatesville and vicinity.

My Real Daddy

"Love never gives up, never loses faith, is always hopeful, and endures through every circumstance."
1 Corinthians 13:7 (The Message)

Two daddies left me through divorce. When a new daddy entered my life, there was no way I was going to love and accept him. I decided the best course of action would be to reject this daddy before he left us.

While my mother was at work, I would be disrespectful and say mean and vile things to my stepfather before my mother got home. No matter how nasty I got or what I said, he would not argue with me. And he never told my mother on me.

I was not easy to love for many years. Somehow, no matter how unlovable I was, he still loved me with compassion and unconditionally. Through his presence and actions, he cared for me and he cared for my sisters. It would be easy to walk away from us, as we weren't his biological children, and I am quite sure he got more than he bargained for with us! But he never abandoned us.

After I came to Christ, I was hurt and saddened by my behavior toward Pop. One day I asked him to forgive my rebellion and ungodliness, and he told me that he had forgiven me long ago. That day I also asked him why he stayed, and he said, "I loved your mother, and I knew that because of that love I would love you girls."

That love and presence was so powerful, transcending every hurt and even biology, so that Poppy became my "real" daddy. His presence brought the security and healing that helped break up the fallow ground of my hardened heart, enabling me to be saved by Jesus and to ultimately receive the Father's love.

Heavenly Father, I thank You for sending my daddy, Poppy, to heal my family with his and Your unconditional love.

Sharon Blantz is the proud daughter of "Poppy & BaBa" and serves as regional pastor of single parents and support and care ministries at The Worship Center.

I Rejoice

"Jesus replied, 'I saw Satan fall like lightning from Heaven. I have given you authority to trample on snakes and scorpions and to overcome all power of the enemy; nothing will harm you. However, do not rejoice that the spirits submit to you, but rejoice that your names are written in heaven.'" *Luke 10:18–20*

I heard my six year old brother, Branton, yelling from the barn. He was crying out to God for help. Branton said he was praying that God would send me to help him. Because he thought he heard a kitten under the lawn mower, he had raised the seat with his foot which slid into a hinged area, smashing the front part of his foot, pinning him there.

After I raised the hood and pealed his foot off the metal we could see how serious it was. There was no circulation going through his foot. My mother rushed him to the emergency room and I was able to get a prayer request on the church phone chain. I found out later that as they waited in the ER, the circulation started coming back into the foot and Branton insisted on going home. They left the hospital without seeing a doctor and Branton's foot healed miraculously fast. "I have given you authority to overcome all the power of the enemy; nothing will harm you."

Father, thank you for Your faithfulness of healing my brother's foot, but most of all, I rejoice that my name is written in heaven.

Tate Warfel is a fullback and defensive lineman for Warwick High School football team. He is a teen who attends Carpenter Community Church and says, "God has been doing amazing things in my life."

Exposed Before God

"No creature is hidden from his sight, but all are naked and exposed to the eyes of him to whom we must give account."
Hebrews 4:13 (English Standard Version)

I've been reading the book of Isaiah recently, and one morning I was reading from Chapter 20. Isaiah has been giving prophetic warnings to various countries and this particular prophecy is against Egypt and Cush (Ethiopia).

The text goes like this: "Then the Lord said, 'As my servant Isaiah has walked naked and barefoot for three years as a sign and a portent against Egypt and Cush, so shall the king of Assyria lead away the Egyptian captives and the Cushite exiles, both the young and the old, naked and barefoot, with buttocks uncovered, the nakedness of Egypt'" (Isaiah 20:3-4).

My mind jumped to this warning from God to people today. The writer of Hebrews has just finished talking (verse 12) about how the Word (*Logos*) of God is living and active and sharp as a two-edged sword, piercing to the division of the soul and spirit, and of joints and marrow. The Word of God, the writer says, "discerns the thoughts and intentions of the heart."

And it's in this context that he says none of us are hidden from his sight. We are all exposed before God. The picture of the kings of Egypt and Ethiopia being marched to Assyria with their buttocks exposed, enduring the humiliation that such exposure brings, comes to mind as I consider myself naked and exposed before Almighty God, and I'm truly humbled.

My thoughts of self-importance, my feelings of great significance, my temptation to consider myself indispensable to the congregation God called me to serve somehow fade into the background as I recognize my exposure to God.

Almighty God, please help me to recognize daily that all of my thoughts and actions that spring from my self-centered behavior are laid bare before Your eyes and exposed for what they are.

Dale Weaver serves as the senior pastor of Sandy Hill Community Church, Coatesville.

Trials

"Who through faith are shielded by God's power until the coming of the salvation that is ready to be revealed in the last time. In this you greatly rejoice, though now for a little while you may have had to suffer grief in all kinds of trials. These have come so that your faith—of greater worth than gold, which perishes even though refined by fire—may be proved genuine and may result in praise, glory and honor when Jesus Christ is revealed." *1 Peter 1:5–7*

In March of 2007 my wife, Donna, and I found out that she had breast cancer. I remember the call from the doctor, standing by her side, as she wrote the word "Cancer." We were devastated. Our children played on the floor as I told Donna I needed to get away a bit to process this. I jumped into the car and drove to the church where I wept bitterly. I asked God why! I was so angry, and I didn't understand why God would allow this. I prayed, "God haven't I served you faithfully?" Little did I know that the journey was going to be long but rewarding in the end.

My faith was tested as we prayed many things for Donna from not needing Chemotherapy, to keeping her hair. It seemed everything we prayed came back the opposite of what we desired.

That summer was the hardest I have ever had. I can't tell you how difficult it was seeing my beautiful wife becoming thin, exhausted and losing her hair. I saw God's grace in her. I also saw God's grace in me, too, as I didn't have anxiety or fear. I was able to be strong for her and the children and was able to minister to her in her time of weakness.

Donna is now cancer free! Her hair and strength have come back and she is feeling great. We praise God for His healing! Our marriage is stronger then ever. Our faith has been through the fire and we have stood firm in Jesus. For we know that there is nothing else that we can stand on but the rock of Christ. We may not always have our prayers answered the way we want them to be, but I know that God will give us the strength to press on, to stand firm and to have victory in the end.

Jesus, I pray that You would help us through the trials today—that we may stand firm in Your promises and know that You are right there with us through the storms of life. Thank you, Lord!

Mike Wenger is executive director of TNT Youth Ministry.

He is the God of Hope

"David said: 'Why are you downcast, O my soul? Why so disturbed within me? Put your hope in God, for I will yet praise him, my Savior and my God.'" *Psalm 42:11*

As I counsel with pastors, sometimes I see the pain, shame and lack of hope in their eyes. I watch them cry tears of regret and repentance. They long to undo mistakes and moral failures. They feel hopeless. My perspective is different. They see failure; I see opportunity for redemption. They see weakness; I see God's grace perfected in weakness. They see loss; through His spirit, I see great gain—gain to their families, gain to the church and gain to the kingdom of God. My hope for them lies in the God of hope, and I encourage them to pray, as David did, "Put your hope in God." I think to myself about the possibilities in the next five to ten years. With restoration, how many people will this pastor touch? How many people will be led to Christ? How many people will he strengthen through his preaching and teaching? God is a God of redemption and restoration. He is the God of hope!

Lord, thank you that You take our mistakes and failures and use them to touch other people's lives.

Dave Wiedis is the executive director of Serving Leaders Ministries in West Chester, a ministry that provides pastoral care to pastors, ministry leaders and their families.

A Smooth Transition

"But thanks be to God! He gives us the victory through our Lord Jesus Christ." *1 Corinthians 15:57*

Nursing homes aren't high on my list of Top 10 Places to Visit, but I've become a regular over the past few years. My introduction was through an elderly friend from church who needed rehab. When she returned home, I continued visiting with her former roommate.

Interestingly, this ninety-year-old Catholic lady became quite interested in the cross I wear. Soon, we began praying together, especially when she was experiencing difficult emotional or physical problems.

As I entered her room one day, I heard a jubilant, "Look, *look*!" There, dangling to her waist, was an enormous crucifix. "My custodian friend found it outside when he was cleaning." Then came the challenge: "Why doesn't your cross have Jesus on it?" Oh no! My comfort zone had suddenly exploded. Lacking boldness in sharing my faith, I inwardly cried, "God, are you asking me to explain the plan of salvation to her? Please give me just the right words!"

We summed up our prayerful discussion by confirming that Jesus no longer hangs on the cross because He conquered death once and for all by paying the ultimate price. Jesus is alive and joyfully waits to welcome us to our eternal home. The cross is empty in glorious victory. "O death, where is thy sting?" (1 Corinthians 15:55).

The excitement in my heart that day didn't come close to the amazement I experienced, when on my next visit the cross was turned over, displaying the "empty" side. Her face was alight with understanding and joy as she ran her wizened finger over its bare surface. "The cross is empty because Jesus *smoothed* the way for me." Smooth!

Thank You, God, for smoothing my transition from mortal life to eternal life by sending Your Son to die for my sins. Thank You, Jesus, for nailing my sins to that cross and for continually covering me with Your precious blood. Amen.

Janet Medrow works for the Director of the National Christian Conference Center in Valley Forge and serves as a deacon at Great Valley Presbyterian Church in Malvern.

Securely Held

"Even to your old age and gray hairs I am he, I am he who will sustain you. I have made you and I will carry you; I will sustain you and I will rescue you." *Isaiah 46:4*

Daylight was slowly beginning to break as I sat in my tree stand with my bow during hunting season. It was the time of morning that "deer" gradually become stumps and bushes, and *actual* deer materialize out of seeming nothingness. Every sense was fully alert as I watched the forest come to life around me.

As the morning progressed and no deer appeared, my mind began to wander, as it so often does when I'm hunting. I shifted slightly on the seat of my tree stand and contemplated how far below the ground was. Looking at the harness that I had carefully strapped on over my clothing before climbing the tree, I thought of how much more safe I felt than if I were without it. I visualized the strap that I had secured tightly around the tree above my head, connecting my harness to the tree. It was good to know that if I fell, I would be caught!

How much is God like that harness system? No matter how precarious my situation may seem, or even how much I get used to having Him there and go through a period of not being as aware as usual of His presence, He's always there, holding me securely. It doesn't mean that I won't ever trip or stumble, but within His grip, I won't tumble catastrophically. Whether I am fully aware of God's presence or not, He is still there, holding me tight.

Though I didn't come out of the woods with a deer that day, I emerged with a valuable lesson learned. At the times when I am tempted to worry about finances, relationships, or other areas of life, I remind myself of that harness, and the security which I have in God. He is faithful, and He has me in His grasp!

God, thank You for reminding me of Your presence and Your faithfulness. No matter how difficult my circumstances are, I know that You are with me, holding me securely. Your grace will cover me. Help me to be continually more aware of your presence.

Ann Rodriquez is the administrative secretary at DOVE Christian Fellowship, Westgate in Ephrata, and leads worship at her home church, DOVE Elizabethtown.

If You don't Go, You won't Know

"...Go into all the world and preach the gospel...."
Mark 16:15 (New King James Version)

I heard someone once say that two-thirds of God is "Go!" On a two-week Extreme Teen Mission Trip to Peru we ministered in Chincha, Peru, the site of the devastating earthquake that occurred in August 2007. Through reconstruction help, children's ministry, and street evangelism, the team encouraged people in a time of great loss.

For many of these teens, this was the first time out of the US on a mission trip. But they conquered their fears and gave up a good portion of their summer vacation to obey Christ's call to "Go." As a result, God met this team in a powerful way. Before the trip, one of the team members received a dream in the middle of the night, which became our outreach drama called "Wake Up Call." Everywhere we went, the youth reached out to hundreds of people with the message, "Wake up! Time is short." Right in the middle of an open market or a soccer field, people would respond to the call to know Jesus. You could literally feel the love of God embracing the people as they came weeping to receive prayer.

Our teens were touched most deeply by the multitudes of children. Because most of the kids are from broken homes, they loved the attention and American candies the youth shared. Many of them made a decision for Christ. The reality of our drama and our message "Time is short!" hit home one night when Marcos, one of the kids attending our VBS, was tragically hit by a car and died.

If this group of teenagers hadn't gone on this mission trip, they may have never known what it means to go beyond their summer vacation and Xbox, truly to live for Christ and a purpose higher than themselves. And if you don't go, there could be a Marcos out there who will never know.

Father, let me truly know You, a God who loves the world, and help me to be willing to go wherever You lead.

Craig Nanna lives in Reading with his amazing wife Tracie and three kids, and they together pastor Reading DOVE Christian Ministry Center. Craig also serves as the director for a group of pastors and Christian leaders called the Reading Regional Transformation Network.

He Will Conceal Me

"For in the day of trouble He will conceal me in His tabernacle; in the secret place of His tent He will hide me; He will lift me up on a rock." *Psalms 27:5*

I can't help but recall playing "Hide and Seek" with our children when they were quite small. It was at that age all five of them could play, but since they were so young, they weren't always clever enough to think of really good hiding places.

So Daddy helped.

He would go along with the one who was "it" to hide him or her in a place where the rest of us would never consider investigating.

And there was the time someone was hidden on the top shelf of a closet. Daddy had to lift that little one up high and put something in front of him to camouflage his clandestine place of concealment.

The psalmist says, "He will lift me up on a rock." Out of reach, out of danger, unable to be found! There's such safety in knowing that the Lord will "hide me in the shadow" of His wings (Psalms 17:8) and a great sense of security knowing that I can "take refuge in Him" (Psalms 64:10).

When trouble comes, He *will* conceal me. Just like my children could count on their daddy to hide them in places where the others wouldn't even think to look, so the Lord will cleverly obscure me from view.

I will run to Him declaring, "You are my hiding place!" (Psalms 32:7).

Thank you, Daddy, that I can depend on You to hide me. I can trust You to keep me from harm. You are continually drawing me into Your tabernacle and closer to You. There's no other place I'd rather be...amen.

Kathi Wilson and her husband Mark, co-authors of *Tired of Playing Church* and co-founders of Body life Ministries, are members of Ephrata Community Church.

A Mighty Work of God in a Small Town

"…Being confident of this, that he who began a good work in you will carry it on to completion until the day of Christ Jesus."
Philippians 1:6

In 1859 a group of Old Order Mennonites were meeting in homes in the area of Fairville (now Terre Hill) Lancaster County, Pennsylvania, for weekly prayer meetings. Since that practice was frowned upon at the time, the group separated themselves from the church and took the name, Evangelical Mennonites. They met in a stable in the west end of town and said just as their Lord started His ministry in a stable so did they. This small group joined a group of other like minded Mennonites, from the Lehigh Valley, headed by William Gehman. They became Evangelical United Mennonites in 1881. After much prayer, they purchased a property across the street and constructed a new church for worship. Early in the history of this church, they were part of a preaching circuit where they shared a pastor with churches in Fleetwood and Blanton of Berks County.

In 1947, they had grown enough to support their own pastor and they built a house for him and his family to live in. The church was very active in their community. Often children would come to the Berean Mennonite Brethren in Christ Sunday school and then go down the street to the other two churches in town. A group of believers in the church felt called to start a "daughter church," nearby Ephrata, in the mid-60's. That church grew into a strong voice for God in that community. Meanwhile, the church changed its name one more time and became the Bible Fellowship Church. The church still desires to reach the lost, in that small town, through many outreaches including a day camp that reaches over 100 children per year. The church God started in a stable 150 years ago continues to give Him glory for all that He has done.

Lord, thank you for the ministry of Berean Bible Fellowship Church in Terre Hill. Please continue to use it to reach the lost in eastern Lancaster County for the next 150 years.

Kevin Kirkpatrick is the current pastor of *that* small church in *that* small town.

NOVEMBER 14

Divine Timing

"Many are the plans in a man's heart, but it is the Lord's purpose that prevails." *Proverbs 19:21*

I planned my day's agenda down to the minute, a habit my husband finds to be less than endearing! My goal was an eleven o'clock arrival, staffing a booth at a health fair as a former dialysis patient and a kidney and pancreas transplant recipient.

The morning progressed as anticipated. I still had the necessary ten minutes to finish getting dressed, allowing for the necessary drive time. I love it when "my plan" comes together! Then, the phone rang, my tension rising as the caller lingered. Hanging up, the phone rang again. Answering the phone, I was ticking off the minutes, realizing "my plan" had crumbled

Aggravated, I raced to my car. *Yeah, the callers needed a listening ear, but why the lousy timing? God, do you have a reason for my delay? Show me who You want me to connect with and encourage today.* A peace washed over me as I continued my drive.

Mary Anne, whose husband recently needed dialysis, was at the health fair. As we talked her eyes revealed fear and anguish, mirroring mine several years prior. A mutual connection formed. I listened to her, encouraging and sharing insight to ease her apprehension as only someone who has "been there, done that" can do. "…He comforts us in all our troubles so we can comfort others…" *(2 Corinthians 1:3-4).*

Then, the "light bulb" moment…Mary Anne was my divine appointment. Her husband's dialysis progressed, as did our friendship. Subsequently, she received another blow, the death of her beloved father. Through divine timing, "His Plan" was accomplished. Mary Anne is now a vibrant part of a Bible study that meets in my home. God has blessed both of us.

Heavenly Father, forgive me when I'm consumed with "my plan." Show me those who need Your love and comfort. I desire to follow and be obedient to "Your plan." I'm Yours.

Nan Schock serves as a Stephen Minister at Manor Church, located south of Mountville.

Divine Appointments

"Now the angel of the Lord spoke to Philip, saying, 'Arise and go toward the south along the road which goes down from Jerusalem to Gaza.'" Acts 8:26

I personally believe there is no such thing as a coincidence, in the life of a Christian. We may not know or understand all that happens in our lives, but God is sovereign and orchestrates meetings or "divine appointments" for His children. Often these divine appointments come when we least suspect them.

For the past two years I have been praying with the leaders of two other churches from the little community of Brickerville, just north of Lititz. We pray and intercede for the community, the region, and the nation, every other Monday evening in the building of Brickerville Grace Fellowship, a Russian congregation.

One week I missed our usual day of prayer, but decided to come the following week, knowing that they usually have their own time of prayer. I waited for twenty minutes in the parking lot for someone to arrive. Just before I left, another car pulled along side mine. It was Elijah, a Russian man that I had not met before. I introduced myself and we talked briefly. We soon realized the prayer meeting was taking place in another location.

During our conversation, I learned that Elijah, a Russian immigrant, was currently unemployed. He had worked various jobs to support his family, but was hoping to be employed in plumbing or a related field, since he had been trained in Russia as a master plumber.

It "just so happened" that one of the small group leaders in my congregation was the head of a local refrigeration company and was looking for quality employees. As we prayed in the parking lot, one of our requests was for the Lord to bless Elijah with a job. That evening I gave his name to my friend. He was soon interviewed and then hired!

If we are willing to be led by the Holy Spirit, the possibilities of divine appointments are endless! My new friend Elijah, was much like the Ethiopian eunuch from Acts 8, "...he went on his way rejoicing"!

Lord, here am I, send me!

Mike Wise serves the Lord as an art teacher at Hempfield High School and as lead elder at New Beginnings Christian Fellowship in Brickerville.

Seated With Jesus

"For he raised us from the dead along with Christ and seated us with him in the heavenly realms because we are united with Christ Jesus." *Ephesians* 2:6 *(New Living Translation)*

The Apostle Paul is in prison. He has suffered terrible persecution and yet he says that Christ has raised him up to sit beside Christ in the heavenly places. We too are seated in the heavenly realms. Where are the heavenly places?

I want you to realize what a rich and glorious inheritance He has given to his people. I pray that you will begin to understand the incredible greatness of his power for us who believe him. This is the same mighty power that raised Christ from the dead and seated him in the place of honor at God's right hand in the heavenly realms. Now He is far above any ruler or authority or power or leader or anything else in this world or in the world to come. And God has put all things under the authority of Christ, and He gave Him this authority for the benefit of the church.

Do you understand your position? You are beside Christ in all those things. Today, ask the Lord to make real to you where he has placed you. Thank Him and praise Him for the victory that is yours because of where you sit.

Lord, open my eyes to see where I am seated. Help me to accept this seat of honor and live accordingly.

David Eshleman is a church consultant for Eastern Mennonite Mission and Lancaster Mennonite Conference.

Great is Your Love for Me

"The heavens declare the glory of God; the skies proclaim the work of His hands." *Psalm 19:1*

You don't realize how many stars are in the sky until you get away from the hustle and bustle of the city and get far out into the country. I experienced this firsthand in a rural village in northern Zambia, Africa. When the sun sets and night takes over, the darkness is almost overwhelming. With no electricity to diffuse the blackness you get a clear glimpse into the heavens.

One night my friends and I went to a nearby field to stargaze and I allowed myself to take in the beauty and majesty of the universe. At that moment I felt very small, yet a part of something too big to put into words. The Lord and I shared some special moments in that field.

I remember asking Him for a shooting star and then, there it was! And another one! And another! Before I knew it I had seen over 10 shooting stars. I have never felt more loved than I did at that moment. It was as if the Lord was saying, *"My daughter, I love you so much that I put on a spectacular display in the universe just for you."* Oh, that I would be able to walk in the knowledge of that love in every area of my life and in every circumstance. The Creator of the universe delights in me and expresses it through the wonder of all that He has made!

Heavenly Father, thank you for speaking to me through the splendor of creation. May my heart remain open to receive the love that You have for me.

Susan Witmer serves with Hope Beyond Borders, a non-profit organization based in Coatesville, that focuses on urban and international development.

Keep Silence

"To everything there is a season, a time for every purpose under heaven...A time to keep silence and a time to speak."
Ecclesiastes 3:1, 7

The woods that night were still, the fall breeze pleasant. Over twenty of us on a prayer retreat were seated in a circle around the fire as we had the evening before. This time was different: our sense of hearing was sharper and our sensitivity to one another was greater. Our bond of oneness was rich. We had been fasting speech for twenty-four hours!

During our "time to keep silence" we had lodged in our cabins, eaten meals together, partaken of communion, and washed one another's feet without saying a word!

In the beginning hours of our fast we tried to communicate with gestures, but the Holy Spirit helped us to realize that doing so was missing the point of fasting speech. Eventually, we came to rest—not trying to communicate.

Rather we communed with the Lord and with one another through simple presence and looking into the eyes and toward the heart. We were led by the Holy Spirit and new sensitivity in our own hearts to act on behalf of others—without human instruction.

As I considered what words I would say first to end the fast, I hesitated to say any, for silence had become such an intimate friend. I wanted these words to be pure, to edify others and to please the Lord.

Through this experience I learned to treasure God's silence and a deeper level of knowing others. I saw anew the power of fasting, of discipline and of community to purify our hearts and our communication.

Lord, lead us into seasons of silence that our speech may be purified in Your presence and what we say may be special to all who hear.

Keith Yoder is the chair of the Regional Council of the Regional Church of Lancaster County and president of Teaching The Word Ministries.

Injured in the Service

"Give, and it will be given to you. A good measure, pressed down, shaken together and running over, will be poured into your lap. For with the measure you use, it will be measured to you." *Luke 6:38*

The congregation and I had a little adventure yesterday morning. I was preaching from Mark 14:1-11, speaking about the life of extravagant sacrifice that God calls us to live if we really desire to have life to the full—life as God intended. This is the story of Mary of Bethany breaking her jar of incredibly expensive perfume and oil to anoint Jesus in preparation for His death on the cross. To close the sermon and emphasize the point, I planned to break a jar and challenge people to truly become people sacrificing for God's purposes.

Unfortunately, as I smashed the jar with great gusto, I put some shards into my wrist and began to bleed rather heavily. So as to not panic anyone (or mess up the carpet), I turned to Dan and told him to close the service as I headed out to clean the wound. It was deep enough that I sent for a nurse sitting in the service, Gwen, who patched me up. In fact, she did so well, that when I went for stitches the doctor on duty declined and proceeded to bandage me up as Gwen had done. He simply charged me a couple hundred dollars for the first aid.

Later, when I repeated the illustration for our second service (this time ensuring that I did not cut myself), I told them about the first service incident. "Today God required a little blood from me. What will you give to Him that is precious because you truly need it, but He needs it more?"

The scripture, from Luke, makes it clear that God looks at the level of our sacrifice to determine his level of blessing in our lives. Do we want to receive an abundant life—the life that He intended? Then we need to surrender our lives to Him—to give it up. The world will think this is extravagant, crazy, even wasteful. But God will honor it.

P.S. Later my wife Dianne remarked, "I have heard of being injured in the Lord's service, but it was never in the *worship* service."

Lord, today may we give abundantly, surrendering our lives to You.

Dr. Steve Dunn serves the Church of God of Landisville as its senior and preaching pastor. He is also a trainer for Becoming a Contagious Christian.

Good Stewards

"God blessed them and said to them, 'Be fruitful and increase in number; fill the earth and subdue it....'" *Genesis 1:28*

As we walked along the road, we would stop every few feet, pick up trash that was lying on the ground, and put it in our trash bags. We found cigarette butts by the hundreds, bottles and various other pieces of trash along the stretch of road that our church adopted. Our youth ministry went out and spent around three hours cleaning up the two-mile stretch of road that we were assigned. One of our youth even said that as she was cleaning up the trash, someone threw a piece of trash out his car window.

All too often, the above passage of Scripture is used to defend the raping and pillaging of our environment. But if we take a closer look at this passage and others within the story of Scripture, we find God's call to us is not abusing His creation, but to be good stewards of what he has created. It means being aware of how our lives impact the environment, whether for the good or for the bad. Taking care of the environment, at its core, is a spiritual issue.

So what does it mean for us, as Christ-followers, to be good stewards of the environment? A first step might be to recycle, if you don't already. What about replacing the light bulbs in your house with compact fluorescent lamps (CFL's) which are more energy efficient? What about signing up to adopt a highway and regularly clean up the trash along that stretch of road? Drive less in order to conserve natural resources. Take shorter showers in order to conserve water. These ideas aren't exhaustive (go to the Sierra Club's website for more personal ideas). May we see that taking care of God's creation is worship.

Lord, may we pray Psalm 24:1, "The Earth is the Lord's and everything in it...."

Ryan Braught is pastor of Youth Ministries and Nurture and a leader of Veritas, an Emerging Missional community of faith.

The Name of Jesus

"And I, if I be lifted up from the earth, I will draw all men to me."
John 12:32

The young man sitting at my kitchen table was whining. He finished his saga and promptly went on to another difficulty. By the time I was finished preparing the dinner we were about to share, I realized that nothing much was right in his life and he now was waiting expectantly for me to solve his problems. I abruptly turned to him and gave the only response that came to mind. "What you need is Jesus. He can help you solve those problems."

I believed that with all my heart, but I wasn't sure it would mean anything to him. He was a totally un-churched young man with no concept of spiritual truth. I wasn't even sure he knew there was a Jesus other than through the swearing he heard in his world.

Four years later, when he testifies that he found God and was baptized, and shares what Jesus means in his life, he refers back to that kitchen table incident—"she told me I need Jesus…can you imagine, that's all she had to say—I need Jesus." And he laughs joyfully at the truth of it!

As time moves closer to the end and as world hunger, AIDs, poverty, natural disasters, social unrest and war seem overwhelming, I see the parallel to the young man's life. The answer still is Jesus. He walked among us in a world that experienced much of the same—leprosy instead of AIDs, storms and winds that drowned and destroyed, the stoning of adulterers. I am left with a sobering thought—those of us privileged to know the answer must proclaim the answer—Jesus.

Father, thank you for Jesus who as we worship Him, draws with a power that supersedes all our own explanations, our wisdom, our works. Help us to know, trust, and evoke that power by exalting Jesus more and more in our daily lives.

Marian Yoder, an assistant professor at Harrisburg Area Community College, leads a Worship Center small group breakfast discussion for women in the marketplace.

Handling Life's Diversities

"Be still and know that I am God...." *Psalm 46:10*

Most mornings, upon arriving at the teahouse, I am greeted by the usual squirrels and birds that always seem to gather in the hollow of the still, quiet morning. And, as usual, when I pull into the parking lot, the birds, without fail, begin to chirp and flap their wings as they prepare to take flight. Meanwhile, the squirrels scurry around in a frantic motion, as they run off to leave me to myself. Each day this ruckus greets me, and because there really is no reason for such a flurry, I find myself getting increasingly irritated over this daily routine.

However, on this one particular morning, I entered the parking lot as usual with the same scenario occurring. Only this time it was a little different; for, as I put the key into the front door to unlock it, I heard this soft quacking coming from my left side. As I turned to see the duck, she was slowly waddling along the side of the house, uttering an occasional quack.

It was then that God brought to mind the question of, "How do I handle life's difficulties?" Am I like the birds, which rather than deal with the problem, fly away and choose not to deal with it at all? Am I like the squirrel running around in circles, trying to solve the problem in my own strength, but ultimately getting nowhere? Or, am I like the duck which quietly stayed strong, and walked calmly into the storm, to wait upon the Lord?

Life comes at us fast. With the dawning of each new day, we never know what lies ahead, or what trials await. But through it all if we wait upon the Lord, we will have a greater reward.

Lord, through life's adversities, help us to surrender and let Your will, not our will, be done.

Janet Young is proprietress of Over The Teacup Teahouse, Camp Hill.

Opening the Door for God to Work

"Let us not grow weary in doing good: for in due season we will reap if we do not lose heart." Galatians 6:9

Prayer opens the door for God to work. He waits to move until we pray. Wesley L. Duewel says in *Touch the World Through Prayer,* "The greatest service you will ever do for God will not be your external ministering, witnessing, or preaching. Your greatest service, whatever your vocation, is to be your priestly intercession."

Prayer opens the door for God to work. So why don't I pray more? "I'm busy." How many times have you heard that? Yes, we all are very busy but prayer is the most important work that I can do.

When someone has a problem or a prayer request, I sometimes say I'll just pray for her. Using the word "just" minimizes the value of prayer. I catch myself saying that often. The best thing I can do is pray.

I sometimes grow weary of praying if I don't see answers in my timetable. Recently I have seen answers to prayers that I've been praying for five years. What a faith-builder that is! Wow! I give Him the praise and glory. I'm so thankful. He is so awesome. It encourages me to pray for the unbelievable. It encourages me to pray often.

My challenge is to pray often. I can pray throughout the day on the run. It is so important to make time for the two of us—God and me—worshiping, talking, listening and interceding together. My God and I. Oh, how sweet!

Lord, I want to pray often whether I see the answer or not. Help me, Lord, to not grow weary in prayer for in due season there will be answers if I don't give up. Thank you, Lord, for hearing my prayers.

Yvonne Zeiset has a passion for prayer, "but oh, has so much to learn." She serves on the Evangelism Commission at her church and as a secretary for Columbia Pregnancy Center.

In the Stronghold of God

"The Lord is my rock and my fortress and my deliverer; my God, my strength, in whom I will trust; my shield and the horn of my salvation, my stronghold." *Psalm 18:2*

We were so excited to bring our second child, another boy, home from the hospital in July of 2008. We were only home for a week when I noticed Connor was not eating right and was getting lethargic. I worried all day, but thought maybe I was overreacting. I was thankful when my husband, an intensive care RN, came home and took a look at him. He noticed rapid breathing and went to get his stethoscope.

He couldn't even count how fast our baby's heart was going. We raced to the emergency room! His heart was beating twice the rate of a healthy newborn. Connor needed to be airlifted to Penn State Children's Hospital in Hershey. Of course, this made me very afraid. Would our baby make it through the night? What is causing this to happen to his little heart? That night, as my husband and I waited, I cried out to God for hope for our precious newborn son. Immediately I felt He reminded me of what Connor means: "Stronghold of God." I pictured Jesus having a strong hold on my baby and giving him the strength to grow and become a man of God.

When the doctors came with an update, they said Connor's heart rate had slowed down but it was severely strained by the rapid rate. He needed to be sedated and on a respirator with IV medicines to help his heart recover. They continued watching him to determine the next course of action so he wouldn't have episodes again.

After eight days, the doctors were able to decipher the proper daily doses of medicine needed. Connor is now doing just fine and hasn't had anymore problems. The cardiologist believes he will grow out of this by the time he's a year old and won't need to be on medication anymore. Praise the Lord! We serve a big God.

Father, thank you for Your strong hold on my life...for holding me even stronger in the times when I feel most vulnerable and afraid. I thank You that I can trust You no matter what comes my way.

Cindy Zeyak lives in Lancaster City with her husband and two sons. She is a full time mom, a worship leader, and a child of God learning to rest in her heavenly Father's strong arms.

Unexpected Opportunity

"...give thanks to the Lord...make known what he has done...let this be known to all...." *Isaiah 12:4*

During a routine day at the greenhouse, I discovered that unexpected events can become an opportunity to testify to God's protection. As I went to load a large bag of potting soil into a customer's vehicle, she hit the gas pedal instead of the brake as she was backing up. I was directly behind her and she hit me, sending me about fifteen feet back into the greenhouse. I remember rolling and my head hitting the concrete floor. I was dizzy, I could not get up by myself and I could feel a large lump forming on my head. I was taken to Hershey Medical Center, where I spent the next few hours being scanned, X-rayed and observed. I was released later that day as no major injuries or broken bones were found. I had a concussion, some cracked ribs, bumps and bruises.

The events of the morning were clear to me. The bag of potting soil that I was carrying helped absorb the impact, she snapped off a steel beam which slowed her down, and a door frame stopped her from running over me. I knew none of these things was a coincidence; each was the mighty hand of God protecting me from serious injury. He was giving me the opportunity to give him praise for what He did for me that day!

As customers asked how I was, I was able to tell them about God's protection and how He had saved me from serious injury. I never want to be hit by a vehicle again, but I am thankful for the opportunity to give God praise. The words of this song have become precious to me, "Be not dismayed what e'er be tide, God will take care of you, Beneath his wings of love abide, God will take care of you."

Lord, thank you for Your protection over each one of us.

Doris Cline, and her husband of 23 years, have three teenagers and enjoy family moments together while juggling schedules.

God's Creative Provision

"And my God shall supply all your need according to His riches in glory by Christ Jesus." *Philippians 4:19 (New King James Version)*

It was shortly after the birth of my fifth child that the economy in the Chicago area went belly-up, and my husband was laid off. God met our needs again and again through His people—a Thanksgiving basket from church, gifts of food and money from those we barely knew, even snow boots for my daughter from one of her teachers.

We were given a gigantic bag of potatoes, which I cooked in every way known to mankind to keep my family fed. But the day came when there was nothing else left in the kitchen, and I despaired of sending potatoes in the lunch boxes of my four children. I cried out to God as I drove to prayer meeting that Wednesday night.

I sat between strangers, with a heavy heart, as the pastor opened in prayer. Then, as I followed his instructions to turn in our Bibles to Romans 8, my heart flew up in my throat in disbelief. There in Romans 8 was a $5 bill! I quickly looked at the young man seated next to me, thinking, *Did he think I looked poor and stuck money in my Bible during prayer? But how would he know to put it in Romans 8? He could have put it in a page where I might not have discovered it till next year's Bible readings!*

I sat in an aura of wonder and amazement, fully knowing that it had never been my practice to use money as a bookmark! I stopped on the way home and bought a loaf of bread, a jar of peanut butter, and a bag of apples. And I praised God all week for putting food in my children's lunch boxes.

Father, thank you for all the creative ways You provide for us.... sometimes through your body, and sometimes directly from Your hand.

Lynne Babbitt is a counselor and speaker who serves as the assistant director of Shepherd's Touch Counseling Ministry.

Hope in Christ

"Let us then approach the throne of grace with confidence, so that we may receive mercy and find grace to help us in our time of need."
Hebrews 4:16

On Thanksgiving Day, 2002, we rushed our fourteen-year-old daughter to the emergency room with symptoms of nausea and vertigo. The attending physician wept as he shared that the CAT scan revealed a terminal brain tumor in her brain stem and that she might not make it to Children's Hospital in Philadelphia where they have specialized care. My wife and I watched helplessly as she was loaded on a gurney and transported by helicopter to CHOP, accompanied only by an EMT and the pilot.

Along the Schuylkill Expressway, my wife and I began to cry out to God for His help and mercy and care for this dear one, the youngest of our four children. We prayed the twenty-third Psalm together as we knew that we were walking through the valley of the shadow of death. The events had turned so critical so quickly.

Our daughter passed from our arms to the arms of Jesus just five days later. It was our desire to have seen the Lord perform a mighty miracle in preserving our daughter's life, but this obviously was not His perfect will. God has given us peace, love, care and He has showed us His grace and His mercy many times over. Through our loss we have come to a greater appreciation of heaven, and we live every day with more of an eternal perspective. He has given us opportunities to share Christ with other families along the way that are faced with losing their precious children, and to offer them hope in Jesus Christ. We would never have written the script of these events to turn out this way; however, we know with confidence that one day we will go to be with our daughter for eternity. Thank you Jesus for that blessed hope!

Lord Jesus, may we always know with confidence Your love for us, and may we always come to You for help in our times of need and experience Your grace and mercy. Amen.

Richard Taylor lives in Coatesville. He and his wife, Jeannette, are with the Navigators Church Discipleship Ministry as full- time missionaries. They minister together in Russia and Dick is on the board of Life Transforming Ministries and has been an elder at Brandywine Bible Church.

Red in the Window

"Look at the birds of the air; they neither sow nor reap...and yet your Heavenly Father feeds them." *Matthew 6:26*

Another shoe dropped. Since I've been the director, a bunch of shoes have dropped. How many more shoes are up there?

Discouragement set in with this latest episode. I began to quote 1 Corinthians 10:13 out loud, almost as if I were trying to convince God of its truth. Then I pleaded with the Lord. In fact, I wanted to yell "uncle" (I've had enough), but I wasn't sure that "uncle" is an expression used at the throne of God.

An hour later I noticed a cardinal alight on the nearest branch outside my window. It sat for a few moments, jumped to another branch and then flew away. Although I occasionally see cardinals, this particular bird landing at this particular spot and time held great meaning. You see, I love cardinals—it's my favorite bird. And, of course, the male is especially beautiful with the brightest hue. The female could be even better if she had a little cosmetic help. Look what it does for human females...but I digress.

As I saw that bird, immediately I thought of the verse for the day and birds not fretting. But I countered with "yeah, but a bird doesn't have people's livelihoods dependent on him, thousands of people who want to come here, an entire denomination watching, etcetera."

The more I thought about the cardinal, the more I realized that this had been a God-moment. I don't know what God told the cardinal or even if there was any debate going on, but that bird showed up to remind me that God is in control.

Lord, I and all those around me are much more valuable than a bird. I'm not sure how You are going to work through this latest situation, but You are faithful. Thanks, Lord, for the red in the window. Amen.

Dr. Dan Allen is a pastor, writer, conference speaker, radio commentator and director of Pinebrook Bible Conference, East Stroudsburg.

He Will Meet Me There

"…Strong God, I'm watching you do it, I can always count on you. God in dependable love shows up on time…."
Psalm 59:9–10 (The Message)

"Are you nervous about the move?" my friend asked. "No," I replied. During an ensuing lull in the conversation, I realized that it was rather disconcerting not to be scared about moving to Indiana to pursue a doctoral degree, especially since I'd experienced the paralyzing grip of fear throughout the years.

I was raised in a family in which sewing, gardening and cooking were viewed as the most important skills to learn. Acting against the cultural norms of my family and church, I decided to go to college. Aspirations, dreams and discernment of God's purpose for my life did not factor into my plans as I had not been taught this perspective of Christianity. The decision was based solely on a quiet conviction that I needed be a good steward of my intellect. Thus, I began my college career humanly alone, scared and wondering if I were smart enough to succeed.

I recall the day when my mentor suggested that I continue on for a doctorate. For those of you from families in which education is valued this may seem normal. For me, in that one moment, the doors to the room of dreams and possibilities swung wide open and turned my world upside down. I began taking more risks because I was convinced that God would use me and convicted that I needed to go outside my comfort zone in order to obey him. At the same time, I was terrified of every new venture.

It's been ten years since that phone conversation, and finally, the fear is gone. I learned over and over again, that every time I moved forward into the unknown, God met me. This instilled a deep confidence in Him—that He will meet me at every new destination and that He will never let me go.

Thank you Lord that Your dependable love always shows up just when we need it.

Tricia S. Groff, M.S., has been a therapist in Lancaster for the last seven years.

Faithful Friend

"Be still and know that I am God." *Psalm 46:10*

The ferret, my daughter, Laura, brought home from college has moved in with us. Boundless energy, primed for adventure; that describes Hunter best when Laura first releases him from his enclosure.

Bouncing along, he glances over his shoulder, "Look Laura, a flower!"

"What's that? Do you feel it, Laura?" he asks. "Is that the wind rustling my beautiful fur?"

"Ouch!" he squeals, serendipitously hopping from paw to paw. "Hot pavement, Laura!"

Fascinated by his reflection in the pond, spellbound, he marvels, "Who's that? Laura, do you see that handsome creature?"

Remarkably, even when Laura frees him to explore outside, Hunter doesn't ever wander too far from her presence, as if to say, "As long as Laura's here, I'm okay." And when he tires he just lies down at her feet with quiet contentment.

I want to walk through life with God like that, with a constant and abiding sense of His presence, guiding me, protecting me.

Instead, I wander from His presence time and again. I forget the most important thing—our time alone together, for He created me for intimacy. Sometimes I get so busy with the things of this life and my service to Him, that I feel like I'm running around in circles trying to get everything done. It's not until I'm exhausted that I finally stop long enough to collapse at His feet, too tired to keep my eyes open, too spent to hear His voice. I've thrown away my time alone with God one more day.

I need to release my agendas, my plans, and come to God with a heart of abandon, filled with extravagant love and devotion that trusts so completely in His love and care for me, that His voice is the only voice I hear, that His path is the only path I follow.

Father, let me not only sense Your presence, but also be transformed by it. Abide in me and change me into Your image, that I may reflect Your glory to others with quiet contentment.

Nancy Magargle is a member of Lancaster Christian Writers group.

Photo by Mark Van Scyoc

December

Proclaiming the Good News

"How beautiful on the mountains are the feet of those who bring good news, who proclaim peace, who bring good tidings, who proclaim salvation, who say to Zion, 'Your God reigns!'" *Isaiah 52:7*

Listening to a spat of bad news the other day, it occurred to me how much we promote the work of the enemy while keeping silent about the ways the Lord is working in our lives and in those around us. The human tragedies, gossip and celebrity "news" tend to overshadow and, more often, move good news to the background or off the news pages.

I know I personally am blessed when I hear reports about how the Lord is working in the lives of those around me or has answered prayer —removing a longtime addiction, restoring a marriage or other estranged relationship, or bringing someone to Himself through a series of other-wise unassociated circumstances.

There is a sense of excitement about His work that cannot be repli-cated by that of the enemy. Let us not dwell in second-rate news when there are so many unreported headlines that need to be broadcast to the world.

Lord, the next time we hear a piece of gossip or about the work of the enemy, prompt us to stop and reflect also on the greater good works that You are doing all around us and to tell others about them. Let the work of the enemy become an automatic reminder to us to let others know about Your goodness. Amen.

Casey Jones, who resides in Parkesburg, is an advocate for development of comprehensive marriage and family ministries, including ministries to the hurting, in churches. He is developer of a Transformation Initiative for Building Healthy Communities Through Healthy Families.

Fill in the Blank

"Now faith is being sure of what we hope for and certain of what we do not see." Hebrews 11:1

I recall taking tests in school with the exam including true and false, multiple choice and essay questions. Often included was a section which required "fill in the blanks" with the correct answers. It was a great knowing the correct answer to these blank spaces and being absolutely certain I answered correctly. I recall anxiety and frustration when the answer was far from me and I could not answer the question. The blank space remained unanswered.

Life brings us many "fill in the blank" questions, doesn't it? Tragic events, unforeseen circumstances, illnesses, human failures, and the mysteries of everyday life can bring us blank spaces as we struggle to make sense or find answers to questions. We naturally find ourselves asking, "Why do bad things happen to good or innocent people?"

If only all of life's questions could be answered so simply as humanly filling in the answers, questions that God alone can answer. The reality is many of these questions may never be answered or understood until we stand before God and we can see through glorified eyes, through the eyes of Jesus.

As a pastor, I often receive questions from persons going through life's difficult journey. Yes, Scripture comforts, counsels, directs, and speaks life and hope into these "blanks," but questions still often remain. As believers, it is in these times we are being asked to rest in the mystery of God. There simply are no easy answers on this side of heaven. This takes great faith. Be assured even in this mystery we have the promise that Jesus will never leave us or forsake us. Our directive is to persevere and to remain faithful in the mystery of life's blank spaces.

Lord, may I rest in Your majestic mystery and faithfulness today even when life's mysterious questions remain. You alone are worthy and in whom I trust.

Brian E. Martin serves as lead pastor at Weaverland Mennonite Church in East Earl. He and his wife Shirley are the parents of four children.

Speaking so that the Dead Might Hear

"As for you, you were dead in your transgressions and sins."
Ephesians 2:1

Pastor Doug spoke from Ephesians 2 one Sunday morning and high-lighted verse 1 where Paul reminds the Christians at Ephesus of their past: "As for you, you were dead in your transgressions and sins. …" And his challenge to us was this: "We need to learn how to speak to the dead in such a way that they will understand."

How easy it is to disregard the audience when our only consideration is whether we are "preaching the truth"! Have you ever asked a ministry worker "How did the lesson (or sermon) go?" And have you received a reply similar to this: "Well, there were three good points with a nice illustration, and it ended with a tear-jerker of a story, so it seemed like things went well." But the real question is "Have the people heard?"

Think of it. When a missionary immerses himself in an unfamiliar society, he will spend time learning the cultural intricacies, the language, and the value system and worldview of the host culture. And why does the missionary do this? He does so in order to effectively communicate the truth of the gospel in a way that can be understood and received by those who don't yet know Jesus. He wants to know the audience with whom he is speaking. And he wants to know how to connect with them in a way that develops trust and merits being heard.

How different things would be as I interact with the men and women at the mission if I understood what they value, how they communicate, what their priorities are and how they view the world! What would a "dead man" want to hear, and how could I communicate with him in a way so that he could receive the gospel for real?

Lord, help me to listen well.

Steve Brubaker is the director of Residential Programs at Water Street Rescue Mission, Lancaster.

Trust and Obey

"Trust in the Lord with all your heart, and do not lean on your own understanding. In all your ways acknowledge him, and he will make your paths straight." *Proverbs 3:5–6*

Becoming a parent was a goal I had for a long time. When it actually happened I didn't realize all the lessons that I would learn as I began the journey of motherhood. Our son was not born into our home, and even though he came to us as an infant we had to develop a bond with him. The biggest challenge in the beginning was to create a level of trust so that he would learn to obey.

It took a long time to work on the bond for developing a secure and trusting relationship with our son. In our eyes we knew we would care for him and thought he should understand that we knew what was best, yet he was insecure and could not trust us to be his "parents."

We must first trust someone before we will be willing to obey. In going through this situation, I was challenged to think about how much I trusted Jesus. If I say I trust him, then I will be willing to obey Him.

I believe that many times as children of God, we want to be in control, and we display our lack of trust in God's way. Our true display of trust in God is to obey Him.

Lord, thank you for being a Father we can always trust. Help us to truly believe that our paths are in Your hands so that obeying You is a security we can't live without.

Jean Boll, her husband, Irv, and son Bruce, attend DOVE Christian Fellowship Westgate in Ephrata.

Shrinking

"He must become greater; I must become less." *John 3:30*

It's becoming a morning ritual. "Mom," my sixteen-year-old calls out as he enters the kitchen, "Take off your sandals. Dad, can you measure us?" My son is attempting to surpass me, and not just in height either. He is growing and expanding. It is his time of enlarging. And he seems to take great joy in reminding me that I am at the shrinking stage of life.

It's true. At my last physical, the doctor measured my height. They hadn't done that for 20 years or so! "What's that all about?" I voiced my question, standing as tall as I possibly could on the scale, "Am I at the age of shrinking?" I didn't care for the doctor's affirmative response! My son is surpassing me in height, strength, skill, and abilities. He is increasing and I am...shrinking!

At first I don't take kindly to this...this overtaking of me. I want to resist it. Then John's words about Jesus echo in my ear. "He must become greater, I must become less." Apparently, I'm not the only one who has experienced this pattern of being overtaken and surpassed. Maybe this isn't such a bad thing after all. John seemed to accept it with grace.

As I ponder this, I find myself actually thanking God that I am at the shrinking stage of life. Everyday as I watch my son surpass me in height and strength, I am reminded to pray and ask God to become greater as I become less.

God, I yield to You. Let this be a season of shrinking in my life, of me becoming less and You becoming more. I want You to surpass and overtake me.

Jenny Gehman, a mentor, speaker and writer, lives in Millersville with her husband and growing son.

Community Service

"Be devoted to one another in brotherly love. Honor one another above yourselves." *Romans 12:10*

One of the blessings of working at Water Street Rescue Mission is to realize that God not only uses the staff to work in the lives of those He brings here, but often God works through fellow residents to minister to those who need His touch.

We had a very interesting chapel this morning. I was sharing excerpts from Philip Yancey's book *What's So Amazing About Grace?* We started out talking about what we think grace is, where it comes from, what to do with it, and moved into things that prevent us from either accepting grace or showing it to others.

I read a quote in the book about "the three common sources of crippling shame": secular society, a graceless church, and un-accepting parents. I said that I knew I had been affected by all of these and asked if anyone else felt they had. Many hands went up at that point, but as they went back down, Stewart's hand stayed up. I said, "Go ahead," and as he started to speak, he completely broke down sobbing and shaking.

Some of the men started encouraging him. One got up and put his arm around Stewart and brought him some tissues. Another gentleman in our program jumped up and asked if we could come around Stewart and pray for him which we did for some time. As we debriefed after chapel, it became clear that Stewart was dealing with some very heavy stuff from his childhood and struggling with the concept that he could ever be forgiven.

The way the community came around Stewart, supported him and helped him understand God's love was a huge reminder to me that God is in control. He will do the work; we only need to be the vessels.

Lord, help us to serve others, as You have served us.

Scooter Haase is the director of operations at Water Street Rescue Mission.

God's Plan

"Nevertheless, you have done well that you shared in my distress... and my God shall supply all your needs according to His riches in glory by Christ Jesus." *Philippians 4:14, 19*

There was a special family event going to be held at our house, so we thought we would spruce up our living room. We had seen a new living room set in an ad and decided to buy it. So the day before the party we sold our old furniture, put the money in our wallet, and headed out the door.

Halfway out the door the Holy Spirit said, "No, this isn't the right time." My flesh was honestly disappointed to set up folding chairs and benches for the party, but my spirit was peaceful that God has a plan.

Almost a month later, a friend was hospitalized and his family was without income. God stirred our hearts to use part of our furniture money to bless them. Another month passed and one day God spoke, "Today's the day." We went to the store to buy the furniture we had desired. Upon arriving, we found it to be very uncomfortable and began to look around.

When we spied a set that we really liked and was comfortable, the price on the tag showed us God's humor. It was marked down by the exact amount we had given to our friends.

We proceeded to pay the salesman but had forgotten about sales tax. Out of cash, we passed on a check we had received in the mail that morning. Change in hand, furniture loaded, we headed home. On the way we realized the change was exactly 10% tithe on the check. God is so faithful!

Father, help me in each situation today to seek Your leading and in following it give my heart fully to trust Your plan for my life.

Al and Mary Ann Hocke founded Freedom Ministry (a prayer ministry for emotional and physical healing with spiritual roots).

Victory at Sea

"So shall My word be that goes forth from My mouth; It shall not return to Me void, But it shall accomplish what I please, And it shall prosper in the thing for which I sent it." *Isaiah 55:11*

Five years in the planning, our family vacation at the Outer Banks was finally a reality. We rose before dawn since my oldest son had arranged an ocean-fishing excursion for the guys. Six of us boarded the small boat—my longtime friend, his son and wife, my two sons and me. As the trolling began, we struggled to gain our "sea legs" while reeling in Spanish Mackerel.

About an hour out, I noticed my oldest son sitting with his head down. As he looked up with his greenish pale face, I knew he was seasick. They say the only cure for sea sickness is dry land and we had another four hours to go. As the fishing dried up, the others became aware of his plight and the fun melted into concern.

I knew that only God could save the day as He prompted me to pray. My oldest son had been away from Christian fellowship for many years, and I assumed he was not likely to expect healing from God, so I took the initiative. I asked my youngest son, who walks with God, to join me in faith and the laying on of hands. We prayed briefly, calling my oldest son's body into order and within a short time, he was back on his feet, catching fish.

Later in the week, as I reviewed the miracle with God, I realized that the others on the boat who witnessed it, were ministered to as well. My younger son's faith was reinforced as he agreed in prayer; my friend, a nonbeliever experienced the hand of God, and his Christian son and wife, who are less experienced in the miraculous power of God, had their faith stretched.

Father I praise You for Your goodness and how Your word accomplishes far more than meets the natural eye.

John M. Hughes is a worship leader and elder at Gates of Praise House Church Network.

Kneading Out the Selfishness

"I was hungry and you gave me something to eat, I was thirsty and you gave me something to drink, I was a stranger and you invited me in." *Matthew 25:35*

It was a crisp, cool, fall morning and I awoke feeling motivated to bake. (It is always good to take advantage of those moments because they are not an everyday occurrence in our household). I energetically began to look through bread recipes to decide what I could make to surprise my family.

I spent most of the morning measuring, mixing, kneading and waiting for the dough to rise. I sensed the pleasure of the Father in the midst of planning my little baking surprise. I reflected on how much He enjoys giving us surprises as well.

By early afternoon the aroma of fresh bread filled the kitchen. Just as the loaves reached perfection, the school bus rounded the corner and the kids came bustling through the door from school. They were delighted that they could enjoy a warm after-school snack of fresh bread…and to my surprise, so were all the neighborhood kids that piled in the door with them!

Immediately I felt possessive of the loaves of bread that I labored over all day. I had intended them to be for my family and not all the other kids that showed up at my door. But then I realized that these precious children were one of the Lord's surprises for me. He had lavished His love on me to extend to them. The Father had to knead out selfishness in my heart and graciously cause love to rise up in its place. With one loaf remaining for our dinner, I was grateful for all God taught me in my kitchen that day.

Father, You are the Bread of Life. Make me faithful to give others from the abundance at Your table. Thank you for gently reminding me, that my love for You is measured by the love I have for the people You place in my path.

Bonita Keener is a wife and mother of four. She serves on the board of directors at the Gateway House of Prayer and as an elder with her husband, Brent, at New Life Fellowship in Ephrata.

A Life of Service

"Knowing that from the Lord you will receive the reward of the inheritance; for you serve the Lord Christ." *Colossians 3:24 (New King James Version)*

Recently I was completing a series on "Serving" which is the fourth purpose of our Christian walk as described by Rick Warren in *The Purpose Driven Life.*

Called to serve is a wonderful reflection of our purpose here. My thoughts went back to the troubled eighteen-year-old woman who had been part of the 60's revolution and had experienced the fruit of that generation's rebellion and excess.

I will never forget how lost and desperate I felt, the sense of hopelessness that gripped my soul. Deep, gut-wrenching, soul-searching had brought me to the brink of destruction—shattered, wounded and seeking refuge from my loneliness and pain.

Peace, a reason to live, a purpose for my existence, was my inner cry. One day alone and disillusioned, I cried out, *"If there is a God out there, I ask that You reveal Yourself to me, because life as I know it is not worth living."*

Two weeks later, my sister who had often tried to share her new faith with me came to visit. Blinded to who she had become, all I could see was who she had been. "Hypocrite!" I sneered, each time she had attempted to share Christ with me. This time, I saw something different in her—a light, peace. It was something that I knew I desperately needed.

I received the message with an open heart. That night, I understood why I was created. I knew that Jesus Christ died to save me, and if I would give Him my life He would give me life, a purpose and direction. I do not regret one day of service.

Lord, thank you for giving purpose to our lives and opportunities to serve You and make a difference in this world. Thank you for Your grace which affirms Your purpose in us.

Mary J. Buch is a senior pastor at Breakout Ministries and serves on the Regional Council of the Regional Church of Lancaster County.

DECEMBER 11

Ministry in the Marketplace

"You are the light of the world. A city on a hill cannot be hidden."
Matthew 5:14

Our wedding date was set for September 12, 1959. Two weeks before we were married, God showed us we were to move to a greenhouse in Brickerville, Pennsylvania. There, Lamar would grow a little business he had started just a few years before.

We were very young and inexperienced, but as we were faithful, God opened doors for us to learn and grow.

During our early years, we continued our business as a secular career. We always tried to keep God at the center of our lives and share Him with employees, customers and salespeople. A few of them came to know Him as their Savior.

Further, we always gave God His portion before we started paying off the money we had borrowed to plant the crops. We were never let down or disappointed through this practice; God always blessed.

In the year 2000, we came into contact with Harvest Evangelism. They taught us that God had placed us where we were not only to give money to "ministries," but that we ourselves were in full-time ministry in the workplace.

We realized being in business was not a lower or higher calling than any other office or profession in life. It is making a difference wherever God has placed you.

Eventually, we hired an intercessor to come and pray a couple of days a week at our business. We had every employee covered in prayer.

We made personal counseling and prayer available to employees, customers and sales people. We helped employees when they got into financial problems. We knew God was interested in every little detail of our lives. He places us where He wants us to make a difference. We knew we were totally inadequate and made many mistakes, but we learned that when our heart is in the right place and we obey God's call, God does the rest.

Lord, help each one of us to be a light in this world today—whether it be in our homes, workplaces, businesses or schools.

Lamar & Nancy Esbenshade are owners of Esbenshade Greenhouses, Lititz.

More than I can Chew

"Ask, and what you are asking for will be given to you...."
Matthew 7:7

Have you ever bitten off more than you can chew and later think to yourself, "What have I gotten myself into?" I think that's the story of the last several years of my life. Recently, these incidents occur with ever increasing frequency.

I felt that way when I set foot in Uganda. I was in an unfamiliar country with new people. Moreover, I was called to an unfamiliar task. I hoped to mentor several young men and help them become mature laborers for Christ, something I'd never really done as a full time job before. Ahhh, the "more than I can chew" feeling struck again.

What do you do in these situations? I'm learning to ask God. Because of my situation in Uganda (unfamiliar people, place and job), I realized, "God, I don't know how to do this. I don't even know how to start!" So I asked God, "Lord, bring the guys alongside of me that you want me to pour into." About two weeks later a student named Moses shows up at my gate and says, "Tom, I really want to know God more, can we meet twice a week to study the Bible?" Talk about answered prayer!

From there, I began to work with more and more guys. Some came to me, others I sought out, but God's hand clearly was in it and directed me. It all began with asking. I realize that the key to a life lived after God's priorities is recognizing my dependence on God, and asking Him for help. Once I've had a "this is more than I can chew moment" and therefore go to Him, He always comes through.

Now I look forward to the "more than I can chew" moments. Why? Because in those times I will ask and seek God, the God who loves to respond to us. Then I will have the privilege of watching Him come through. I may not be able to chew huge mouthfuls, but my God can. He'll help us all chew those big mouthfuls if we simply ask Him.

Lord, help us to go immediately to You and ask for help when we seem to have more than we can chew on our plate!

Tom Kline serves at DOVE Christian Fellowship Westgate Celebration in Ephrata.

God's Love in the Details

"Now to him who is able to do immeasurably more than all we ask or imagine, according to his power that is at work within us, to him be glory." *Ephesians 3:20–21*

After a whirlwind three-week Christmas visit to the States, we anxiously eyed the new departure time listed for our delayed flight to Dallas. Our time with family and friends had been wonderful but exhausting. Now, I was traveling home to Germany four pounds lighter because of amebic dysentery, while my husband felt like his head was four pounds heavier because of a terrible sinus infection.

Our late arrival in Dallas necessitated us running, lugging our carry-on baggage the length of the airport to the international terminal. Why did the Lord allow this to happen when we were both feeling so miserable?

We arrived, out of breath, only to have to wait in line at the ticket counter—and, then, be told there was a mix-up about our e-tickets. The agent could only find two widely separated seats in the smoking section—a disaster for two sick, allergy-plagued missionaries.

The agent told us to wait, even though we knew the plane was now boarding passengers. She kept searching data on her computer as we silently prayed for God's mercy and wished we could sit down somewhere. Finally, she shocked us by placing us in first class at no extra charge!

We felt like royalty as we melted into the recliners, enjoying the luxury of delicious food, special service and amenities. Our Father had fulfilled a lifelong dream to fly first class at a time when we really needed it. God still had another surprise for us. The plane entered a jet stream, so we reached Frankfort two hours early, in time to catch an earlier flight to our home in Cologne.

Thank you, Father, for the love You lavish on us, taking care of every little detail of our lives.

Donna Faehling has served as a missionary, Bible teacher and speaker and enjoys writing.

An Orphanage in Brazil

"A generous man will himself be blessed, for he shares his food with the poor." *Proverbs 22:9*

When my wife and I were first married we were living in an apartment building. Like many young couples we were starting to save for the down-payment to purchase a house. We were just starting to put money away, and we realized we had a long way to go. We felt like we should take a seed and sow it. Since seeds reproduce after their own kind and our goal was to own a house, we wanted to give the money toward a building project of some kind. So we gave $500 from our meager savings to help build an orphanage in Brazil. Sure enough, a few years later, we moved into a new home that we had designed. God just brought the right people into our lives at the right time to help with the construction and purchase of the home. Amazing!

We have lived in a farming community for most of our lives, so we have been able to watch what farmers do. I don't know of a single farmer that plants corn and doesn't expect to harvest corn. No, they start planning for the harvest during the winter, long before they even plant the seed. I would dare to say that any farmer who planted seed but didn't expect to harvest it would be the laughing stock of his peers. This is a biblical principle to expect to receive a return from the Lord when we plant our seed. Givers are blessed in this way.

Lord Jesus, thank you for faith to sow financial seeds when it looks like we don't have much to give. Let us never grow weary in well doing as we are faced with multiple opportunities to sow money into Your kingdom and into people. And Lord, we expect each seed to grow and bear a harvest. Amen.

Brian Sauder helps provide oversight and direction for DOVE Christian Fellowship International's network of churches and is the author of the book *Prosperity With a Purpose.*

Help Me Be a Witness

"Therefore since we are God's offspring, we should not think that the divine being is like gold or silver or stone—an image made by man's design and skill. In the past God overlooked such ignorance, but now he commands all people everywhere to repent." *Acts 17:29–30*

I had been ministering in Bulgaria and was on my way back to the USA. I boarded a plane in London bound for Washington, D.C. and found myself in a seat which was in a row of two. After a while a Muslim lady, with her head, but not her face, completely covered walked down the aisle and took her seat next to me.

How can I communicate with a Muslim lady? I am sure she has strong religious convictions which are opposed to mine! How do I, as a man, initiate conversation with a Muslim woman in an appropriate way? These were some of the questions going through my mind in those first few minutes. But I had eight hours in front of me and I just knew that I needed to tell her about the Lord Jesus. I prayed for an opening to communicate with this women.

After a while she began to cry. She eventually turned to me and told me that she was very upset and preceded to tell me that she was leaving her husband behind in another country and would be separated from him which pained her greatly. We talked for two hours, and we were able to speak of bringing Jesus into the situation. I offered to pray for her, making it plain that the only effective prayer was through Jesus and that if I prayed it would be a Jesus-centered prayer. She readily accepted, bowed her head, and opened her arms as was her custom in prayer. There we were, high above the Atlantic ocean, praying to Jesus!

God is working in the lives of many people, whatever their race or religion. This incident taught me never to assume that people will not be open to God's truth, whatever their appearances tell us. God desires all people everywhere to know Him through His Son, Jesus.

Heavenly Father, help me to deal with all that is in me which hinders me from telling people about Jesus. Help me to be a witness to all with whom I come in contact, regardless of their culture, race or religion.

Peter Bunton, serves as the director of DOVE Mission International, based out of Lititz.

I Laugh

"There is a time for everything, and a season for every activity under heaven…a time to laugh." *Ecclesiastes 3:1, 4*

People think I'm funny; but it is not my fault! My family is famous for laughing. In fact, we can laugh and cry at the same time. It is not a very pretty sight. Tears stream down our faces, and our noses start dripping and we can't catch our breath.

I must be completely honest with you. I am just like my dad. He was a class clown and loved being the center of attention. My dad would be sitting in his old Lazy Boy chair and when the grandkids came for a visit, he would spontaneously pull out his air trombone and play John Phillips Sousa songs for them.

We're made for laughter. It's fun to laugh. What happens when we laugh? New research says that our T cells are all ramped up, and our endorphins really explode, and our entire muscular system relaxes. That's what happens. That's the science and the health benefits of laughter.

It's really not *new* research, because the Bible told us long ago in Proverbs 17:22, "A cheerful heart is good medicine."

Throughout His Word God has told us that the earmark of a Christian, the sign that we know Jesus Christ, is outrageous, contagious joy. And a by-product of joy is what? Laughter. So it's good to laugh. I choose to laugh.

Lord, You said laughter is like medicine in our lives. We pray for a healthy dose today!

Dan Houck is the pastor at The Table Community Church, Lancaster.

Take a Risk-Today!

"Then the man who had received the one talent came, 'Master,' he said, 'I knew that you are a hard man, harvesting where you have not sown and gathering where you have not scattered seed. So I was afraid and went out and hid your talent in the ground. See, here is what belongs to you.' His master replied, 'You wicked, lazy servant!' ...Take the talent from him and give it to the one who has the ten talents.'" *Matthew 25:24–26, 28*

When retired persons were asked what they regret, or if they were given the opportunity to live their life again, what would they have done differently? Eighty four percent said they regret not taking advantage of opportunities. Only sixteen percent said they were sorry for things they had done.

Think back on your life. Do you say, "I wish I would have gone to school? I wish I would have shared the good news with my neighbor? I always wanted to do...." Jesus wants us to go out on the limb. Without faith you cannot please God (Hebrews 11:6). Why are we so afraid? "For, God did not give us a spirit of timidity, but a spirit of power, of love and of self-discipline" (2 Timothy 1:7). The New Testament instructs us to be bold twice as often as it instructs us to be humble.

The Good Samaritan risked his life for the man who was robbed. The four men who brought the sick man on a mat and lowered him through the roof took a risk. Peter risked walking on the water. Did they regret their action? What is God asking you to do today? Step out in faith! Do what the Holy Spirit is nudging you to do. As the popular slogan says, "Just do it!" Jesus loves risk-takers!

Lord, forgive me for being timid and fearful. I have missed so many opportunities. Help me to be obedient to Your still, small voice. Help me to walk in obedience to You today.

David Eshleman is a church consultant for Eastern Mennonite Mission and Lancaster Mennonite Conference.

Even the Small Things

"For nothing is impossible with God." *Luke 1:37*

While Christmas shopping during the first year of our marriage, I was awed by a lovely tree decorated in blue and silver. "It's so beautiful! Oh, how I would love…." But, I stopped in mid-prayer, since I felt it was wrong to bother God with such a trivial request. After all, I did have my old decorations.

A week or so later I got so excited as I began to decorate our home. But my excitement soon turned to discouragement when a search through still-packed boxes produced not one ornament. I must have accidentally given them away prior to our wedding! Later that day Doris, one of Jeff's sisters, called. After hearing that I had no Christmas decorations, she offered to drop off a box of ornaments she no longer used. I thanked her and uttered a prayer of gratitude to God for having produced such a timely solution and one that would not cost Jeff or me anything. Then I left the house to do some errands.

When I returned, there was Doris's box on the porch. Quickly I took it inside and tore open the flaps. Tears came to my eyes and I uttered an, "Ahhh." There were blue and silver ornaments! And I hadn't even mentioned anything about the lovely store tree I had admired. "Lord, you are so gracious and loving. You care even about the small things."

Now, eighteen years later, I can see how the Lord used that to build my trust in Him. I learned that since He cares enough to supply unimportant decorations, how much more I can trust Him to supply my real needs.

Lord, thank you for being such a loving Father. Help me to remember You want me to bring all things to You; nothing is too small or too big.

Linda Lilley and her husband are members of Calvary Church. Linda endeavors to use her gift of encouragement using art, writing and acting to point others to the Lord.

You Can't Out-Give God

"Give, and it will be given to you." *Luke 6:38*

Our seven-year-old son, Bryce, had been saving his money to buy a new PlayStation 2 game. The game cost $30, and after saving his change for quite some time, at last the final dollar came. Shortly after (before we had chance to get to the store) the topic of stewardship came up in his schoolwork. The lesson presented the concept of giving to God, saving and spending.

As we finished reading the lesson, Bryce became agitated and almost cried. When I asked what was wrong, he said that he thought God wanted him to give all his money to church. I explained that God doesn't necessarily expect us to give all our money to church, but sometimes he does ask us for all we have, and that he should pray about what God was really wanting from him.

My husband and I shared with him the different times that God had given us specific directions, including selling our house and quitting a job in order to focus on our new church plant. We reminded him of all the ways God had provided for our family. As we talked of all that, Bryce got quiet. Tears filled his eyes as he said, "I'll do it! I'm going to put all my money in the offering at church. That Sunday, he joyfully deposited his bag of change into the collection.

The next morning our daughter came into the house calling, "Look what I found on the windshield of the van!" She was holding the very game Bryce had been saving for. Attached was a note that read:

"Bryce, you cannot out-give me. I will always give you back more in return. Love, your heavenly Father."

My husband and I looked at each other, stunned. "Do you know who did this?" I asked.

"No, don't you?" he replied.

Then Bryce chimed in, "Guys! It was God! It says, 'your heavenly Father'—that's God!" That experience is one neither he, nor we, will quickly forget. Our son now knows he can hear God's voice, and that God honors joyful obedience.

Thank you Lord, for speaking to us today. Help us to be obedient to what You say.

Jessi Clemmer is a church planter at Koinonia House, Pottstown.

Working for Your Good

"For this reason I say to you; do not be anxious for your life, or for what you shall eat or what you shall drink, nor for your body, as for what you shall put on. Is not life more than food, and the body than clothing?" *Matthew 6:25*

It was around 10:00 p.m. on Thursday, December 20, 2007, just five days before Christmas. The phone rang, and I received one of those calls no parent wants to receive. "Mom, I've been in an accident. I'm okay, but the car is totaled." I was so grateful my daughter was not seriously hurt. However, that was the only vehicle I had. I'm a single mom with no money to buy another vehicle or to make payments. I had no idea what to do. I did the only thing I could. I took the situation to the Lord.

I had to decide what kind of vehicle I wanted. I chose a minivan. With my daughter in college, I figured it would be more practical. On Saturday, my parents took to me around to different car lots looking at vans. At the last place we stopped, I saw a van I was interested in. The place was closed. All weekend I kept praying that if this was the van for me, that God would work it out. If not, direct me to the vehicle that was for me.

On Monday, Christmas Eve, I had to work. My parents went to the car lot to check out the van and see what kind of deal they could get. They got a good deal, loaned me the money and had the van ready for me to pick up after work. God gave me the new van for Christmas. If my parents would not have loaned me the money, there is no way I could have afforded the van. My parents are allowing me to pay whatever I can each month. Two blessings have come from this whole situation: I now have a reliable, practical vehicle, and my parents and I have been brought closer together. God really knows how to work things out for our good.

Thank you, God, for taking bad things in our lives and turning them into blessings.

Julie Gehman attends Ephrata Community Church.

Practicing His Presence

"Jesus said to them, 'My Father is always at his work to this very day, and I, too, am working.'" *John 5:17–18*

It was the mid seventies and many of us were experiencing renewal in our hearts with a hunger for God's Word and power. I would take extended times studying the Bible and waiting on the Lord in prayer. But after my second child was born, I found it more difficult to have those extended times. I remember asking the Lord how I could possibly retain those times with two small children needing lots of attention.

I remember so well His words to me, "LaVerne, practice My presence all day long." It was during that season that He taught me to see Him at work in my life every minute of every day and to acknowledge Him, even as I was changing a diaper, feeding the baby or going for groceries. Although my extended "quiet times" were much shorter and some days I barely had time to sit five minutes, I discovered great joy in practicing His presence in the daily routine of life.

It was years later that I read a book by a monk, Brother Lawrence, who revealed the need to practice God's presence—and it does take practice—daily learning to see God at work in all details of our lives, knowing that Christ in me can be just as real when I am changing a diaper as when I am leading a prayer meeting or preaching. It's not about getting our God-stuff out of the way each morning (although those quiet devotional times are imperative), but it is learning to know and experience Him at work in every detail of our lives.

Heavenly Father, we thank You that You are always at work in our lives. We receive grace to see You at work, even in our daily routines and to practice Your presence each moment of the day. In Jesus' name, amen.

LaVerne Kreider leads a house church with The Network and serves with her husband Larry in DOVE Christian Fellowship International.

A Future and a Hope

"For I know the plans I have for you, says the Lord, plans for good
and not for evil, plans to give you a future and a hope."
Jeremiah 29:11

That has been my life verse for many years, as the Lord has taken
me through difficult times and showed Himself very real to me. But on
July 27, 2006, He showed Himself to me in a tangible way.

It was a pleasant summer day as I accompanied my husband, John,
on a day trip. We made good time on the way, not even stopping for
lunch. I noticed that the weather was changing as the day progressed,
and by the time we were starting back, it was getting dark. I have only
faint memories of what happened next, but as I drifted in and out of
consciousness, I realized we had been in a serious car accident.

I watched the nurses and doctors working on me in the emergency
room, as I felt myself peacefully slipping into the arms of my Savior.
Suddenly, I heard the voice of Jesus saying, "I am not finished with
you yet, you have to go back."

I was prepared to meet my Lord, and it was bittersweet to go back
because I wanted to be with Him. However, I knew He had a plan for
me and a purpose and I needed to fulfill it. I have learned to live the life
the Lord gave back to me and I desire to serve him.

About one week later, I was talking with John about the accident. I
remember saying, "Wasn't it nice of that guy to stand beside me at the
car? He talked so comfortingly saying, 'Yea, though I walk through the
valley of the shadow of death, I shall fear not evil.' I felt such peace."

It was then that John said, "Honey, there was no man standing
there." I had had a visitation from an angel!

*Papa God, thank you for a new chance to serve You and to fulfill my
purpose on earth before I meet You in heaven. Love, your daughter.*

Mary E. Miller, a very blessed wife, mom and nana as well as an LPN, serves
Jesus through children's ministry at Carpenter Community Church, Talmage.
She lives in Farmersville with her husband of 32 years.

God, I Just Have to Know!

"For if we sin willfully after we have received the knowledge of the truth, there no longer remains a sacrifice for sins." *Hebrews 10:26*

I have the annoying habit of needing to know—what, where, why, how and when—now!

I've not been able to just accept the work that God is doing without understanding the details. One night while wrestling about some issues, I asked Him, "Why doesn't everyone just believe in You? What needs to happen for the world to accept You? Why don't You just wave Your hand and make everyone live happily ever after?"

Sometime after our discussion, I fell asleep. I had the most interesting dream. I was in the room where Little Red Riding Hood had walked in on the wolf that was masked as the grandmother.

I remember thinking to myself, what if the grandmother had talked him into eating some of the cookies she had made for Red and then he wouldn't need to eat anything else. What if Red noticed who he was from the time she walked in and showed him kindness instead of fear? What if the wolf would have had a change of heart and admitted his deception? How would the story end, if all this would have happened?

God showed me that the end of it is still that good overcomes evil. The characters make up the story, but the moral of the story never changes.

Okay, I realize that this walk with God is not a fantasy story. Yet, I did wake up with the answer I needed. People make up this world and every one of us has choices to make and a God-given free will. Not every one is going to decide to do the right thing. The end of all this will still be the same—good overcomes evil. However that plays out—God is still in charge!

Give me the desire to do Your will and not my own.

Linda Keller is an outreach leader, musician and songwriter for Breakout Ministries.

Papa's Faithfulness

"...Listen carefully to Me, and eat what is good, and let your soul delight itself in abundance." Isaiah 55:2

I remember well the moment when, three years into a new ministry, I heard Papa request, "Give this city two years." God was asking us to sell our lovely suburban home and become "urbanites." We obeyed —sort of.

We moved into a home just on the edge of the city limits. After six grueling months, we repented, put that house on the market and prepared to move again. The house sold quickly. Papa supplied a great rental for us, just in time. We signed the lease on February 25, 2006. The clock on Papa's request started ticking.

As January 2008 arrived, we decided that we were fine living right where we were. We let our landlord know that we would stay for a third year unless, of course, the Lord provided just the right house at just the right price. He agreed to be flexible with us.

One Sunday morning as I glanced through the newspaper, an open house caught my eye. I showed the listing to my husband and off we went to take a look. Unbelievable. Though it would need some TLC, the house had everything we wanted, at just the right price. By the next evening, we had signed the sales agreement.

We hadn't paid much attention to the date, until a close friend asked, "When did you sign the lease on your current house?"

I responded, "February 25, 2006."

"What did God tell you about moving into that house?"

I answered, "Give the city two years."

"And what was the date your offer was turned in and accepted on the new house?"

I let out a delighted gasp, "February 25, 2008!"

Ever faithful Papa! Once we "listened carefully," He was more than happy to keep His word—exactly.

Papa, thank you for Your faithfulness to me. May I always eat the goodness of Your words for me and find delight in Your blessings.

Deb Munson is a writer/artist and the director of Artists' Junction in Lancaster.

Food-Shelter-Warmth

"For I was hungry and you gave me something to eat, I was thirsty and you gave me something to drink, I was a stranger and you invited me in, I needed clothes and you clothed me, I was sick and you looked after me, I was in prison and you came to visit me."
Matthew 25:35–36

One frozen December night a homeless man was asked by a WGAL news reporter what he wanted for Christmas. I recall the urgent answer, "food-shelter-warmth, food-shelter-warmth, food…" Not only was this suffering man desperate for mere survival, it jolted my perspective on material needs. That report motivated my wife and me to volunteer to help serve the Christmas meal at Lancaster's Water Street Rescue Mission a few weeks later. This experience helped me to see how selfish I am.

I am privileged to have nutritious food, fresh, drinkable water, and reliable shelter from the elements and clothing to preserve adequate body heat. Is not any other material possession I have a luxury? I like my food to be tasty, my clothes reasonably fashionable and my shelter architecturally appealing. But these are psychological pleasantries not essential to my survival. I realized Christ called me to feed the hungry, not merely to have tea parties for the full-bellied. He called me to clothe the naked, not add to the tie rack of the clothed.

At Water Street that year we served Christmas turkey alongside an extended family group. Rather than open gifts, these siblings and spouses spend Christmas day each year serving together at a homeless shelter.

Many of us across this county hold food, shelter and warmth in our hands to be either consumed or shared. How will we help someone survive this year's Pennsylvania winter?

Dear God, I am humbly grateful that I have adequate food, shelter and clothing. Today I renew my commitment to share with others in these necessities of which I have so much. Amen.

Dave Witmer, church planter, writer, musician, husband and father, serves leaders with HopeNet Fellowship of Churches.

Restored

"O Lord my God, I cried unto thee, and thou hast healed me."
Psalm 30:2 (King James Version)

T. J. sought counseling for some very personal struggles. After a period of time and self-examination, he took his query to God. Those questions, when answered, brought about an understanding of the traumatic events of his life. He was able to face the fear, anxiety, depression and total loss of self that had resulted in the destructive behaviors that robbed him of years of productive living and destroyed many relationships.

It was a powerful discovery for T.J.—that through faith and trust in Jesus Christ alone, God's forgiveness, forgiving others and forgiving oneself was not only possible but the way to true healing. T. J. was enabled by the truth and power of the call of the gospel to cry out to God, "Lord, is it easier to heal me, or just forgive me? Please God, please forgive me!"

While there was a process leading up to this moment in God's perfect timing, within two weeks after his prayer, dependency, fear, and the anxiety were gone and T. J.'s health was restored. Pleasantly surprised and amazed, T. J. pressed on with a miraculous new inner strength to serve God in the newness of life.

Lord, if we surrender to anything today, let it be to You!

Thomas R. Miller B.A. M.A. is pastoral counselor and minister of Grace For Life Ministries. www.godswordforlife.com

Graduation to Glory

"For to me to live is Christ and to die is gain." *Philippians 1:21*

In early January of 2008, my sister, Cindi Farr, a career linguist with Wycliffe Bible Translators in Papua New Guinea, along with her Baruga language helpers had just completed the translation of Philippians 1:21, *"For to me to live is Christ and to die is gain."* All agreed that the Baruga rendering of this verse was clean and "sharp like a knife blade."

On the morning of January 15, Cindi and her husband Jim had an extended time of prayer with some of those translation helpers and close family friends in the village of Erika. Cindi laid hands on each of the participants, praying a blessing over them. Then as Jim concluded the prayer time, she excused herself and went over to her village house to make the daily radio contact with Ukarumpa, the center for Wycliffe operations in Papua New Guinea. After turning on the radio, she gave an audible gasp, fell back on her bed and went immediately into the presence of Jesus. Attempts to revive her failed and just like that she graduated into Glory.

Cindi often questioned what she had really accomplished for her Lord, yet she, along with her husband Jim, completed the Korafe language New Testament, finished work on the first ever Korafe dictionary and translated several books of the Baruga New Testament. In honor of Cindi's lifetime of Commitment to them, the Korafe people requested that her body be buried in the village square of Baga at the exact spot where their New Testament had been dedicated in 1984. By example and precept, Cindi reflected Christ in her living and in her dying she gained the ultimate prize of God's upward call in Christ Jesus.

O death where is your sting? O grave, where is your victory?
Thanks be to You Father God for the victory You give us through our Lord Jesus Christ. Amen.

Fred Moury and his wife Miriam reside in Lititz, and Fred serves as conference minister for the Susquehanna Region of the Evangelical Congregational Church.

Stability

"For I was hungry and you gave Me food; I was thirsty and you gave Me drink; I was a stranger and you took Me in; I was naked and you clothed Me; I was sick and you visited Me." *Matthew 25:35–36*

"Jesus Christ is the same yesterday and today and forever." *Hebrews 13:8 (New American Standard Bible)*

When I first came on board in my new position as director of the Lancaster Pregnancy Clinic, I resolved that I would bring some stability to the office. It seemed that as God was, forever, expanding the boundaries of our ministry, He was also moving many people into different positions in the space of a short time. I had this sense of arriving and staying. I was here for the long haul and determined to provide a stable office environment.

Several months after I started, we began to consider adopting a new database. I was all for the database and knew the great things it could do for us; but, at the same time, I knew that it meant converting data, changing forms, changing reports—lots of new things! About the same time, the board also approved a new curriculum. It was one that we were excited about, and yet it meant learning a new program. I cringed inside and thought, what happened to the stability I was working on?

I emailed my boss at headquarters and shared my concern with her. Were we taking on too much at once? I desired to create a sense of stability within our office after so many other changes, though I was also excited about these new directions.

She responded to my email with five simple little words: "Our stability comes from God."

What could I say to that? Indeed she was right! He is our stability. He is the same yesterday, today and forever. We look to Him for ministry direction, and as we follow Him, He is our rock and our stability.

Thank you, dear Lord, for always being there and providing that steady strength we need in our ever-changing world.

Lisa Hildebrand works for Susquehanna Valley Pregnancy Services and ministers as a teacher and speaker in local churches.

God Teaches Us

"I will instruct you and teach you in the way you should go: I will counsel you and watch over you." Psalm 32:8

I was part of a group of believers who were meeting for three days of prayer and fellowship. During this time I experienced feelings of being inadequate for a new assignment that I was planning on taking. A large part of the problem was that I was comparing myself with others and telling myself that I did not measure up to others in people skills, wisdom, intelligence, etc..

The last morning of the three days we were together, I woke up early and asked the Lord to give me a word for the fears and anxieties that I was facing. I read from the Bible, but nothing seemed to speak to how I was feeling. I closed my Bible and walked outside and started praying.

It was not long before the phrase from Psalm 42, "Put your hope in God," came to my mind. This simple phrase turned my troubled mind and spirit into one of rest and hope. I was so amazed at how differently I felt. God taught me a lesson that morning, which has given me a strength for living I did not have until that point. It is simply this: in the stresses of life, don't look to yourself or anything else; put your hope in God. He loves us and He will give to us whatever we need.

I have found that God often speaks to me through His Word when I am experiencing a difficult time in life. They become times of learning lessons that have lifelong value.

Lord, thank you that You care about us and You teach us lessons that we need to learn through the difficult times of life.

Daniel Miller pastors Freedom in Christ Fellowship in Lebanon.

High Seas Adventure

"He got up, rebuked the wind and said to the waves, 'Quiet! Be still!'
Then the wind died down and it was completely calm." *Mark 4:39*

Since fishing is a favorite activity during our vacations, my husband, our three teenage children, and I were twenty-eight miles off the coast of Sanibel Island in the Gulf of Mexico. We always begin our fishing days with a time of prayer asking God for protection and wisdom for ourselves and the other boaters. It was a rough two-hour ride to our fishing spot, with the seas measuring two to four feet. Soon after we arrived, we caught several large grouper, but we were troubled by some storms, which seemed to be moving closer.

After about an hour or two, my husband declared that we should head towards shore. I thanked the Lord for His answer to my prayer to grant my husband wisdom. After all, our boat is over thirty years old and has a single, twenty-year-old outboard motor. I was glad we were heading in, but now the seas were four to six feet, making it a slow, rough trip. I knew that God could hold the storms back and calm the wind and the waves, and I asked for His protection. When my husband informed me that in addition to the dark skies, rain, wind, and rough seas, our motor was not working properly, my prayers took on a new level of intensity. I could imagine our fate if the storms closed in and our motor failed. We motored slowly for more than three hours until we were able to see land, and then for another two hours until we were safely at the dock.

Under normal conditions, our return trip would have taken two hours rather than the five-hour adventure we had experienced, but God answered our prayers. The motor continued to run; the storms did not get very close to us; the wind and the waves decreased. We were all safe and had a God Story to tell.

To the One who creates and commands the wind and the seas, we give You thanks and praise for Your loving care over Your children.

Cheri Miller is a wife, mother, teacher at Lancaster Mennonite Schools, intercessor for SVPS, and member of Middle Creek Church of the Brethren.

Light Prevails

"I tell you the truth, when you did it to one of the least of these my brothers and sisters, you were doing it to me!"
Matthew 25:40 (New Living Translation)

Our team loads up in two vehicles and heads to a neighborhood of Philadelphia. Years ago it was a nice place to live, but now its streets are comprised of boarded-up factories with the working poor living in row homes and their children playing among discarded needles and trash. It's nighttime, and this area is where the shipwrecked ones wash up, the marginalized with generational cycles of continuing despair. Crack is cheap here. We see the ones strung out on heroin—they have that gray look of the walking dead. We see young women, once beautiful, driven to prostitution to support their addictions.

At Kensington and Somerset, a busy drug corner, we set up to serve a hot dinner to these precious ones. We proclaim the love of Jesus over them, we listen, we weep, we love.

I meet a man who is bent over and stumbling. He is middle aged and incoherent. He becomes very quiet as we pray for him. I suddenly realize something is wrong. His breathing gets more and more shallow. I call 911. Emergency folks are slow to respond in this neighborhood. Bullet proof vests do not protect them from AIDS contaminated needles.

We pray. I tell the operator, "Hurry, he's coding on us!" A crowd starts to gather. Unfortunately this is an all too familiar scene, one repeated daily in this neighborhood. An ambulance arrives. They give him several shots of Narcane, a new drug that counteracts the effect of the drugs.

Tonight, this one was ripped from Satan's hand. This one, made in the image of God, created for God's pleasure, someone's son, someone's brother, probably someone's father—was dying, lying on a pavement among strangers. However, the Holy Spirit came and said, "Not this one, not tonight." Life reigned. The Light prevailed over the darkness.

Jesus, give us a heart of concern and compassion for those who are left out and forgotten today.

Joetta Keefer serves with Hands of Hope, a ministry to the homeless in Philadelphia, meeting physical, emotional, and spiritual needs of hurting people in a practical way.

A Celebration of Partnership

The following regional networks within South Central Pennsylvania partnered in publishing this volume of devotionals. We invite you to contact them to learn more about how God is at work to bring transformation in your local region.

The Regional Church of Lancaster County

Keith Yoder, Chair, and Lisa Hosler, Assistant Chair
Box 311, Leola, PA 17540
Phone: (717) 625-3034   www.theregionalchurch.com

Our mission is to build relationships and ministry partnerships which position us for the answer to Christ's prayer that all God's people be one in a way that transforms the region. Our strategies are to:

PRAY To blanket the region with continual prayer and worship
WITNESS To saturate the region with the gospel witness of Jesus Christ
TRANSFORM To mobilize initiatives to transform our communities with God's love
GUARD To guard the well-being of the church through reconciliation, relationship, accountability, intercession and spiritual discernment

Many partnerships; one mission: Lancaster County transformed by the kingdom of God

Reading Regional Transformation Network

Craig Nanna, Director
P.O. Box 8188, Reading, PA 19603
Phone: (610) 371-8386   Email: craignanna@readingdove.org

Reading House of Prayer

Chad Eberly, Director
Phone: (610) 373-9900   Email: ChadE@rhop.net www.rhop.net

Uniting leaders together in strategic kingdom relationships for the purpose of transformation in the Reading region. Our priorities include advancing the kingdom of God in the Reading region through relationship, the unity of the body of Christ, the house of prayer, and strategic initiatives that will produce transformation.

Life Transforming Ministries: Coatesville Regional
Bill Shaw, Executive Director
643 East Lincoln Highway, P.O. Box 29, Coatesville, PA 19320
Phone: (610) 384-5393   www.QuietRevolution.org

A catalyst in the movement for church unity and community transformation. Generated out of humility and united prayer the mission of LTM is to feature the Lordship of Jesus by being a conduit for the development of trusting cross cultural relationships and incubator of collaborative ministry initiatives.

Lebanon Valley Prayer Network
Stephen J. Sabol, Executive Director
825 North Seventh Street, Lebanon, PA 17046
Phone: (717) 273-9258

This Network exists to lay a foundation of worship and intercessory prayer for the purpose of birthing transformation in the Lebanon Valley.

Lebanon 222
Jay McCumber, Director
515 Cumberland Street, Lebanon, PA 17042
Phone: (717) 279-5683

The Lebanon 222 Team exists to discern and implement God's heart for the Lebanon Valley.

Capital Region Pastors' Network
Dave Hess, President
P. O. Box 9, Camp Hill, PA 17001-0009
Phone: 717.909.1906   Email: c.reg.pastors@pa.net

We are a network of pastors in the Capital Region of Pennsylvania committed to Christ and to developing relationships among pastors, rooted in prayer, which lead to partnerships in ministry bearing the fruit of revival.

York Prays
Jim Herbert, Pastor of Emmanuel Christian Fellowship
2309 East Philadelphia Street, York, PA 17402
Phone: 717-840-0840   Email: jimherbert@ecfyork.com
www.yorkprays.com

The York Coalition for Transformation is a collaboration of men and women of God who are committed to *sustained Godly transformation* in York City and County.